On Jordan's Stormy Banks

On Jordan's Stormy Banks

Religion in the South
A Southern Exposure Profile

Edited, revised with new materials, and
introduced by

Samuel S. Hill, Jr.

Mercer University Press
Macon, Ga. 31207

ISBN 0-86554-035-7 [softcover]
ISBN 0-86554-060-8 [casebound]

All books published by Mercer University Press are produced
on acid-free paper that exceeds the minimum standards set by the
National Historical Publications and Records Commission.

Library of Congress Cataloging in Publication Data

Main entry under title:
On Jordan's stormy banks.

"A revised and expanded edition of On Jordan's
stormy banks: religion in the South, edited by Jim
Sessions, Sue Thrasher, and Bill Troy, that appeared
as volume 4, number 3 of Southern exposure"—T.p.
verso.

1. Christianity—Southern States.   2. Southern States
—Church history.   I. Hill, Samuel S.   II. Southern
exposure (Durham NC).

BR535.06 1983   280'.0975   82-14524
ISBN 0-86554-035-7 (pbk.)
ISBN 0-86554-060-8

Table of Contents

Religion in the South
Introduction

"*I am bound for the promised land,*
I am bound for the promised land,
O, who will come and go with me,
I am bound for the promised land."

Introduction

by the Editor

Quite a variety of descriptions of the religious life of Southern people appears in this collection. These in their rich diversity shed light on why Southern religion has been studied too little and why it has such deep human significance—also why it is an endlessly fascinating topic.

These pieces, many of them simple and direct testimonials, reflect the faith of the common people. As such they may not appeal to the intellectual community, historians or theologians or even sociologists who attend to ideas and behavior patterns, and the relationships between them.

And so the articles that follow are more to be enjoyed than to be "studied." Academic slants on human experience are not the only valid ones after all. In this material we are invited to listen, to share, to become a part of the experiences and concerns. In a real sense, this material is more like poetry than prose. The reader should drop his guard, not work at it too hard, move with the flow of the human spirit, Southern style. So authentic are these reports of life that one adapts rather easily from black experience to white, from poor to middle class, from low-country rural to mountain isolated.

There is remarkable power in the experience of the Southern faithful. What is sometimes stereotyped as shallow or corny or quaint or out-of-date may instead be seen as having a genuine richness and complexity and wide applicability. Plain-folks Southern religion sustains a few million souls, providing direction, comfort, and incentive for many people for whom life presses in hard. Instead of serving as an opiate, it often enlivens the faculties and the feelings, and issues in a call to responsible behavior. The observer may or may not find familiar and appealing the particular forms all those qualities take. But the person who makes the effort to participate is apt to wonder at the resources and be impressed by the power.

Take some simple examples, such as mottoes and roadside signs. "Only one life, 'twill soon be past, Only what's done for Christ will last." "Prepare to meet thy God." "Christ died for your sins." "Don't ever stop telling people what Jesus has done for you." Not elegant, perhaps, not blessed with subtlety, scarcely alluring and inspiring to all. Yet these have an aphoristic quality and they are genuine. For they bring significance into focus, impel you to discriminate between high stakes matters and all else, and remind you of what "good" in "good life" is really all about.

The religious faith of the Southern common people stacks up pretty well. Religion is supposed to do just those things.

Observers have frequently noted that the South acknowledges an informal established religion. To the degree that this is so, this pattern departs from both the casualness of true establishmentarianism (as in state church societies) and from the high-level intensity of authority-minded faith. What the reader will find here (and quite generally in Southern society) is best described in other language than "casual" or "intense"; rather it is "expressive," "permeating," "taken for granted"—so important that it is simply *taken for granted*. It *is* casual in that your faith is the air you breathe. It *is* intensive inasmuch as it requires you to play for keeps. Nevertheless this kind of religion is closer to being "expressive" and "permeating." Southern folk religion is quieter, less aggressive, and better integrated into one's life than much sophisticated opinion would have it.

There is a certain true-to-character, natural, uninhibited, and even unconscious quality to this kind of practice of faith.

Southern religion is famous for its personal expressions. But the religion of these folk lives in public as well as in private. Some stories in the pages that follow show its revolutionary capability, suggest how much of an irritant it can be in a society with quite fixed notions about race, caste, and consensus values. On another front, it can harden into solid institutional form. Part Five below reveals that religion is big business in the South. Few cities are more Vatican City-like than Nashville. Few organizations match the Roman Catholic Church as well as the Southern Baptist Convention does for centralized and effective planning and financing.

The astute observer can readily see that the personal and the public, the informal and the bureaucratic, the spontaneous and the stylized are at home under Dixie's dome. Moreover, the distance between them is often short. Accuracy is compromised and social reality is misrepresented by anyone with a bias in favor of "folk religion" at the expense of "organized religion."

The regular staff and the invited onetime contributors of the 1976 issue of *Southern Exposure* of which this book is largely a reprinting are due much credit and many thanks.* Only a little has been omitted here from what appeared then. A few pieces have been added in order to fill in some gaps and provide a wider coverage.

Finally, the photographs selected through the genius of the original editors enable us to see the expressions of faith contained in the words of the text. It is to be hoped that readers of *On Jordan's Stormy Banks* will look, see, and feel—all three—since each of those sensory responses is appropriate to this collection and the marvelous phenomenon that it seeks to portray—Southern religion.

---

*The editor is especially gratified over bringing back to public access the fruits of the labors of longtime friends, Jim Sessions and Bill Troy, who with Sue Thrasher were the three original editors.

Part One

Religion in the South
Its Preachers

"On Jordan's stormy banks I stand,
    And cast a wishful eye
To Canaan's fair and happy land
    Where my possesions lie."

The Call

by Will Campbell

Thad Garner was, I suppose, the most profane man I have ever met. And, in a way, he was also the most profound. Whatever he was, he made a deep impression on me at the time. He was a preacher down the road from where I was a preacher. He had been there for a long time when I got there and he sort of took me under his wing.

Both of us were Southern Baptist preachers. When we first met it seemed easy for me to think of him as a Southern Baptist preacher. He was older, had a much larger church, held lots of revival or protracted meetings, was popular with the young people, played a small harmonica in his nose while playing a larger one in his mouth, played golf, was an ardent hunter and Chaplain of the Volunteer Fire Department, had been a professional boxer, had been to the Holy Land, attended the Baptist Seminary in Louisville, spent two years at Yale, and had recently hosted the state annual meeting of the WCTU.

I did not do any of those things and was just out of a liberal Yankee divinity school. Not only was I younger than Thad, I wore white buck shoes and a tweed cap—even in hot Louisiana summers—smoked a calabash pipe, committed sermons to manuscript, had never held a revival, conducted a building campaign, or spoken to a Sweetheart banquet. I had not been to the seminary in Louisville, a sort of union card in those days, and did not even have a map of the Holy Land.

Then I discovered that Thad had once worn white bucks and a tweed cap, still smoked a pipe, conducted revival meetings for money, had gone to the Holy Land only because his congregation had lifted a surprise love offering for that purpose, and had bought in the Tel Aviv Airport the set of color slides he brought back to show to youth groups around the state. He also disliked teenagers, drank a lot of wine—though he only had one kidney and couldn't handle it very well—and cussed a lot.

Learning these things made it easy for me to think of myself as a Southern Baptist preacher and increasingly difficult to think of Thad as one. I believed some rather definite things about Jesus and the Faith while Thad would not admit to believing anything. Yet, somehow, I never got the feeling that I was in the presence of a fraudulent or deceitful person. He did not remind me of Elmer Gantry. Marjoe was barely born at the time and he wouldn't have come to mind anyway. I was totally fascinated; I had simply not met anyone quite like this before.

Sometimes I would go hunting or fishing with him. I was not really a hunter but he taught me how to shoot and how to avoid copperheads and quicksand, taking full advantage of the opportunity to compare both those enemies to various aspects of the pastorate.

On one occasion we were about to conclude an all day, totally unproductive bird hunt. The dogs had pointed at everything from rabbits to starlings but not one quail had been flushed. Thad had excused them by saying the weather was too dry, and he had maligned them as stupid, useless mutts. He had pampered and cajoled them, and had dragged one of them by the tail across a barbed wire fence as punishment for pointing a brown thrasher. Finally the three of them were frozen in a hard-point position at what was sure to be the biggest covey of quail in the parish. At least that was what Thad allowed. And

Will Campbell is a preacher from Amite County, Mississippi. He now lives in Mt. Juliet, Tennessee where he is the Director of the Committee of Southern Churchmen, publishers of *Katallagete*, a quarterly journal of religion. He is the author of *Race and Renewal of the Church*, and coauthor with James Holloway of *Up to Our Steeples in Politics*. This selection is taken from his book *Brother to a Dragonfly* © 1977 by Will D. Campbell, and used by permission of the Continuum Publishing Company.

when the flush signal was given, that proved to be the case. Even when I am expecting it, even when I have seen the movement of the little critters through the underbrush, I am always startled by the sudden fluttering of quail wings, lifting their fat bellies like giant bumble bees from the earth and away from their pursuer. Consequently, I seldom got a shot before they were well out of range. This time Thad got off three quick shots, each BOOM! blending with and echoing the last. As his last shot was dying away I jerked the trigger and waited for the jolt against my shoulder and the ringing in my ears. But nothing happened. The thing was not even loaded. Despite the three volleys in such rapid succession nothing lay

Photo courtesy of Baptist Home Mission Board

dead for the dogs to retrieve. Thad had missed as surely as I had with an empty gun. (Or "piece", as he liked to call any weapon.) Though I had not led what one would call a sheltered existence during the past several years and my own language did not always measure up to garden-party standards, I was not familiar with some of the words my friend could spit out. For a full sixty seconds the big Louisiana field was filled with his expletives. At the dogs, at the birds, at me, at the gun, at the manufacturer of the shells, at the Almighty—all were profaned and reviled because of this misfortune. When he had quieted down, he sank backward onto an eroded levee. I sat on the ground not far away. It was an occasion for a question I had wanted to ask him for some time.

"Thad, why did you ever decide to be a Baptist preacher?" He looked puzzled and not just a little hurt. He pondered my question for a long time, sighting and squinting down the barrel of his shotgun. Finally he looked me straight in the eye and answered my question: "Cause I was *called*, you goddam fool!"

And who's to say? I have met a lot of preachers since then. But none of them could preach with such assuring certainty, claim to believe so little, or be as convinced that he was indeed *called* to do exactly what he was doing.

Thad had a lot of notches on his Bible. He called it "drawing the net," or "gettin' em ready for the waters." He made fun of every organization in the church but promoted and organized as if his very life depended upon their success. (And maybe it did.) When I called him a hypocrite for making the rounds of country churches, preaching his fundamentalist brand of religion because he knew what would sell, he countered that I was the real hypocrite because if I really believed all that I said I believed about Jesus and the Gospel I would not be working for one of those rich edifices masquerading as the house of the Lord.

I am not so sure now that I was right about Thad. But I am very sure now that he was right about me. When I castigated him for taking money to preach something he didn't believe, his answer was that a man had to make a living for his family.

But he always added something else. "Don't watch me in the church house, boy. Watch me on the street." I guess that he was telling me that his Sunday antics were a tent-making operation, and had nothing to do with his professed vocation, his call. And I guess he was telling me that if we really believed in grace then the chief sinner might well be the preacher. And apparently St. Paul would have concurred. And whether he was telling me or not, I was learning from him that the Gospel does not depend for its efficacy upon the personal habits of the preacher.

Privately, Thad called himself his congregation's mascot. "They feed me well. They even love me. They pat me on the head and brag about me. They show me off before the other teams. There's only one thing wrong with being a mascot. Just one little inconvenience. They keep you on a leash. Otherwise, it's a great life."

There was one term that always sent him into a rage quicker than any other. A pet name for the minister who was liked and approved was "the little preacher." "We just love our little preacher," he would say mockingly. "We have the cutest little preacher." He had a comic routine about the term which began with a guy who was six feet four, weighed nearly three hundred pounds, was a weight lifter in the Olympics, and still his congregation called him "our little preacher." The routine ended with Mary Magdalene running up to old man Zebedee after the crucifixion exclaiming, "Did Jimmy tell you what they've done to our little preacher?" And sometimes he would launch into a discourse about a college somewhere that had a fine registered dog for a mascot. A neighboring school stole him one night, bred him to a mongrel bitch, kept him until the puppies were born and then returned him to the campus with his mate and whelps. He never explained his story, but the way he would shrug and wink his eye the listener was led to believe that it meant that even a mascot can't be controlled absolutely, that once in awhile the Lord will steal him away, get him involved with what the world calls common and use him to mess up their pretty system.

Anyway, after a time I learned to watch him on the streets and not in the pulpit.

Once it was a bond issue before the voters of Granny White to build a swimming pool for the children. Since this was long before civil rights days, the matter of whose children would get to use the pool and whose would not never came up. Nor would Thad bring it up. At least not directly. "I operate like a rubber band," he liked to say. "I stretch things just so far and when it's about to break, I let it snap back in place. Only every time I stretch it, it's a little weaker." Thad was, of course, very active in the Lion's Club International, the most influential civic club in Granny White. Clown that he was, it was only natural that he should hold the office of Tailtwister. That's the one who cuts off ten dollar neckties of a member who comes in late, makes a shy guy a solo for not joining in Club sing-songs, and playful little things like that.

On this day the Club was discussing whether or not to make an all-out effort on behalf of the bond issue for the swimming pool. The sentiment was strongly in favor of doing so. Most everbody had said his piece. Then Brother Thad takes the floor, tells a few stories—like the one about the airline stewardess on a transoceanic flight who kept *insisting* that he have a drink, not knowing that he was of the cloth. "In complete disgust and annoyance I said, 'Lady, I'm a dry alcoholic. If I had one little drink I would rip this whole airplane apart and send it diving into the sea if you wouldn't give me every drop on board.' " (This was very funny to the Club because just the thought of anyone pulling a social error like offering a Baptist preacher a drink was hilarious.)

Thad called himself his congregation's mascot. . . . "They pat me on the head and brag about me. They show me off before the other teams."

And I believe that was the occasion when he told about the "ole colored preacher" who went to a church for a trial sermon and at the dinner table of the head deacon passed his glass instead of his plate when the good sister asked if he wanted more corn. And things like that.

Then the last throat was cleared and the last chortle faded because everyone knew that Brother Garner had some little something serious he wanted to say. "Brethren," he said, "I want us to have a swimming pool. I have two little boys as all of you know and they want a swimming pool. And they asked me at the breakfast table just this morning if I was going to vote to have one. And I told them what I'm fixing to tell you. 'I just can't vote for water for my own children to swim in when there are children in this town who don't have water to drink'." And he sat down.

Now there were a few more throats cleared and the president fondled his gavel. But no one wanted to get into a discussion of that. Everybody present knew that two years earlier a bond issue had been defeated which would have extended water lines into a part of the black community where dozens of families still got water by hand from a single hand-dug well.

Going back to the house I chided him about the propriety of telling "ole colored preacher" jokes. "That's the trouble with you shithook liberals, Willie. You had rather see a hundred children die of dehydration than have the sound of nigger heard from your lips. Whether I say nigger don't matter a damn. If one of those young'uns die of thirst, he ain't nothing but one more dead nigger, whether I say the word or not, or whether I go to hell for saying it or not. But if he lives to get grown maybe he can lead his people out of this godawful Egypt and there won't be no more niggers." I sort of just changed the subject to something else.

On another occasion it was a papermill strike in a small town more than a hundred miles away. The president of the company, who lived in Jacksonville, Florida, said that weekends were the only time he could be present for negotiation sessions. When the union said they would be glad to go to the table on weekends, the president said he couldn't come on Sunday either because he had to teach his Sunday School class. This had made the local press and for me it seemed a perfect springboard for a Labor Day sermon—straining at a gnat and swallowing a camel, whited sepulchres, and all that. But Thad took another approach. There had been a lot of violence accompanying the lengthy strike. Almost every night a gas line leading to the plant would be dynamited far out in the swamps. The union version was that armadillos were stealing dynamite in the mill, burrowing under the fence and storing it under the gas pipes and accidentally igniting it with their teeth. Management did not quite buy that explanation. On the same Sunday I was preaching my Matthew 23 sermon, Thad mounted his pulpit and delivered a stinging indictment against violence. And it was against every form of violence—war (we weren't in one at the time), racial floggings, fist fights between children (always throw something in for the kids), cock fights (there hadn't been one within a hundred miles of Granny White for thirty years) and of course, destruction of private property. All the rest was lagniappe, a redundancy heard by no one. Everyone knew that the sermon was directed at union violence. And everyone approved.

Next morning he called to compare notes. After I accused him again of hypocrisy, dishonesty and moral inconsistency, he asked me if I wanted to go down to Oakville with him that night, the scene of the strike. Of course I did.

There was a giant Labor Day rally of all the strikers and their families. The country high school auditorium was filled beyond capacity. Thad was introduced as a courageous prophet, long known as a fearless friend of organized labor, his body bearing the scars of battle. As I wondered about the scars, he proceeded to preach a sermon the delivery of which would have made Billy Sunday blush with envy. And the words he spoke would have convinced Diogenes to blow out his lamp. Taking his text from Exodus 14, over and over again he pounded home his point, comparing Moses' looking back to see the Egyptians lying dead on the seashore to contemporary labor leaders' looking back at the sinister mill owners, lying rotting on a sea of decadence and injustice. Pharaoh became Robert Taft, the Israelites were the rank and file of working people, and Moses was the president of the State Labor Council. He was so convincing that it was reported by one of the organizers that two company "spies" sent from the scab ranks had expressed keen interest in joining the union. At the end of his homiletical excursion, he exorcised the demons from the ranks of management, then lapsed into a long and pious prayer that God forgive them all for they did not know what they did.

When we left neither of us spoke for twenty miles. He insisted that I drive while he sat on the back seat of his Chrysler blowing gales of smoke over my shoulder from a cigar he had fished from a glass container looking like a test tube. "Willie," he bellowed above the noise of the motor, "Do you know what the church of Jesus Christ is?" I said I sort of thought I did. "Well, I'm going to tell you anyway. The Church is one cat in one ditch and one

nobody-of-a-son-of-a-bitch trying to pull him out." When I acknowledged that I had no serious disagreement with that, he continued.

"Yesterday was to pay the rent for tonight. If your integrity was giving you trouble, well then maybe your sermon did something for it. But I don't have any trouble with my integrity 'cause I ain't got none. And yours is probably an idol. I didn't push anybody in the ditch with my little sermonette yesterday. And I didn't pull anybody out. Everybody broke even. But tonight!!"

He slapped the back of the seat with one hand and knocked my cap into the windshield with the other. "But tonight!! Man, the ditch was full." By now he was screaming at the top of his voice. "The ditch was full! And I sat 'em on *my* ass and took them to town!" He waited for me to respond. When I didn't he started again, this time in a much lower and slower tone. "And if you don't believe it was *my* ass, then just wait til my people find out I was down there and you'll see whose ass it's going to be." He began to laugh and make funny noises in his throat, beating both knees with both his fists until it seemed one or the other would break. Stopping this, he reached in his pocket and dug out a little bottle of pills, swallowed two of them dry. Then he pulled a bottle of Mogen David wine from under the seat, took several long and noisy gulps, finally gargling his throat with the last swallow. Feigning drunkenness he slurred, "Man, if I didn't have milltowns and Mogen David to prop up Jesus Christ, I never would make it."

Again there were miles of silence. He was down. Finally he reached over the seat into the glove compartment for his harmonicas, the tiny one for his nostril and the larger chromatic one to be played in the usual way. Beginning with "Amazing Grace," he played us on into Granny White, stopping only once to say, "Yea, Wee Willie, the Church is one cat in one ditch, and nobody-of-a-son-of-a-bitch to pull him out."

Despite his seemingly simplistic definition of the Church, the study of the church history was an obsession with him. He knew the dates and outcome of every council from the beginning, the issues of every controversy, the reasons for every split, the ground of every new denomination. And sometimes he would speak nostalgically and even sympathetically of "the old whore." And on occasion he would vow to restore her to some imagined day of purity and glory. But generally his ambivalence listed in the direction of hostility and revenge.

He came one day with a grandiose scheme for church renewal. It was complete with charts, budget, timetables, and a written foundation proposal. "Willie, what's the biggest wasted manpower resource in the world?" I said I didn't know. "Well, I'm going to tell you. The greatest wasted manpower resource in the world is preachers." He explained at some length that as a professional group we were better educated, more sensitive to human needs, had more insights into what the world is all about, were better

Photo by Jim Thompson

country. Christianity ain't! But religion is. And as soon as the news hits that any preacher who wants out of his cage has a job waiting for him, security for his family, and a chance to really *be* the Church, man! They'll jump out like martins to their gourds. I'll empty two-thirds of the pulpits in a month."

"And then what, Thad?"

"And then what? You stupid fool! Then we'll have some ministers abroad in the land. Folks making a living because they have to and doing what they are called to do because they want to. And then those dead souls who have been sitting in those rich pews for fifty years with their mascots minding their altar fires and tea parties will have to start asking some questions. Then you'll see some church renewal. Then you'll hear some folks singing the Psalms for the first time in their lives. Then you'll see some idiot church bureaucrats from Nashville and Chicago and Atlanta and New York and wherever they hang their fat hats beating their ecclesiastical swords into plowshares if they have any degree of humanity left in their bones—which most of them don't—and then you'll see Jesus Christ get a fair shake in this world for the first time in a long while. That's 'and then what!' "

There was the usual long silence when one of us came out with something the other thought too far out to merit discussion. And as usual, it was he who broke it.

"There's only one thing wrong with being a mascot. Just one little inconvenience. They keep you on a leash."

organizers, and a lot of other things I don't remember that we were supposed to be.

"And the world thinks we are a bunch of eunuchs. They tried to make us eunuchs. But they didn't pull it off. At least not with most of us. We have something to offer this world, but we'll never be able to do it as long as we're in this box. Now, here's what I'm gonna do."

And then he outlined the most detailed scheme of how he was going to renew the Church and at the same time make it possible for preachers to be ministers to the world. First he would hire a staff which for two years would go to industry, agencies, business, and everybody who employed people. He would convince them that the biggest single wasted manpower resource was waiting at their doorsteps. Then he would get a commitment from them as to how many they would hire and in what capacity and at what starting salary. All this would be filed away until he had seventy-five thousand jobs available for preachers. All this would be done in secret.

When that job was complete he would hold a press conference with the announcement that he had the biggest religious story since Wittenburg. "It'll get the coverage. Don't worry about that. Religion is big news in this

"Man, it's got the Armageddon idea beat all to hell." And then another long period with only the sound of his foot and mine tapping out a brotherly cadence upon the ground.

"Naw, Wee Willie, you're right. Yea, you're right. It wouldn't work. As long as they're rich, they'll get the technicians. It's just too good a deal for a fellow to give up. Aw, we'd empty some pulpits. But they would see it as the providence of God, getting rid of the uncommitted riff-raff. They would turn the whole damn thing right around on us and rip out our emerods. Yea, *they* would call it church renewal—getting rid of all the false prophets in their midst. Man, ain't it a bitch!" I allowed as how it was and we went on to something else. But after awhile he came back to it. But not for long. "You know, Wee Willie, I don't hate anybody. 'Cause the Bible says it's a sin to hate. But there are some folks I hope dies of cancer of the tonsils." Thad had a way of putting things.

It wasn't long after that that he showed up at the door one morning too early for anybody to be stirring. In fact, it wasn't even four o'clock. Sometimes he would do that if he wanted to harangue me into going hunting with him. But it was clear that he wasn't dressed for hunting. It was Monday morning and he still had on his preaching suit, a garment of which he always divested himself as soon as he reached the parsonage. There was a sort of confused look in his eyes, and when I beckoned him inside he didn't move. Usually he walked in without even a knock. He was whimpering softly, like a small baby coming off a crying trip. I was so baffled and frightened that I joined him outside in my underwear, not even noticing the cold. As I did he turned and buried his face in the crook of his arm, leaning forward into a giant sweet gum tree. His whimpering became loud, uncontrollable sobs. I had never seen him cry before and didn't know what to do. (Women can cry together but men have not yet attained that freedom.) I slipped my arm around his waist and he turned quickly around, my shoulder replacing the tree. He kept muttering something I couldn't understand and his tears were not quick in stopping. His body shook and trembled. But then suddenly he stopped, placed one thumb and then the other against each nostril and blew his nose, kicked the ground lightly over the droppings. We went inside.

Now he was well composed, steady and seemingly calm. "Willie, I'm quitting." "Quitting what?" "Quitting it all. I'm tired. I'm tired of lying. I'm tired of being a whore. I just want to be a human being. I'm tired, brother. And I'm sick."

The courses in Pastoral Psychology, Counseling and all that had not been among my best or my favorites. But it took no Menninger to know that he was, for a fact, sick. He slumped down in a big arm chair and began to roll out a self-analysis—the things one new to the couch might think it necessary to blurt out in his first session. Conversion at an early age, growing up in a round of revival meetings, church camps, "surrendering to preach" (he always said when one *decided* to preach under a modern-day steeple, he was for a fact surrendering) at the age of twelve under the urging of a fast-talking, high-powered return missionary, life with father, life with mother, life with brother and no sisters—all the things I suppose one talks about to his therapist. But I was not a therapist. I had no way of evaluating what he was saying, only the good sense to bring him coffee.

It was a long day. There was the secret call to a good mutual friend, a parishioner of his who was a doctor in Granny White. There was the doctor's visit to Thad's wife and their secret call to an analyst in New Orleans and finally their arrival to take my friend, brother and mentor away.

But there was no problem. He was more than willing to go. He helped with the quick decisions which had to be made. He agreed that he was having what they call a real, old-fashioned nervous breakdown. And he knew that it would take some time and a lot of money to get over it.

Guns, camping equipment, insurance policies, a piece of retirement land, furniture, the big Chrysler—all of it would be turned into enough money to make the move and begin paying the doctor. (A bit of the old Thad returned as he grinned with devilish delight when he was told that the analyst was a woman.) The doctor friend would resign for him on Wednesday night at the Church's business meeting, with dignity and in good taste. He would ask for six months full salary for Thad.

At six that evening they drove away, Thad crying softly in the back seat as he said good-bye, the strong wife at the wheel, the doctor at his professional best.

It was a long time before I saw him again. I heard that he and his family moved in with his mother, that he was in a hospital for three weeks, and then settled in for two years of unemployment and a complete analysis.

When he surfaced again it was as chaplain of a large metropolitan hospital. I saw him by accident while visiting a relative. It was as if we had been together the day before. "This is it, Willie. Yea, man, this is where it's at. I've found it and I've found myself. Ain't it a bitch. I'm a counselor, a natural born counselor. That's what I am and always was. Tell the boys old Thad is back on the yard." And there was no doubt that he was back, and higher than ever.

Not only was he back on the yard, he was back in the fields, the swamps, the forest, wherever there was game to be stalked and killed. Nothing got him as excited as hunting or just talking about hunting. "Yea, Wee Willie, I'm a killer. A born killer. 'Course, everybody is a killer. Me, I just kill animals. Not people."

On one occasion one of our friends was in his office when he was about to leave on one of his island safaris with two of his rich planter friends. Everyone was dressed in camouflaged denims, rubber boots, wide gun belts around their shoulders and waists, each one trying to look the most like Ernest Hemingway, or Humphrey Bogart in *African Queen*. Thad was in complete charge, telling the funniest jokes, the biggest lies, and getting all the laughs. Going down in the elevator Thad was still talking, still entertaining in anxious preparation and anticipation of the hunt. An elderly black man was sitting in a wheel chair. A young, well dressed, collegiate looking black man was standing behind the chair. Thad noticed the pair and looked down at the old man. "Well, Uncle, so you're going home today. I know you'll be mighty proud to get home."

The old man grunted and nodded in the affirmative. The young man pounced as if he had been waiting since 17 May 1954, for this moment. Feigning a dialect which obviously came hard for him, he moved a bit closer to Thad in the elevator.

"He yo uncle? Why, he my uncle, too. That done make me an you cuzzins." Then, looking around the elevator, he addressed everyone there. "Hey, everybody. I wants y'all to meet my cuzzin, Chaplain Garner. What you know 'bout dat! Me an' the Chaplain cuzzins. Ain't dat sumpin'!"

The warts and moles on Thad's nose and face seemed almost to disappear against the redness of his skin. The laughter of his two friends was uncontrollable. Thad made a feeble comeback by patting the old man's shoulder and telling him he hoped he wouldn't get sick again for a long time. The old man had not changed expressions and again nodded in the affirmative. As they left the elevator, the young man was guffawing like Gildersleeve, slapping his thigh in hambone fashion, stomping a light buck and wing before rolling his own Uncle down the hall.

Out of sight, Thad was even more humiliated. He knew better than to call the old man "Uncle," but he knew better still than to try to explain it in the presence of his rich planter friends. As they left for cigarettes our friend said, "Looks like somebody in one family or the other has been messing around."

"That smart aleck son-of-a-bitch. After all I've done for the Negroes. He knows who I am and what I stand for. What did he have to do that for?"

"Because you called a black man, 'Uncle,' Thad."

Will Campbell

Photo by Al Clayton

"Well, hell. I call *all* old men 'Uncle.' "

"Naw, Thad, you call all old *black* men, 'Uncle,' in the presence of rich white folks who take you on all expense paid hunting trips."

"Well, he's still a smart aleck son-of-a-bitch."

Then never to be outdone, he started to laugh and turned the whole incident into one more funny and entertaining story, kidding the friend about his knee-jerk liberal embarrassment, adding it to his vast repertoire.

He stayed four years as a counselor. He was too active politically for the hospital board, and serious disillusionment had set in quite early in this phase of his institutional journey.

The next time I saw him, he was some kind of a college administrator. He had just received a letter from his seminary informing him that his Bachelor of Divinity degree could be traded in for a Master of Divinity degree with no additional work. He was highly indignant. "Now that's their contribution to the social crisis. A stupid war going on, prisons running over with our brothers and sisters, millions of people starving to death, black people no better off than they ever were, a nut in the White House and their response to the Gospel is to rename a crock-of-shit diploma." Suddenly all institutions of theological learning were a giant punching bag and he danced and sparred around, jabbing all over like he used to do as a boxer. He held the letter in his hand, all crumpled up in a tiny wad. Students stole quick glances at us as they went to and from classes.

He began to laugh. "Willie, we got took. You know that! They never should have called our degree Bachelor of Divinity. It should have been a Bachelor of Sophistication. They took our country asses up there and filled us up with New England culture, sent us back playing Bach Fugues on hundred thousand dollar pipe organs, smoking calabash pipes, wearing tweed caps and white bucks. Man they did it to us. They gave us the treatment." He began to make jokes about the way you could tell where a professor had done his graduate studies by his campus manner. "Now if he went to Edinburgh he always wore a tweed jacket, complete with coat of arms. And smoked a big pipe and had a yachting cap or braided tam. If he rode a three-speed Raleigh bicycle to school, you could bet he was an Oxford or Cambridge man. He generally wore a tweed cap, too. And carried his books around in a sack with a neck strap on it. If he studied in Germany he had returned with a Volkswagen. That was before *everybody* drove Volkswagens. And they all, no matter where they went, would eat with the fork in the left hand, pushing their food onto the upside-down fork with the knife. And sometimes they would forget and drive on the left side of the road. Man, what a crock." He began to rave again. "Willie, the whole screwed-up world is going to hell in a bucket and this is their commentary. Jesus Christ! Where's your nervous breakdown?"

I said I was just waiting around.

Billy Graham: Superstar

by Bob Arnold

Back at the turn of the century, when hundreds of itinerant preachers worked "the sawdust trail" to standing-room only crowds, evangelism meant miraculous healings and mass conversions in tent-meetings. Hell-fire and brimstone oratory poured forth from an army of men and women mobilized to beat the devil. As a result of their insatiable appetite for publicity, evangelists soon acquired a reputation as Bible-thumping, hysteria-prone, super salesmen for God.

Many years have passed, and the number of communities able to point to a successful tent-meeting in recent memory is small indeed and getting smaller. But the image has prevailed. Until recently. One man, and a Southerner at that, has done more than any other single individual or organization to recast that image in a form more acceptable to modern American culture. Though firmly rooted in the hell-fire and damnation school of Southern fundamentalism, William Franklin (Billy) Graham, Jr. has exchanged the shirtsleeves and histrionics of the "Hot Gospeler" for the tailored business suit and toned-down eloquence of a religious moderate and political conservative.

Yet Billy Graham has hardly renounced his heritage. In fact, the organizational techniques and sophisticated public relations methods employed by Graham and the association that bears his name (The Billy Graham Evangelistic Association) stand as proof of the huge debt which he owes to the rich legacy of the evangelists and evangelism of an earlier age.

Mass revivalism on a national and international scale was a highly developed exercise by the time Graham had spiritually come of age. Even before he was born, Reuben A. Torrey, successor to noted evangelist D. L. Moody, had successfully concluded a four-year campaign which packed the largest public facilities available in China, Australia, India, and the British Isles, and netted 102,000 converts to Christianity in the process.

One of the most significant features of Torrey's approach was his adroit use of community leaders. In each of the cities targeted for a crusade, the evangelist established "executive committees" of socially prominent laymen. The committees raised money for the evangelistic campaign and used the status of their members to gain free coverage from the press and enthusiastic endorsements from sympathetic pulpits.

In Chicago, Henry P. Crowell, president of the Quaker Oats Company and a trustee of the Moody Bible Institute, organized The Layman's Evangelistic Council to lead the Torrey crusade. At the top of the stationery used by the committee, Crowell had printed the explanatory note, "A Businessman's Movement." The Council had charge of everything connected with the crusade, save the actual delivery of the sermon. Graham learned from later revivalists that a full-time staff was more dependable, but he still relies heavily on wealthy, powerful businessman to provide the financial and moral support so necessary to his crusades. As we shall see, under Graham evangelism continues to be "a businessman's movement."

Eventually, Torrey became concerned about the growing commercialization of the crusades; Charles Alexander, his soloist and chorister, was making a mint from sales of his songbooks (selling songbooks, records, and books by Billy Graham continues to be a regular feature of his crusades) and the different approaches to finances led to the end of the Torrey/Alexander team in 1908. Alexander immediately joined John Wilbur Chapman and the Chapman Simultaneous Evangelistic Campaign.

Chapman spent ten years mastering the technique and enjoyed varying degrees of success. But soon Chapman's

Bob Arnold is on the editorial staff
of *Southern Exposure*.

Photo by Carter Tomassi

crusade no longer drew the large crowds or prestigious invitations. A new star had appeared on the horizon, young and more dynamic than any who had gone before him, the man whose name was to dominate evangelism for the next fifteen years—Billy Sunday.

Sunday's style was remarkably similar to Billy Graham's early "windmill preaching." Sunday would run up and down the stage, telling Bible stories in popular language with a hoarse, rasping voice, challenging members of his largely lower-middle-class audience to "be a true patriot" or a "manly man" and make a decision for Christ.

And like Graham, Sunday tried to keep the emotional pitch of his audience at a manageable level. He discouraged people from yelling even simple "Hallelujahs" or "Amens" and instructed his ushers to remove those who insisted on continuing these relatively mild emotional indulgences. Sunday was evangelism's top showman and he didn't want any competition—not even from his own audience.

At the heart of Sunday's revival corporation was the Sunday Party, a corps of more than twenty experts, each of whom specialized in some aspect of revivalism. The members of this Party were called directors, and most of them had assistants. Many of these directors and assistants were in charge of organizing delegations from various constituencies in the community and bringing them to the crusade. Sunday's staff and volunteer canvassers would grant blocks of reserved seats for any group that requested them in advance, and the staff made sure there were plenty of requests. Every night of the crusade there would be as many as fifty delegations on hand, some as large as 3,000. Homer A. Rodeheaver, Sunday's chorister, would warmly welcome each delegation and would then have them compete against each other during the singing program. By the end of the service, when Sunday appealed to each delegation to step forward, entire delegations often made the trip up the center aisle. The same delegation system is still used very effectively by Billy Graham.

Sunday gradually lost touch with his audience as his attacks against the "decadence" of the Roaring '20s became more irrational and extreme. By the end of his career, Sunday's message had degenerated into pessimistic resignation and a conviction that the Second Coming of Christ was the only hope for the human race. His constituency dwindled, and he was reduced to working one-church revival services in small rural towns like his birthplace of Ames, Iowa.

Anointed to Preach

Graham gave his life to Christ at a revival led by Mordecai Fowler Ham, a fire and brimstone evangelist who had made his reputation in the South during the Depression. Graham's father, a strict Presbyterian, had helped organize the revival on some farmland just outside of Charlotte, N. C., Graham's birthplace.

The story of his conversion is important in understanding the way he structures his services today. In an interview with Myran Blyth in *Family Circle*, she described the incident: "There's a great big sinner in the church tonight!" (said Ham). The boy blushed, ducked behind a woman in a big hat and thought, "Omigosh, my mother must have told him I was coming."[1] At the end of the service, Graham, moved as much by feelings of guilt and shame as by his love for Christ, went forward to give his life to God.

Like Billy Sunday, Graham's conversion experience was fairly calm; not a single tear was shed by the sixteen year old when he went forward that night. And like Sunday, he re-creates his conversion experience at his crusades today, relying on a message that is often riddled with remarks that Graham has consciously chosen to make the *individual* sinner in the audience feel his or her burden so heavily that they must come forward and have it lifted. The atmosphere is solemn, heavy with the "presence of God"; though the emotionalism isn't as theatrical as Billy Sunday's, the effect is just as powerful.

Graham graduated from high school in 1936 with no particular career ambitions. He had seriously considered attending the University of North Carolina, but his mother, a deeply religious woman, had decided that he should go to Bob Jones College in Cleveland, Tennessee (now Bob Jones University in Greenville, South Carolina).

The summer before Graham left for Bob Jones, he joined the summer sales staff of the Fuller Brush Company. His experience selling door-to-door had a tremendous impact on his career. Before that summer, he had considered himself a bit shy with strangers and was uncertain of his speaking abilities. But when he broke all sales records for his area, he found new confidence in his general personality and presence. Many years later, that same sales ability exerted for the Lord's gospel instead of Fuller's brushes, prompted the Sales Executive Club of New York to dub Graham "Salesman of the Year."

Disturbed by the lack of athletic facilities and the constraints upon independent thought and lifestyle, Graham left Bob Jones after only one semester, and transferred to Florida Bible Institute (now Trinity College), where he had the freedom to mature at his own pace with individual guidance and counseling from faculty and staff. He changed from a happy-go-lucky, gangly boy to a young man determined to be "an ambassador for God." And he met evangelicals like Homer Rodeheaver (Sunday's enterprising musician), Gypsy Smith, and W. B. Riley. John Pollack, Graham's official biographer, describes Graham's meeting with these leaders as an anointing:

---

[1]Myrna Blyth, "An Interview with Billy Graham," *Family Circle*, April 1972, p. 72.

"These old stalwarts who had seen the fires die down had one theme: we need a prophet. We need a man to call America back to God."[2] Under new tutelage, Graham began to preach everywhere he could—on street corners, in small churches, or to the stumps and alligators at a nearby swamp. He would often preach seven or eight times in one day, coming home thoroughly exhausted. He pursued his studies seriously, determined to get a firm grounding in the Bible.

The Florida Bible Institute was a small school and, in his new passion for knowledge, Graham soon exhausted its resources. Consequently, when he was offered a free year's room, board and tuition at Wheaton College in Illinois, he decided to move north. But before leaving the South, he became, with his parents' approval, an ordained Southern Baptist minister.

Wheaton and the Bells was "that any minister who was a strong evangelical should focus his vision on the entire horizon of American Christianity." It was 1943, the year Youth for Christ International was founded. Graham had abandoned doctrinistic fundamentalism, but still retained his earlier style.

He plunged into his evangelistic career with the same energy and dedication he showed his studies. Torrey M. Johnson, another Wheaton graduate, gave his popular Chicago radio ministry, "Songs in the Night," to Graham and his Village Church. Graham convinced George Beverly Shea, a well-known Christian soloist and broadcaster, to assist him and the show soon became popular enough to pay for itself.

At the invitation of George M. Wilson (now executive vice-president of the BGEA), Graham began to work with

Photo by David Massey

During his stay at Wheaton, Graham met Ruth Bell (daughter of Dr. Nelson Bell), who was to have a moderating influence on Graham's religious beliefs. As Pollack notes, "Ruth and her family, loyal Presbyterians, eased Billy Graham from his unspoken conviction that a vigorous Scriptural faith could not dwell within the great denominations." Graham's most important lesson from

the Youth for Christ movement. For three years, he gained valuable experience as field representative for Youth for Christ, organizing and speaking to rallies rang-

[2]John Pollock, *Billy Graham, the Authorized Biography* (New York: McGraw-Hill, 1966), p. 16.

ing from 3,000 to 5,000, traveling to Europe, and meeting the leaders of the National Evangelistic Association, which strongly supported Youth for Christ.

Then, W. B. Riley, a frequent visitor to Florida Bible Institute, asked Graham to accept the presidency of Minneapolis-based Northwestern Bible School. Riley had found his prophet. Graham had reservations about becoming associated with the orthodox fundamentalist but took the offer anyway. However, Graham rarely spent his energy exercising the presidential duties. He left the school in the hands of George Wilson and others while he continued to devote most of his time to evangelism.

In spite of all this activity, Graham still didn't have a regional following, much less a national audience. He had long thought of himself as a poorly-educated Southerner, lacking poise and sophistication, and felt that this placed definite limits on the potential effectiveness of his ministry. At times, he seemed almost resigned to the mediocrity seemingly imposed by his "indifferent background." But, after his 1949 Los Angeles crusade, he never had to think about that again.

The Big Crusade

The Los Angeles Crusade had run for three weeks and though it was time to fold the tent, many of the staff protested, citing the rising attendance and interest. Graham decided to wait for a "sign" from God, a "fleece" that would convince him that it was God's will that the tent revival continue. The sign came from Stuart Hamblen, a famous singing cowboy, but it would be hard to call it a miracle.

Graham met Hamblen before the revival started at a meeting of the Hollywood Christian Group. Graham was attracted to Hamblen and because Graham was a Southerner, Hamblen took a liking to the earnest young evangelist, inviting him to appear on his radio show, and encouraging people to attend the crusade, saying, "I'll be there, too."

Hamblen attended with regularity, but soon began to feel defensive about the content of Graham's sermon. Hamblen believed the evangelist's sermon, his standard fare about the sinner in disguise, was aimed straight at him. At the last night of the crusade, as Graham said, "There is a person here tonight who is a phony," Hamblen shook his fist at his erstwhile friend, and stalked out of the tent. But the power of Graham's method was clearly evident in the events which followed. In a sudden reversal, the singing cowboy called Graham at two o'clock the next morning and came over to his apartment. By five o'clock, Hamblen had given his life to Christ.

The effect was sensational. Hamblen told his radio audience that he had given up smoking, drinking, and horse racing, that he had given Christ control of his life, and that at the invitation he was going to "hit the sawdust trail."

Jim Vaus, a high ranking accomplice of underworld czar Mickey Cohen heard Hamblen on the radio and decided to stop by the tent and see just who this Graham fellow was. Vaus accepted the invitation the first time he attended, providing Graham with more free publicity.

Louis Zamperini, a 1936 Olympic star who had since become a penniless, heavy drinker, attended the revival at the request of his Christian wife and went forward at the invitation.

In addition to individual guilt, Graham preached a message that took advantage of the Cold War sentiment in his California audience: "Russia has now exploded an atom bomb. Do you know the area that is marked out for the enemy's first atomic bomb? New York! Secondly, Chicago; and thirdly, the city of Los Angeles. Do you know that the Fifth Columnists, called Communists, are more rampant in Los Angeles than any other city in America? We need a revival."

William Randolph Hearst heard about the famous converts and Graham's warnings and sent a telegram to the editors of all Hearst newspapers ordering them to "Puff Graham." Henry Luce, the publisher of *Time*, *Life*, and *Fortune*, was so impressed with the message, according to a Graham aid, that he "pledged the cooperation of his magazines to support subsequent Graham campaigns in other cities." The Graham crusade was becoming a national media phenomenon.

The next five years were a dynamic period for the North Carolina native. He started his Hour of Decision radio program, founded the Billy Graham Evangelistic Association, held successful tours all over the country and was publicly seen and photographed with some of the most famous people in the United States. The lesson of Los Angeles had not been lost.

But Graham still hadn't matured as an evangelist. Stanley High, another biographer, described his early preaching style as "pretty much in the tradition of the 'Hot Gospeler.' His voice was strident. He inclined to rant. The same sound effects in politics would, in most places, be called demagoguery."

Indeed, Graham's sermons of that period often smacked strongly of demagoguery. In a 1953 radio sermon on "Labor, Christ, and the Cross," he said, in an obvious reference to McCarthy, "I thank God for men who in the force of public denouncement and ridicule go loyally on in their work of exposing the pinks, the lavenders, and the reds who have sought refuge beneath the wings of the American Eagle and from that vantage point try in every subtle, undercover way to bring comfort and help to the greatest enemy we have ever known— Communism."

Willis G. Haymaker, an advance man for Gypsy Smith, Bob Jones and Billy Sunday, had been with the Team since 1950 and introduced many changes in the Team operations. He organized prayer meetings before crusades, coordinated publicity, and taught the basic facts of organization.

According to William McLoughlin, author of an extensive study of revivalism, Graham's image "... shifted from the Hollywoodish, flamboyant revivalist in the direction of the conservative, but fervent, Protestant minister. His crusade atmosphere became less like that of a circus and more like that of a cathedral. He ... directed his associates to keep up with the best means of advertising, office efficiency, promotion, small group evangelism, and follow-up."

The real test of the Team's growing organizational expertise came in New York in 1957. In the course of the three and one-half month crusade, 61,148 inquirers came forward from an audience of 2,397,000. Follow-up work, guiding and directing people who have decided to follow Christ, became unmanageable. The Team acquired the services of former Air Force Colonel Bob Root, who eventually organized the follow-up procedure.

The success of the New York crusade, highly visible in the American media fish bowl, firmly entrenched Graham as a national religious figure and celebrity, establishing him as the friend of politicians, religious luminaries, sports stars, etc. After the New York success, the challenge was to expand and deepen his organization and public support.

The Medium of the Message

Crusades, the source of Graham's support and publicity, are masterpieces in the application of the latest techniques in public relations and organization.

Once Graham decides to accept a city's invitation to conduct a crusade (usually one to two years before the projected opening date), an advance group goes to the city and begins to mobilize every Protestant church willing to support the effort. An executive committee is established (a la Sunday) and ministers of the participating churches are appointed to a variety of committees.

In his early career, Graham, like Sunday, made sure a sum large enough to cover costs was pledged by private subscription as a guarantee should offerings during the crusade fail to bring in the needed support. Crusade expenses have since soared to over $1 million and now Graham supplements local offerings with television and radio appeals and direct mail solicitations.

Graham has pioneered work in follow-up of inquiries, publicity and financing—the three most controversial aspects of mass evangelism. Follow-up is done by a group of young Bible school students called the Navigators who work in a city up to six months after the crusade has ended, trying to connect "inquirers" with a local church.

Publicity has been developed to the highest possible degree, using every conceivable means. Thousands of volunteers conduct door-to-door canvassing operations, mobilizing the local church community (and involving them in the success of the crusade) and spreading the word that Billy Graham is coming to town. And when he broadcasts over television, he blacks out the local area to insure high attendance.

After successful crusades, public explanation for success is that the Spirit of the Lord, working through Graham, his Team, and the local churches provided the inspiration to reach new converts and backsliding Christians. Any reference to the importance of a hightly efficient organization is saved for private interviews. But God has never taken any of the blame for those crusades which fell short of their goal.

In kind, Graham's entire crusade apparatus rivals that of any multinational corporation.

The Hour of Decision, Graham's weekly radio program, started in 1950 at the suggestion of Fred Dienert and Walter Bennett of the Walter Bennett Advertising Company. Prompted by a $2,000 gift from two Texas friends, Graham decided to make the additional $23,000 he needed to begin broadcasting a "fleece" for his Portland crusade, stipulating that the $23,000 had to be raised before midnight. Graham took the regular offering, not mentioning the radio program; after the money had been collected, Graham told the audience he needed $25,000, inviting those that wished to contribute to meet him in the office at the end of the service. The draw of meeting Graham personally probably had as much to do with the long line as the appeal to higher Christian service. At the end of the night, Graham had $23,500, including the $2,000 from the sympathetic Texans. When he returned from the crusade, he found $1,500 in pledges waiting at the hotel from people unable to stand in line, giving Graham the $25,000 and a new radio ministry.

Due to income tax laws, Grady Wilson couldn't put the money in the bank under his name or the Billy Graham Radio Fund. George Wilson (no relation) flew from Minneapolis with articles of incorporation for a non-profit Evangelistic Association that he had drawn up over a year ago, foreseeing the need for such an organization. Billy and Ruth Graham, Grady Wilson, Cliff Barrow, and George Wilson signed the papers to create the Billy Graham Evangelistic Association (BGEA). Graham asked for a radio ministry and got an institution, too.

Today the Hour of Decision is aired by over 900 stations around the world (including the one owned by the BGEA in Honolulu, Hawaii).

The Good Word is also spread through Graham's "My Answer" syndicated newspaper column appearing in 200 dailies, through purchased television broadcasts of the crusades, and through the distribution of films produced by the BGEA World Wide Pictures based in Burbank, California.

The monthly magazine of the BGEA, "Decision," now has a circulation of 5,000,000 (at $2/year)[3], a sizeable increase from the initial run of 253,000 in 1960. "Deci-

---

[3]Lois and Bob Blewett, *Twenty Years Under God* (Minneapolis: World Wide Publications, 1970), p. 127; and from an interview with Don Bailey, executive assistant with the Billy Graham Evangelistic Association (Atlanta office), September 1976.

sion" promotes Graham's theology, runs testimonies of the saving grace of Jesus Christ, solicits funds, sells books, and reports on the activities of Graham and the associate evangelists.

Books, phonograph records, and radio-sermon leaflets are distributed by the Grason Company, a taxable business started in 1950. The BGEA cannot legally distribute these materials, but Grason donates its profits to the Association.

Finally, there are the crusades. Graham has reached approximately eighty million people through his revivals where he peddles materials like the "Authorized and Authentic Biography of Billy Graham," "Billy Graham Songbook," and the thirteen books he has authored.

The BGEA employs over 300 people worldwide with headquarters in Minneapolis and offices in Paris, London, Hong Kong, Sidney, Winnipeg, and Atlanta. The staff has grown to seven associate ministers and five full-time musicians. The BGEA has an annual income of $14 million controlled by Graham and a 25-member board of directors that meets four times a year (the seven person executive committee meets once every six weeks). No director receives monetary compensation. The BGEA would not divulge the names of the people on the board saying "it might create too much of a hassle for the directors to have their names made public."[4]

The proceeds from all the "ministries" provide the bulk of the income for the Association, the rest coming from direct mail solicitation and anonymous gifts. The Association also uses this income to pay Graham's $25,000 salary. He has always been sensitive to criticism of personal profit from preaching the gospel; consequently, he has let it be known that "I personally do not receive any money, honorarium or stipend for any of my appearances anywhere in the world. My annual income is solely from a salary paid by our corporation in Minneapolis and by royalties from my books." The royalties are no small sum: *Secret of Happiness* (1955) has sold 906,357 copies; *World Aflame* (1967) 1,027,976, with an additional special run of over 600,000."[5] Graham keeps a percentage of the royalties and donates the rest to the Association and other religious organizations.

He can well afford to be benevolent. The Association pays all his travel expenses; he receives free food and lodging at Hilton hotels; he often receives chauffeured cars from Ford Motor Co., and he has received gifts ranging from a jeep to a new home in the mountains of North Carolina.

Apparently the size of the organization and the comfortable affluence Graham has attained hasn't reduced his personal involvement or interest in the operation of the Association. "Billy Graham receives daily reports by telephone. Each month he runs his eye down the list of checks, large and small, paid out from every office, and asks for the detail of any he can't understand."[6]

Politics and the Preacher

Carl McIntire is more rabidly anticommunist, Bob Jones more harshly critical of liberal ministers, and Garner Ted Armstrong more apocalyptic, but Billy Graham is more influential and his politics are, essentially, as conservative as the other gentlemen above.

The recurring theme in Graham's political statements is "Yes, do good works, but winning souls to Christ is more important." John Pollock says Graham is "more convinced than ever before '. . . that we must change men before we can change society. . . . The task of the evangelist is not merely to reform but to stimulate conversion, for conversion puts man in positions where God can do for him, and through him, what he is incapable of doing himself'."[7] Graham restated the same theme in *World Aflame*: "If the church went back to its main task of preaching the Gospel and getting people converted to Christ, it would have far more impact on the structure of the nation."[8]

Photo by Dan Dudenbostel

An example of this logic comes from *Billy Graham Speaks*: "Reno can give you a quick divorce, but Christ can give you a quick transformation in your home. The tempers that have flared, the irritations that are evident, the unfaithfulness that is suspected, the monotony and

---

[4] Interview with Don Bailey.
[5] Blewett, *Twenty Years Under God*, p. 127.
[6] Pollock, *Billy Graham*, pp. 243-44.
[7] Ibid., p. 222.
[8] Ibid.

boredom of existence without love can be changed and transformed in the twinkling of an eye by faith in Jesus Christ."[9]

This optimism barely surpasses his patriotism; Graham believes that "America is the key nation of the world. We were created for a spiritual mission among nations. . . . America is truly the last bulwark of Christian civilization. If America fails, Western culture will disintegrate." He strikes the same note on a personal level in his sermons: "If you would be a true patriot, then become a Christian: If you would become a loyal American, then become a loyal Christian."[10]

Three of the most influential social movements in the past twenty-five years have been the civil rights, antiwar, and women's movements. The first two shook the conscience, structure, and politics of the nation and the third is still being hotly debated. Graham has definite opinions on all three.

In the early and mid-50s Graham took a moral stand towards the issue of integration in his crusades. By 1953, he would not allow segregated seating, even in the South, opening himself to attacks by more close-minded evangelicals. He changed the site of the 1954 Columbia, South Carolina, crusade from the segregated statehouse grounds to federal property to have an integrated rally. Ten years later, however, he was on the conservative end of the civil rights question. He deplored boycotts, marches, and protests stating "the position he has maintained consistently: conciliate, and strike at the root of the problem, which is basically spiritual."[11] Graham seems incapable of understanding the need for struggle outside of that required to become a better Christian and resist the temptations of Satan.

Graham's conviction that communism is the work of the Devil laid the foundation for his unequivocal support for the war. At a 1966 Presidential Prayer Breakfast, Graham made it clear that his Christianity helped his support for the slaughter in Southeast Asia. "There are those who have tried to reduce Christ to the level of a genial and innocuous *appeaser*; but Jesus said: 'You are wrong. I have come as a fire setter and a sword wielder.' He made it clear to them that His coming, far from meaning peace, meant war. . . . Those who hate tyranny and aggression will take sides when little nations suffer terror and aggression from those who seek to take their freedom from them. To preserve some things, love must destroy others." Perhaps this is why John Connally has called Billy Graham "the conscience of the nation."

Since then Graham has made the typical excuses that his stance only reflected the mood of the nation at the time, that he couldn't possibly have known Vietnam would become such a divisive, bitter, embarrassing question among Americans. But that is exactly the point. Graham keeps a wet finger to the wind of the powers that be, only mellowing his position on Vietnam when it was comfortable and acceptable for him to do so. The opportunism and lack of morals he demonstrated on this issue is one of the most graphic examples of the true role Graham plays in our society—legitimizing the war policy and ingratiating himself to its leaders.

On the question of women's rights Graham relies on a literal interpretation of the Bible. God created man and then woman with a definite plan for each. "The biological assignment was basic and simple: Eve was to be the child bearer, and Adam was to be the breadwinner. Of course, there were peripheral functions for each, but these were their fundamental roles, and throughout history there has been very little deviation from the pattern."[12]

He makes it absolutely clear that he does not support the women's movement. "I believe the women's liberation movement is an echo of our overall philosophy of permissiveness." Since Graham doesn't believe the women's movement is constructive, he points to the Bible and its three-part plan for woman in society. "Eve's biological role was to bear children—'in sorrow thou shalt bring forth children' (Genesis 3-16). Her romantic role was to love her husband—'Thy desire shall be to thy husband' (v. 16). Her vocational role was to be second in command—'and he shall rule over thee' (v. 16)." That, says Graham, is true freedom. "God frees us to be what we are created to be—each with a separate identity and purpose, but both sexes one with God. That is true liberation."

Billy Graham is not unmindful of his own special identity and the freedom that comes with courting the rich and famous. The acquisition of wealth is required by salvation because it is a powerful means of benefiting others. Private gain donated to the great crusades can lead one to believe that the exercise of private and personal virtues is the totality of public responsibility.

His roots are in Southern fundamentalism, but he has built upon that foundation a vast smooth-running corporation that adapts to the social and political climate of the American status quo. In so doing, he has gained what his evangelical forebears never did: respectability—and a carefully calculated plan for his own organization's survival.

---

[9]Cort R. Flint, *Billy Graham Speaks* (New York: Grossett and Dunlap, 1966), p. 62.

[10]"Our Bible," sermon distributed by the Billy Graham Evangelistic Association.

[11]Pollock, *Billy Graham*, p. 224.

[12]Billy Graham, "Jesus and the Liberated Woman," *Ladies Home Journal*, December 1970, p. 42.

Black Ministers Speak Out on the Black Church

interviews by Jim Sessions, Sue Thrasher, and Bill Troy

"To Be Prophetic"

To understand the Southern movement for social and political justice, it is necessary to understand the black church. Throughout the civil rights movement of the '50s and '60s, it served as the nurturing institution for the new mass movement. Its structures were used for meetings, freedom schools, voter registration drives, and community centers. Its members were often the foundation upon which local movements were built and sustained.

Nor is it a recent phenomenon. Since the time black people were brought to this country under slavery, the church has been the one institution they have controlled and used as a tool for their own liberation. W. E. B. DuBois, writing in *The Souls of Black Folk* described a

Photo by Robert Ballard

"First Baptist" congregation in Virginia during the post-reconstruction period: "Various organizations met here—the church proper, the sunday school, two or three times insurance societies, women's societies, secret societies, and mass meetings of different kinds. Entertainments, suppers, and lectures are held beside the five or six regular religious services. Considerable sums of money are collected and expended here, employment is disseminated and charity distributed. At the same time, this social, intellectual, and economic centre is a religious centre of great power."

In the following pages, three ministers talk about the vitality of the black religious experience. One theme emerges again and again: that the black religious experience is based on the "totality" of life, the melding of the physical and the spiritual in a way that has forged an institutional expression altogether different than its white counterpart. It has been a place where the political and social needs of the community could find collective expression and where the personal anguish of an earthly existence could find spiritual release, a place where personhood was affirmed rather than denied, where hope and faith in the future found solid expression in the here and now.

"Right Here On Earth"

[We found Rev. James Corder on his tractor at the far end of an Alabama cotton field. It was the first day without rain for quite a while, but anxious as he was to get the earth turned, he graciously spent two hours talking with us about his life in Pickens County.

Rev. Corder pastors four Primitive Baptist churches within a fifty-mile radius of his home near Aliceville, Alabama. Moved by the events of Selma in 1965, he became an active member in the Selma Project, a statewide civil rights organization.

Photo by Bill Troy

Selma, Albany, Jackson, Montgomery, Birmingham, Atlanta, and Nashville were all well known for the drama of the civil rights struggles. Aliceville, Alabama, and numerous other small towns across the region were hardly noticed, and sometimes their very isolation made the struggle much more dangerous.

The most blatant forms of discrimination are no longer as apparent as they once were in Aliceville, Alabama, thanks to Rev. Corder and his organization of sinners. As we left, however, we got the impression that the good Reverend was keeping a watchful eye.]

At the time of the Selma March, it was quite dangerous to organize because Pickens County hadn't had no type of demonstration, and they was doing things that was keeping people from taking a part or standing up talking to anybody that appeared to identify themselves in a civil rights way. Therefore I used strategy. I organized under the name of Rural Farm and Development Council. I let them know that they just had to stand up and take some chances, that some of us might get hurt, but even getting hurt was going to help somebody. And if I was brave enough to stand there and tell them what was necessary to be done, and not begging nobody not to tell it, they ought to be brave enough to be a member of the organization 'cause it was good for everybody.

After I got that organized, I got a group together and we decided that we would group around the city hall of Aliceville. I knew if I could get a group standing to hear what I had to say, I would get the message over to the administrators of the town. Course they all came with billy clubs and shotguns and everything. I let them know that we was tired of the way that the county and the elected officers was taking all taxpayers money and turning all the evil against the black and protecting the white. I pointed out that whenever a big day come, any officer that had any lawful rights at all would be out on the road stopping all the blacks and waving to whites to pass. I said that if they had any reason to be checking, we would be very interested in their checking everybody or nobody. We won't have it no more! And I didn't go into detail to say what would be the results, and really I hadn't figured out what would be the results, but it was just in me to say. There wasn't no fear there.

When we started off, most people that was religious at all was altogether agin it. I had one friend. We're in different fields—when I say fields, I mean different denominations—he's a Missionary and I'm a Primitive. Bue we works together.

The people that belonged to the church were set in their ways—just old religious practices that they got out from under the slave master was all they would accept. The type of activity that went on in the black church was about the type of activity that the slave masters would allow them to practice.

See, church work is like any other kind of work; what people were trained to think was church work, that is all they would accept for church work. But if they don't fight against wrong, who will? And so I started, and we had a church fight. That's one of the biggest fights I believe I had. The deacons at the church would get so mad, they would want to put me out. I just kept approaching it in many ways until I got some to see what I was talking about—that justice has got to come from a person that has justice in him. When a person who is not just, do just, he do something that he didn't aim to do.

And I reached the conclusion that that was one of the chief reasons for Christ setting up a church here on earth—to establish His will, to change the minds of wicked people into righteousness. And it was going to take the preachers to do it, and if he wasn't going to do that, he wasn't a preacher of God, he was the devil's preacher. You know, the devil's got some good preachers, too. Sure! Any man who fights against the cause of God and thinks how to prevent the will of God, he is working for the devil.

I preached that for six or eight years as much or more than I did anything 'cause that was more on my mind than anything. It was more urgently current that I had to show the people. I couldn't show them heaven and couldn't show them the way out of trouble here. I be like the man who was preaching and tore his pants, and he had a habit when he got in his high keys of holding his hands high and pointing to heaven and mentioning to the people about heaven. And a little boy was there and he said he couldn't see heaven for looking at Africa.

*Here is sweetmilk and honey
—cows giving milk, and
bees making honey—why am I
going to wait till heaven to get it
—Rev. James Corder*

What I am saying is, if I couldn't show the people what was right here, I don't believe I could do a good job showing them something that was out of sight. And if I couldn't change them to benefit themselves to do something right here, why point them to heaven? Here is sweetmilk and honey—cows giving milk, and bees making honey—and why am I going to wait till heaven to get it? When God told Moses to lead the people into a land that flowed with milk and honey, he wasn't talking about heaven no-way. He was talking about a land of plenty, and that land is right here on earth. He was leading them out from under their slave master to a land where they would be free and a land that produced.

Finally, the members of my church, they didn't join the organization, but they gave me the privilege of holding the meeting in the church. And I built the organization more out of sinners, people that didn't belong to the church. I had them acting more religious than the people that belonged to the church.

"A Free Platform"

[Rev. Joseph L. Roberts, Jr., is the minister of the historic Ebenezer Baptist Church on Atlanta's Auburn Avenue. It is a symbol of the movement for black equality and of its most powerful, respected, and charismatic leader. Older church members remember holding Dr. Martin Luther King, Jr., on their knee when he was a child. It was in the basement at Ebenezer that he helped form the Southern Christian Leadership Conference (SCLC), and it was here that his body was brought home for the final time in 1968. Today, Ebenezer still serves its local Atlanta congregation, but it has also become a shrine to thousands of tourists who visit each year. It stands now within the new complex of the Martin Luther King, Jr., Center for Social Change.

Joe Roberts is excited by the possibilities and the challenge of his ministry at Ebenezer. He feels that precisely because of its historically prophetic role, the black church can remain the "focal point where political, social, economic, and theological issues can be discussed."]

I graduated from seminary in 1960 when integration was still big. I was the pastor of two integrated churches—trying to help people live together as Christians—and almost denigrating the black experience in so doing, compromising by allowing the church service to be what I had learned in seminary: a modern version of the English Puritan worship of the 17th and 18th century. And then sort of disavowing who I was as a black person.

When Stokely Carmichael and others broke forth—Dr. King did it, but Stokely did it more dramatically because he said we've got to liberate the turf we occupy—that made me wonder what I was doing in a predominantly white denomination. Was I really selling my services to perpetuate a basically racist system, or was I in a ministry with which black people could identify? To be honest, it caught me. It resonated with something that was deep in all of us, and I think we were able to sort of move on from there.

Photo by David Jenkins

When I was pastoring in New Jersey, I was involved in the denominational hierarchy in New York as a volunteer on a number of boards and agencies actively involved in church and race. The cities were going up in smoke; Stokely had given the black power sign in '66, and the National Committee of Black Churchmen had met in New York to sanction the validity of the black experiment. I think the black church, at that point, was trying to put some religious sanction on blacks calling for separate black power—*before* they integrated—believing that it was impossible to integrate an elephant with a mouse. I was in the business of trying to interpret to conservative black congregations why the whole business of black identity was a valid pursuit and how it wasn't antithetical to the Christian gospel.

In 1970, I was called to do Church and Society for the Presbyterian Church, South, and I decided to give it a try. It is a church where one half of one percent of its constituency is black, and I was the highest black bureaucrat; naturally I had the church and race portfolio. I insisted when I came that I have some money to do some social change strategies.

We were right in the sweep of all the stuff that Nixon was talking about when he tried to get the Department of Commerce to push black capitalism. I had some feeling of satisfaction because I was in the train of James Forman (author of the Black Manifesto, demanding reparations from the white church). We were getting white people's money and giving it to black folks. I have some real questions about that now. In the first place, we did not have enough money to make black entrepreneurs successful. But I think the basic tragedy was that we never questioned the assumption of capitalism. We just said we are going to replace white entrepreneurs with black entrepreneurs and never did deal with the moral issue.

I traveled for the church in 16 states; I would be off maybe once or twice a month. A mutual friend introduced me to Dr. King, Sr.; he was getting older, and said, "I need a little help now and then. Can you help me?" I said, "It would be an honor to preach at Ebenezer." And that's how I started. I preached for about a year when I could and just got close to the congregation. One evening he just got up in a church meeting and resigned and told them, "I know who you should choose for your successor," and put my name forward. They unanimously elected me.

I feel it is an honor for me to come here, and then I also feel, not being overly modest, uniquely prepared for the ecumenical thrusts that are needed now. I wouldn't have come here if it were just another local church. I felt this was a chance to give some personification to the ecumenical movement; I mean what difference does it ultimately make—all this noise about denominations? I saw it also as an attempt to speak out on some international issues that are very close to me, involving the violation of human rights in Latin America and Africa in particular. Those two places concern me. I knew here I would be able to have a platform to actually say something and do something.

Because this is a tourist spot, I have the opportunity to make it more than a tourist spot, to heighten the consciousness of a lot of people about the problems of Third World folks, and get them to see how they might affect those problems. We had 1,400,000 tourists last year. From April through October, they came by reservation. I would say easily a third of the congregation are tourists in the summer.

Then, to a very real extent, this place will always be something of a shrine to black people and it is very important for us not to let it die with Dr. King, but to at least make it the place where the issues are looked at and where folks can gather to do something about them.

Now I haven't romanticized the position. I don't plan to lead anybody down the street. I am not Dr. King, and I do not presume to be. I respect him for who he is and realize that he comes along once in a millennium. But there are still a lot of things to be done. Ninety percent of all black Protestants in this country are in Baptist or Methodist churches. The black church still has what the white church has seldom had because it didn't need it—the reputation of being the focal point where political, social, and economic as well as theological issues can be discussed openly. Here I have a free platform. We lay out Angola; we criticize the state legislature for cutting welfare, and with no apologies. In the Presbyterian Church you had to tip softly on some very, very fragile egg shells because some of the folks had the misconception that all welfare folks are lazy and black. But you don't have that here.

I think the black church has been far more political and theological, even when it did not realize it. The spirituals had theological as well as political overtones. "Let us break bread together on our knees." That had to do with when a meeting was going to be held for taking off; the line "when I fall on my knees with my face to the rising sun," meant "in the morning, on the west side of the river is where we are going to take off." The old spiritual "Wade in the Water" had to do with slaves escaping and hitting the water to kill the scent when the dogs came after them.

Always there was this feeling that another message was being carried. What the black preacher was trying to do was deal with the fact that black people had no place where they were called sane, or no place where they had any dignity. I've got women in my congregation who go out five days a week wearing white uniforms, which says they are nobody, but when they dress on Sunday morning and come to Ebenezer, they are dressed to kill, naturally. This is the only place where a nobody can be somebody. It doesn't matter to the people where they work who they are, and the uniform is a sign that they do not belong in that community, that they are only there to serve it. But when they come here, it means something altogether different.

How do you get your dignity? That is what black folks talk about; white folks didn't need to talk about that because, for better or worse, by whatever means necessary, they were able to get some power, and that was power over somebody else. But the struggle of black folks is how to get equality. And that is where *this* church has been very meaningful, from the time King supported the bus boycott and Rosa Parks.

I basically think the white Protestant Southern church serves a constituency that is interested in maintaining the status quo, and therefore is far more guarded and far more ambivalent than the black church. In contrast, the black church is not afraid of being prophetic because it's been on the bottom. In this congregation, people will applaud a strong statement for justice, will break out in a round of applause. If I said the same things in a white church, I would be fired. If I talked about multinational corporations, if I talked about ITT and Chile, if I talked about Brazil and the heinous things going on there and, as I did, call for missionaries to leave because they were really perpetuating a bad system, I would just be out on my ear. That is the real difference; the white congregation is to tied in with the white power structure to be critical of it. The danger for black people is that they are tempted to pick up some of those same values.

...the white Protestant church serves a constituency that is interested in maintaining the status quo. . . . In contrast, the black church is not afraid of being prophetic. . .
—Rev. Joseph Roberts

The black church has always been willing to admit that a person is not only cerebral but visceral. The white church has not. From the Greeks on, the white church has made a bifurcation between mind and body, so that everything that didn't fit into western, rational, logical categories could not be dealt with. So, how do you deal with a feeling? The white church just isn't able to deal with that. The psychiatrist is, and so you get psychiatry and religion as twin ministries. A person goes to a white church and stays for one hour on Sunday morning bleeding inside and then beats it to the analyst that afternoon or all the next week to try to get it together. The black church always was able—sort of in the Hebraic concept—to keep body and mind together. For example, I had one guy who just said one Sunday morning, "In spite of everything that has happened to us, I'm so glad trouble doesn't last always," which is from an old spiritual. There were people who screamed, literally screamed, screamed as an act of jubilation because that was an affirmation of the faith. Now a white preacher would have said, "Rest assured that ultimately in the eschaton, there will be the assurance that the resurrection will be affirmed." You know, I don't know what that does for somebody whose kid got ready to jump off the roof, or spit in their face, or someone who had a fight with his wife. The black church has always been able to identify with the idiom of the people; it's known its people pretty well, and has had to deal with the underside of its people. The white church has always

come, not to hear that stuff, but some religious sanction for what it was.

I do think there is a psychology of poverty and oppression that is pervasive and transcends racial barriers. There has always been a fairly good relationship between poor whites and poor blacks in the South, because they were thrown together. They all lived in the same kind of shanties; they had relationships, albeit covert, on all sorts of dynamic lines. There has always been an attempt on the part of those who were in power to keep those two groups from coming together, to pit them against one another. Wallace plays to a mentality that itself is powerless; its only claim to fame is whiteness, so there must be a tenacious holding on to that in order to say I am better than the only person I see under me, who is black.

I don't see any revolution that was sustained by mass movements. You get to the point where you have got to take advantage of the gains that have been made, and then implement them into a new system. It is much easier when you have a tangible goal to go after and you knock it down. But that is always a means to an end and not an end in and of itself. I am unapologetic about saying that we don't have anything to pull people into—King would not have had. In Memphis, he was trying to take on the economic power in this nation and say that poor folks have to be organized to get what they want. It is the same thing that Caesar Chavez said, and that is the reason Mrs. King supported him; she could see the farmworker's struggle as a follow-through on what her husband was doing in Memphis with the garbage strikers. But he would have had to change tactics.

The '70s are a time when we have to figure out the new Easter egg hunt. When you take kids on an Easter egg hunt, you hide all the eggs. The next Easter, the kids go back to the same spots, but if you're slick, you hide them in a different spot. Well, what this nation does is hide all the eggs, and you learn where they are, and then the next year they are somewhere else. That is what Nixon and Ford have done. OEO money has either been cut out or shifted to HEW. It's no longer Selma, it is Washington. Or it's the state capitol where they do three cuts on welfare recipients! It's any issue that pertains to old folks. That is the new Easter egg hunt. The eggs aren't on the Selma bridge anymore, they are just not there. You can go anywhere you want to in Selma. You can eat at any restaurant. That is irrelevant. That has nothing to do with poor folks who get cut off of medical assistance. That has nothing to do with welfare mothers who get cut.

The point is that you go find the eggs this Easter, and then because history is dynamic, you have got to find out what the new scheme is. You know, they are going to shift it to maintain power, and the job of those folk who have a social conscience is to find out where they are and deal with it everytime it comes up. You know, we are out of Vietnam, so now it is Angola. We're out of Angola, so now it is Rhodesia. But it's the same thing, the exploitation of poor folks in the interests of those that have vested interests in multinational corporations.

I see a high correlation between domestic and international problems, and I don't think America is ever going to be serious about helping poor folks as long as it is pouring any money into Angola. If we can cut the poverty program yet continue high military expenditures, when part of that money might be used in Angola or Rhodesia, that has a direct correlation to black folks. When Roy Innis tries to get black Vietnam veterans to go fight in Angola, that is no longer simply an international issue because I have black Vietnam veterans in this church who do not have work because they are a part of that eight-and-a-half million unemployed. So, that is a very critical, domestic, international issue. I say, "Hell no, you don't go over there and fight black folks. We will feed you first before you start destroying your own people."

I wax warm on these things, because I think they are critical to what the black church is actually doing. If they can continue to subject workers in the Republic of South Africa to low wages, that means that black folks in this country are still in trouble, because those same corporations will refuse to hire people here as long as they can exploit people somewhere else. So, I have got to stop exploitation over there so that the man cannot run away and leave me starving here.

I think the problem with the '60s was that people didn't face the fact, when you get involved with social change you have to deal with failure and death. That is what Kent State taught the white community. You see, white folks didn't believe when they saw the dogs and the horses in Birmingham; but when they shot those kids at Kent State, that revealed a lot. They were then able to see that it was true what black folks were saying, that you cannot just stand up as if there is "freedom of speech" and say you do or do not believe something, because they will get you. They really will. Now, that's enough to throw people off and leave them disillusioned for a long time.

But the whole history of the black experience has been a history of having to deal daily with failure and death, so we didn't get that sure. We didn't have to go into transcendental meditation or anything like that. The very essence of the Christian experience had already incorporated that. See, we didn't have any psychiatrists to go to. We had to deal with death and failure and "I am not a man" and they will shoot you and burn down your house whenever they want. So, I think we could make the transition much more easily than those who had invested too much in the American dream.

White people have always been used to winning. We just don't have a good, practical theology of winning. That's the history of American imperialism. So, how do you deal with the fact that kids get shot at Kent State? That was a mind-blowing thing; that shook me.

When you look at the '60s, we paid the price. The two Kennedys and King are gone. The hope that we all had for this nation—and black people had that hope too when they looked at Kennedy—you really saw that you could get a good guy up there and they would kill him. Somebody would kill him. And that just says, what the hell, why should I care, why should I get involved? What's in it for me other than dying? And it's just better to survive.

Black folks have always known that when you can't eat steak, you eat fatback. Fatback might be working for a full employment bill; fatback might be pushing for national health insurance. Black folks have always been more practical in their politics.

So, I'm trying to pull some things together. This is a great church to be in. It gives me an opportunity to see if I can shape the ways some things are going. I'm excited about what could happen.

"Mind, Body, and Soul"

[Dr. Cecil W. Cone grew up in the small town of Bearden, Arkansas, and started preaching at the tender age of thirteen. He has been a pastor, an administrator, and a professor of theology. He is now the Dean of Turner Theological Seminary in Atlanta, and was recently a candidate for Bishop in the African Methodist Episcopal Church. He is the author of *The Identity Crisis in Black Theology* (AME Press, Nashville) in

Photo by David Massey

which he argues that the point of departure for black theology must be the black religious experience.

We found our conversation with Dr. Cone to be both engaging and disconcerting. He is charismatic and at times overwhelming, with an intellect that is far ranging and probing. He has a sense of play in his thoughts, but is deadly serious in the main points he wishes to make. The following excerpt is only an indication of his provocative analysis of the black religious experience.]

Most people believe there is little distinction between a black Methodist church and a white Methodist church, a black Presbyterian church and a white Presbyterian church. Organizationally, they belong to the same institution, but there is a definite distinction. They approach Christian religion in a different way, and the result is a different phenomenon altogether.

Black Christianity is the only mode of experience in America that is consistent with the revelation of God as expressed in the Exodus event of the Old Testament and the Christ event of the New Testament, which is to say that black Christianity is the *only* Christianity that is Christian. White Christianity is not Christian. It does not grow out of the Old and New Testament concepts of what the Christian religion, or the Christian way of life, is. White Christianity should not be called Christian.

The difference is in the way each looks at life; it has to do with the Greek and Hebraic world views. The tradition of Christianity got messed up when it moved into the Graeco-Roman world. It left behind its Hebraic understanding and approach to life. Instead of approaching God and life in a Hebraic way, the Greek way became dominant.

Black religion has a world view that is closely related to the Hebraic way of looking at life. It also has to do with the African tradition. There is an element of divine understanding and truth that can only come to people who are at the bottom, people who are oppressed, people who cannot look to any earthly reality for their salvation. They become open to the divine revelation in a way that people who can depend on the political order cannot.

When black people were brought to this country, they had no rights and no hope within the structure of society, and they could not free themselves from this predicament. As a result, they were open to God in a way that they could not have been had their approach been Greek and rationalistic. It would have been absurd to talk about hope in a situation where the impact of your whole being is directed against the stone wall of slavery, and not only does it not come crumbling down, it does not even crack. Because of their African understanding of life, black people opened themselves up to a reality that was beyond rationality, and they were therefore able to get an insight into a divine reality even they had not been aware of before. If they thought that slavery was something, they soon discovered that this Almighty Sovereign God was

something else! As a result of encountering him and embracing him and giving their total lives to him, they became free because they knew he was far more powerful and awesome than the structure of slavery itself.

Now, it's true that as a result of this freedom they were not oblivious to the fact that they still had to do what the man told them to do. They were in the same predicament, but now as different persons, free beings with hope in a situation where hope was not even possible. They began to create a new kind of religious experience and way of life that was made possible both by their world view and their encounter with this Almighty Sovereign God in the midst of slavery. For some, it meant the creation of spirituals where you could sing, shout, and talk about God and freedom. It created a community and brought them together and made life possible.

This African-Hebraic tradition includes the *total* life—the spiritual, the economic, the social. There are political implications, but the starting point is not political. It is political because that is part of the total way of life. Within the white religious experience, the spiritual, economic, social and political are all separate. That reflects their Greek heritage which separates the mind from the body, the rational from the spiritual. For black people, life is a *total way of being*. It isn't just science, a strictly rationalistic process. Notice a black baseball player, how he approaches life; he approaches it mind, body and soul, which is very Hebraic. Football, O. J. Simpson doesn't just run; he *RUNS!* In singing the blues, Aretha Franklin doesn't just sing, she *SINGS*—her mind, body and soul.

There is an element of divine understanding and truth that can only come to people who are at the bottom
—Rev. Cecil Cone

When you examine the black experience as black religious scholars are now doing, you see a way of life and a religious experience that was far superior to what existed in the white community. Black people were dealing with the Bible and the Christian religion in a more creative way than the folks who were supposed to be trained in theology and the Christian tradition.

I would not say that everything within the Western tradition has no connection whatsoever with the Hebraic tradition or the African tradition. But for Western Christianity to fully incorporate this tradition, white folks would have to be converted. The situation is analogous to the one Jesus confronted when the Syro-Phoenician woman came to him for her daughter to be healed. She went to Peter and the disciples and said, "Look, tell Jesus I have a daughter I want him to heal."

So Peter went up to Jesus, touched him, and said, "This woman is out here." Jesus merely turned his back and continued to deal with black folk. She was persistent, so Peter went back to Jesus and said, "You talk to the woman; I can't deal with her." So Jesus said, "I have come for the lost sheep of the House of Israel and furthermore, you don't take bread out of the mouth of black folk and give it to white folk; you don't take bread out of the mouth of children to give to the dogs." Then the Syro-Phoenician woman got on her knees and said, "Yes, Lord, but the dogs will receive the crumbs that fall from the table."

Jesus looked at this white woman and said, "My God, I haven't seen faith like this among black folk. As long as you stay in that position, go your way; your daughter is healed." I say that because if white people want to become a part of the African-Hebraic tradition, they must have the right attitude, the attitude of being on bended knee to be taught.

I don't see white folk willing to embrace black religion in this way. I see white folk who are interested, but there is still an unwillingness to be circumcised, an unwillingness to embrace a whole new way of looking at life, even if that means the only way of being Christian. I still hear white folk saying, "Well now, Lord, I'm going to follow you, but on my own terms." White people have to come to the point where they say, "I am lost, I know not which way to go unless you tell me." There's a refusal to admit that one is totally lost, and unless someone provides the means for that light, it will not come. I think the Lord has his way of eventually bringing that about. I don't know whether that is in the near future or the far future, but I think eventually it will come, and I think black religion will be the main instrument to bring it about.

That is the reason that black religion has not become anti-white. It hasn't because there is always that universal appeal within the black community, even at times when there were groups within the church who wanted to institute a "no whites allowed" policy. You can't get that across in the black church; the black church won't hear of it. Now, they won't allow white folks to come in and take over, but at the same time, there will be no strict "anti" sentiment throughout the black church against white folks. That just can't be. There is always that universal appeal of saying, "Well, maybe white folks will change."

Part Two

Religion in the South
Its Call to Action

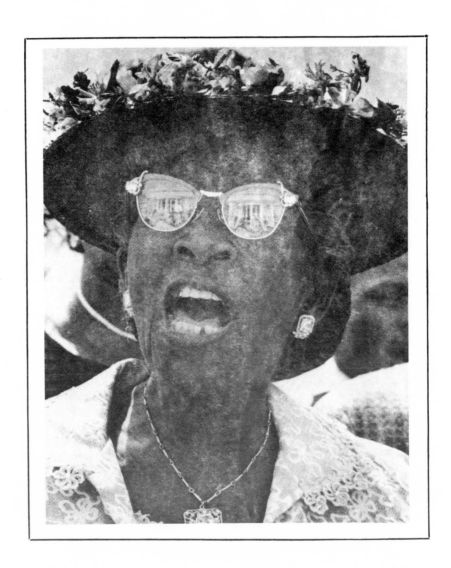

"O, the transporting, rapt'rous scene
    That rises to my sight!
Sweet fields arrayed in living green,
    And rivers of delight."

A Place of Their Own

by Thelma Stevens

In 1895, at the age of 80, Elizabeth Cady Stanton published *The Woman's Bible*, a critique of woman's role and image in the Bible. Pointing out that the Scripture itself was a source of women's subjugation and dismissing the story of Adam's rib as a "petty surgical operation," *The Woman's Bible* was considered scandalous and sacrilegious, arousing protest from clergy as well as women suffragists.

For centuries, the theological view of woman which undergirds the policies and structures of the church has followed a strictly conservative interpretation of the Bible. Consequently, no other institution in society has more overtly and more consistently kept women in their "place" than the church. Whenever women attempted to become involved in the social movements of their day, they met swift and harsh response from the clergy.

A pastoral letter from the Council of Congregationalist Ministers of Massachusetts is typical of the reaction to women's involvement in the Abolitionist Movement:

> The appropriate duties and influence of woman are clearly stated in the New Testament. . . . The power of woman is her dependence, flowing from the consciousness of that weakness which God has given her for her protection. . . . When she assumes the place and tone of man as a public reformer. . . she yields the power which God has given her . . . and her character becomes unnatural."

The women abolitionists persisted, however, and were soon drawing their own parallels about liberation. South Carolinian Sarah Grimke was among the most outspoken:

> All history attests that man has subjugated woman to his will, used her as a means to promote his selfish . . . pleasure . . . but never has he desired to elevate her to the rank she was created to fill. He has done all he could to enslave and debase her mind . . . and says the being he has thus injured is his inferior. . . I ask no favors for my sex . . . All I ask of our brethren

is that they take their feet off our neck and permit us to stand upright on the ground which God designed us to occupy."

Forced to beg, and occasionally demand their rights, first as professional workers, then as laity, and lastly as clergy, church women have consistently been in the position of having to do battle for their own rights in order to carry out their moral concern for the rights of others. In the course of these struggles, women began to discover their own capabilities as well as the restrictions they faced. Though they were able to operate effectively through separate "women's work" organizations such as the ladies aid and missionary societies, they continued to find them-

Thelma Stevens, originally from Mississippi, has been a "full-time church worker" all her adult life. While a student at Hattiesburg State Teachers College in the late 1920s, she became involved in the YWCA and organized interracial meetings between the students from the college and black school teachers in the town. The meetings had to stop when she was ordered by the college president to "stop building a climate for training yankee school teachers." After graduation from Scarritt College, she became the director of the Bethlehem Center in Augusta, Georgia. When the varrious branches of Methodism united in 1939, she became the executive director of Christian Social Relations for the newly created Women's Division of Christian Service and remained in that position until her retirement in the early 1970s.

selves in the position of the powerless and the petitioner in regard to official church policy.

Methodist women in the South have long played a leading role in this fight to gain a position within the church from which they could express and implement their own concerns. At the Methodist General Conference in 1880, Frances Willard, newly elected national president of the Women's Christian Temperance Union (WCTU), requested ten minutes to bring greetings to the body. A two-hour debate on the request followed. One delegate threatened to use all parliamentary measures to block her appearance even after two-thirds of the delegates voted to hear her speak. Finally, she sent a note "to her Honored Brethren" saying that she declined the ten minutes they had been so kind to allow her.

Eight years later, Frances Willard returned to the General Conference as one of five elected women delegates. The Committee on Eligibility voted eleven to six against seating women, stating that the vote to permit lay participation had referred only to men. The ensuing floor debate continued for one week, and the women eventually lost by 39 votes. The gentlemanly delegates then voted to pay their travel expenses.

Attempts to become a part of the larger church structure continued unsuccessfully, despite the fact that women continued to carry the weight of the Methodist Church's local programs and missions. Their community work went practically unnoticed in the larger picture; records of the participation of women in church history are as scarce as hen's teeth.

But participate they did—funnelling their energies into separate women's organizations that became vital to the church as a whole. At first, men viewed the Ladies Aid Societies as a welcome right arm, a "service arm" of the church, functioning at the behest of the male pastor, with no share in making church policies. But under the effective leadership of women like Belle Harris Bennett and Lucinda and Mary Helm, local women's mission societies, which had sprung up all over the South, were united in a region-wide Woman's Home Mission Society. Autonomous and democratically organized, this new structure gave Southern women an unprecedented opportunity to gain administrative skills, self-confidence and experience in running their own affairs. Under it auspices, Methodist women introduced the settlement house movement to the South and sought to implement the concerns of the social gospel.

Feeling the need for full-time workers, the Woman's Home Mission Society petitioned the general conference in 1902 to create the office of deaconess thus providing

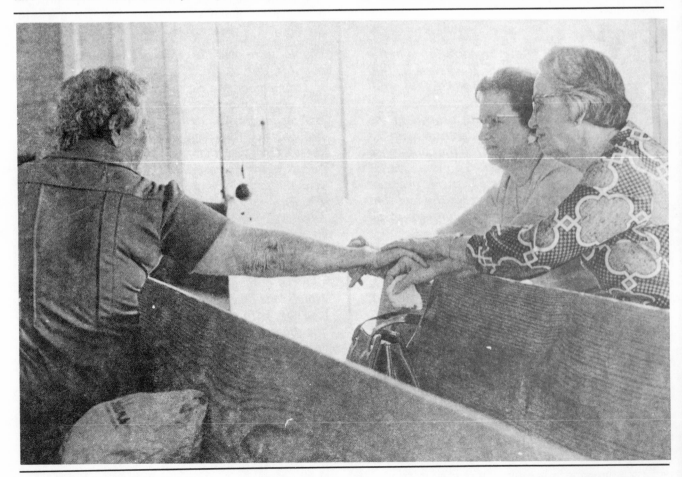

Photo by Baldwin-Watriss

recognition for a new breed of professional women church workers. When the request was presented to the conference, the delegates feared that such official recognition would lead to women aspiring to the ministry, others thought it would replace the minister entirely. One man simply said, "This is heresy."

In order to allay their suspicions, Mary Helm wrote an article in *Our Homes* magazine (the official publication of the Home Missionary Society) explaining in part that a deaconess is *not* a preacher and *not* ordained. She also felt compelled to explain further that a deaconess does not wear a nun's habit and is not a begger. Typically each new gain was won only against the bitter opposition of those who feared that women's work in the church might serve as a dangerous foothold for feminism.

The movement for laity rights for women in the Southern Methodist Church was given impetus by an attack on the hard-won autonomy of the Women's Home Mission Society. Without consulting the women, the Board of Missions combined the Society with the more conservative Foreign Mission Society and subordinated both under its male-dominated administrative structure. Without a voice in church policy, women leaders had no choice but to submit or resign. In response, they launched a campaign for laity rights which paralleled the larger, secular movement for woman suffrage. After winning the right to serve as voting delegates to the General Conference in 1918, Southern women began the long struggle for ordination.

When the Methodist Episcopal Church, South, convened with the Methodist Episcopal Church, North, and the Methodist Protestant Church in a unifying conference in 1939, women were still battling for the rights of clerical ordination. The 1938 General Conference of the Southern Methodists had left intact its church policy that "Our church does not recognize women as preachers, with authority to occupy the pulpit, to read the Holy Scriptures, and to preach as ministers of the Lord Jesus Christ; nor does it authorize a preacher in charge to invite a woman claiming to be a minister . . . to occupy our pulpit to expound the Scriptures as a preacher. Such invitations and services are against the authority and order of the church."

Following the union of the three branches, the newly created Women's Division of Christian Service included within its structure a standing committee on the role and status of women, with similar committees on all organizational levels. One of its major objectives was to secure full clergy rights for women. It was seventeen years later, in 1956, after extensive debate, that clergy rights were finally granted. The General Conference that year had little alternative—it had received some 20,000 resolutions from women's groups across the country.

The organization of the Women's Division provided a valuable and effective channel for women's full participation in the church structure. The Division became one of the most powerful and active arms of the United Methodist Church, particularly in the realm of Christian social concern.

It is in the area of racial justice that the Women's Division has perhaps had the most impact. A Commission of Race Relations was created as early as 1920 in the Southern church, at the urging of Belle H. Bennett. The Commission helped lay the groundwork for women's involvement in the interracial movement after World War I. In the '30s, Methodist women were active in the Association of Southern Women for the Prevention of Lynching, founded by Jessie Daniel Ames, a Texas Methodist.

Following World War II, the Division organized "demobilization workshops" across the country. Among other things their goals were to develop strategies for transforming defense industries into peacetime industries, to conserve gains achieved for minorities and women in job opportunities, and to insure the continuation of integration efforts.

In the late '40s, Dorothy Tilly of Atlanta was the moving force in initiating and promoting an organization known as The Fellowship of the Concerned, an ecumenical and inter-religious group with members from 13 Southern states. The Fellowship was primarily concerned with achieving justice in the courts, and later, with mobilizing support for the 1954 Supreme Court decision on school integration. Mrs. Tilly, who served as jurisdiction secretary of Christian Social Relations in the Woman's Society of Methodist Women in the southeastern region, had a ready-made base of many hundreds of Methodist women who played a major role in the organization.

When Truman created the Commission on Civil Rights, Mrs. Tilly was among its nine members. The Commission released its report in 1947; in December of that year, she reported its findings to the annual meeting of the Women's Division. As a result of her report, a special study on human rights was initiated for Methodist women in 1948-49 to help prepare Methodist women for the changes coming in the '50s.

As the decade of the '40s drew to a close, the nation was beset with McCarthy's witchhunts and Communist labels. The Women's Division, sensing the need for an informed and concerned electorate, authorized a National Roll Call for Methodist Women urging their political participation at all levels. The call that went forth stated in part:

I have set before you life and death . . . choose life . . . World peace, freedom, justice for all mankind are not achieved by apathetic, indifferent Christians. Conflicts in ideology are not resolved by failure to face controversial issues. Community practices are not changed by worshippers of tradition—born too late. Good laws are not enacted and enforced by citizens who fail to vote. The rights to food, a home, a good life will not be guaranteed the children of the world by society geared to materialism and personal profits. The UN will not be strengthened by people with no knowledge of its achievements nor of the issues confronting it.

In 1951, the Women's Division published an 800-page volume of *State Laws on Race and Color*. This marked the first time any effort had been made to collate the state and local laws of the nation in regard to race. The vast resource was compiled by Dr. Pauli Murray, a young, black woman lawyer from North Carolina. Following the 1954 Supreme Court decision, Dr. Murray prepared a "Five Year Supplement." Her distinguished work was hailed as an important landmark in providing factual data about such laws. For Methodist women it provided needed information about their own state laws and local ordinances.

The Women's Division adopted in 1952 its first "Charter of Racial Policies," a commitment to full and equal participation that was later ratified by all the participating conferences. When the 1954 decision of the Supreme Court was announced, the Methodist women, who were in session at their Quadrennial assembly, immediately adopted a resolution of gratitude and support, and called for Methodist women throughout the country to work for its implementation.

As the Women's Division moved into the decade of the '70s, it renewed its emphasis for the full and complete integration of women into positions of lay and clergy on all levels. The 1972 General Conference created a Commission on the Status and Role of Women, mandated to work with all the agencies of the church to build structures that provide equal participation and responsibility of women in every part of the church's life. The Division has also established new channels for encouraging women, both lay and clergy, to develop and utilize their skills for effecting change in the present male-oriented church and society.

[The following recollections of the Women's Division of Christian Service are excerpted from an interview with Thelma Stevens conducted by Jacquelyn Hall, director of the Southern Oral History Program, University of North Carolina at Chapel Hill.]

The strength of our organization is in the power of the volunteers. If we have 36,000 societies, that means we have 36,000 presidents. If we have 600 districts, we have 600 district presidents with officers in the district. There are 73 conferences with 73 conference presidents and all the conference officers of that region. So, you see, if there's any strength at all in the program that we create, it comes from the fact that you've got alert, trained volunteers at all the steps of the organization.

This is one of the reasons why Methodist women work effectively many times—not always, I'm sorry to say—but many times, more times than not. It's because they've got a channel of communication, you see, step by step. And the most important is the local, when the news gets home, gets down to the local church.

Over the years some very wonderful policies have been set by the Women's Division, and we've taken action on things that upset the apple cart a lot of times. People were awfully troubled and upset about it, But, in due time, it worked out.

I remember the first annual meeting we had after I moved to New York. Two of the recommendations that our department brought to the Women's Division were these. One was that we work for Social Security for domestic workers. The other was that we demand a union label on all the printed material of the Women's Division. Now, those two recommendations, in December of 1941, really rocked the building. You just can't imagine it.

We had one old lady, about ninety years old, the outgoing president of the Woman's Home Missionary Society, that had merged, you see, with the Division. And she was on the board on a temporary basis for the transition. Well, she just had forty-eleven fits about the recommendation for union labels. But she was all for the payment of Social Security to domestic workers. Another older woman from Kentucky, who was also there for the transition quadrennium, she stood up and said, well, she didn't know that she minded union labels, but she couldn't bear the thought of paying Social Security to domestic workers. So that body of some sixty women had one big discussion. Finally they tabled both recommendations.

After the session adjourned, I was in my office. I knew they wouldn't accept them, but you see, it was an education to bring up the recommendations, and have them discussed. This woman from Kentucky came into my office. She stood in front of my desk and said, "Thelma, I know you think I'm awful."

"No, I don't," I said.

"Well, I'll tell you what I came in here for. I want you to give me some material to read on this Social Security for domestic workers." She said, "I'm not just plumb down on it, but I just don't know anything about it. I don't think I like it, but I want to know what it's all about. And I'll be honest. If I find out I think it's all right, then I'll come back and tell you, and I'll vote for it."

Well, nearly a year later she came in and said, "Well, I've got something to tell you. I want you to bring that recommendation back in on Social Security for domestic workers, because I want to speak for it." And sure enough we did.

We brought the union label one back too and we got it passed, years later, modified. The only thing they would be willing to say was that the Christian Social Relations Department could have its materials with a union label on it. So we did, from that day on. We had all our materials that were published specifically for the department, with union labels. We had to have all our materials printed outside the Methodist publishing house.

A NEW DAY BEGUN

interview with John Lewis

by Jim Sessions and Sue Thrasher

Life every voice and sing
Till earth and heaven ring
Ring with the harmony of liberty
Let our rejoicing rise
High as the listening skies
Let it resound loud as the rolling sea

Sing a song, full of the faith
that the dark past has taught us
Sing a song, full of the hope
that the present has brought us
Facing the rising sun
of **a new day begun**
Let us march on, till victory is won.

[In the winter of 1959-1960, the nation was mesmerized by a group of young, black college students in Nashville, Tennessee, who appeared at a segregated lunch counter one Saturday afternoon and asked to be served. All that spring, they filled the jails and the nation with their freedom songs, sparking similar actions and demonstrations across the South. Although an earlier sit-in had been held in Greensboro, North Carolina, it was the small coterie of Nashville students who gave impetus to the concept of nonviolent direct action, and continued to provide critical leadership as the Movement spread.

By the spring of 1963, many of the students had moved on to help organize other Southern cities. Still the Nashville movement persisted. The Nashville Christian Leadership Council (NCLC) held mass meetings regularly, and the local chapter of the Student Nonviolent Coordinating Committee (SNCC) continued to demonstrate for open public accommodations.

One of the demonstrations stands out clearly in my memory. It was a chilly spring afternoon. The demonstrators were mostly high school students; the target was one of downtown's "fancier" restaurants, the kind that most of the students would not

be able to afford once it was opened. They left the First Baptist Church holding hands and singing, showing not the least sign of fear. They returned almost immediately, some hurt and bleeding, running to avoid the violence that had awaited them. They were cared for and sent home. They were also asked to return the following day for another demonstration at the same location.

A few of us were left in the front of the church, talking quietly, trying to make some sense of a situation where none existed. There was a commotion in the back and we looked up to see four or five young white guys. No doubt, they had been partly responsible for some of the blood that had been shed earlier; their hostility had apparently only been whetted by the confrontation. They stood now in the doorway, threatening, yet showing some signs of discomfort and wavering bravado, a little unsure that it was cricket to make trouble in a church.

I had been more than slightly shaken by the events of the afternoon, vulnerable to all the feelings of ambivalence and helplessness that were all too familiar to white Southern students of my generation. And now, I sat stunned by the fact that they had actually come into the church, obliterating by their very presence my make-believe lines of *us* and *them*. They could easily have been the good old boys from my high school, the ones who had joined the army or gone to work in the local paper mill because that was what everyone expected them to do.

Wanting desperately to put some distance between myself and them, I muttered something about "how dare those thugs come into church." I had expected at least a murmur of approval. What I got was a stern, but gentle reprimand from John Lewis. He looked me straight in the eye and said, "Don't call them thugs. You have no right to do that. They are human beings just like you and me." For the first time I understood clearly what it meant to accept nonviolence as a way of life.

Later that spring, John became national chairman of SNCC. He was in and out of jail constantly over the next few years, and was beaten badly at the Edmund Pettus bridge in the first attempted Selma to Montgomery march. Yet, I never saw his commitment to nonviolence waver.

For the early civil-rights movement, indigenously Southern, and deeply rooted in the black church, the philosophy of nonviolence and the Christian ethic were totally complementary. In the following interview, John talks about that early Movement, its deep commitment to the philosophy of nonviolence and its integral ties with the Christian faith.

John Lewis is now the Director of the Voter Education Project in Atlanta, an organization that has continued the work of registering black voters in the South. For John it is a continuation of the work he started in the early '60s, a Movement that has progressed from lunch counter sit-ins to the attainment of black political power.

—Sue Thrasher]

I'm the third child in a family of ten. I grew up on a farm near Troy, Alabama. When I was four years old, we moved from where we worked as tenant farmers to a new farm about a half a mile away. My father had saved enough money in 1944 to buy 102 acres of land for a little more than $300; they still live there today.

When we got settled at this new house on the swamp, it became my responsibility to raise the chickens. At the same time, I had a growing interest in religion and going to church so I started playing church with the chickens. This is the truth—I tried to baptize the chickens, and in the process, one of them drowned. I felt very bad about it, but it did not discourage me. I did not lose my great interest in raising chickens, in a sense, my love for them.

I really don't know where my interest in religion came from. It could be my family; we all went to a Baptist church—my mother, my father, most of my first cousins. My grandfather was a deacon. See, in rural Alabama, we only had church once a month. So every third Sunday we

John Lewis leads sit-in march in shadow of Tennessee State Capitol.

Photo by Frank Empson/
The Tennessean

would go to a regular church service; that's when the preacher came. When he wasn't there, we went to a Methodist church that was right down the hill below our house.

During that period, when I had a belief in Santa Claus, one of my uncles had Santa Claus bring me a Bible for Christmas. It had an impact. And somewhere along the way I grew up with the idea of wanting to be a minister. It was well known in the family. One of my aunties would call me preacher.

I have six brothers and a host of first cousins about my same age; we all sort of grew up together. It was like a big fellowship—really an extended family. When we went to Sunday school and church it was the whole family, not just the immediate family.

Religion, the whole idea, played a tremendous role in my family. We all had to learn a verse of the Bible at an early age. We *had* to do that. Before meals we had to say grace and then we all had to recite a verse; it's still done even today. On special occasions like Thanksgiving or New Year's or Christmas, my mother or my father or one of us had to lead a prayer.

My interest in the chickens and my interest in the church sort of came together. In addition to helping my family raise the chickens because we needed eggs—it was a necessity, being poor in rural Alabama—the chickens became part of an experiment. I would preach to the chickens each night when they would go into their coop, or what we called the hen house. It was my way of communicating to them. When a chicken would die, we would have a funeral. My younger sisters and brothers and first cousins would be the mourners. We had a chicken cemetery where we buried them and had flowers and everything I recall a large pecan tree that's still there today; we had a swing and benches under it, and we would gather there to have the services. People would line up like they were in church. The service would dismiss, and we would march off to the cemetery below the house.

The grade school that I attended for the first three years was in the Methodist Church, just below our house. It was a public school, but they used the church building. Next door, there was another one-room school where we went to the fourth, fifth, and sixth grades. After the sixth grade, we took a bus to a little town called Banks, Alabama; I took junior high school in Banks. The high school was located in Brundidge, going on down toward Ozark. We passed the white school on our way. We had this old, broken-down bus. Many of the black families in this area owned their own land, and the county actually skipped parts of the road—the area where blacks owned land was not paved. So, some morning when there was a lot of rain, the bus would run in a ditch and we would get to school late. Or coming from school, the bus would get stuck in the red mud coming up a hill, and we wouldn't get home til late at night. That happened on several occasions.

We were very, very poor, like most of the black people in this area. And I wanted to go to school. I wanted to get an education. On the other hand, we had to stay out of school to work in the field, to pick cotton or pull corn, or what we called "shake the peanuts." From time to time, I would get up early enough in the morning to hide. On two or three occasions I actually went under the house and waited until I heard the bus coming; then I ran out and got on the bus, so I could make it to school rather than work. My parents used to say I was lazy, because I didn't want to stay out and go to the field. But I saw the need and I wanted to go to school. That was particularly true during my junior high and high school years.

We didn't hear much discussion about civil rights. It was strictly two separate worlds, one black and one white. When we'd go into the town of Troy, we saw signs, "Colored only," "White only." The water fountain in the five and ten store. At the courthouse. Couldn't use the county library. I don't recall hearing anybody speak out against it. The closest thing was to hear the minister say something like, "We are all brothers and sisters in Jesus Christ." Or through the Sunday school lesson, particularly those lessons based on the New Testament, it came through: "In Jesus we are one." That had an effect. That influenced me, no question about it.

We didn't hear much discussion about civil rights. It was strictly two separate worlds, one black and one white.

In 1955, at the beginning of the Montgomery bus boycott, when I started taking note of what was happening there, we didn't have a subscription to the Montgomery paper. But my grandfather had one, and after he read his paper, we got it two or three days later, so we could keep up with what was going on.

We didn't have electricity during those early years. We didn't get it until much later. We had a large radio, one with these huge batteries, the kind that have to be knocked open with a hammer when they decay. There was a local station in Montgomery, a soul station, black-oriented, but I don't think it was black owned. Every Sunday morning a local minister in Montgomery would preach, and one Sunday I heard Martin Luther King. Now this was before the bus boycott. The name of the sermon was something like "Paul's Letter to American Christians." He made it very relevant to the particular issues and concerns of the day. That had an impact. I also heard other ministers on the station. Our own minister was very aware and talked about different things.

The bus boycott had a tremendous impact on my life. It just sort of lifted me, gave me a sense of hope. I had a resentment of the dual system, of segregation. Because I saw it. You could clearly see the clean new buses that the white children had that were going to Banks Junior High and the buses that were taking white children to Pike County High School. You see, in the state of Alabama, most of the black high schools were called training schools. So in Brundidge, my high school was called Pike County Training School, and the white school was called Pike County High School. That was true of most of the counties in Alabama at that time. In Montgomery, they were saying something about that dual system.

I remember in '54, the Supreme Court Decision, I felt maybe in a year or so we would have desegregated schools. But nothing happened. Then Montgomery came in 1955. It was like a light. I saw a guy like Martin Luther King, a young, well-educated, Baptist minister, who was really using religion. The boycott lasted more than 300 days; it had a tremendous effect.

During that period, I think it was February of 1956, I preached my first sermon. I must have been about a week short of being sixteen. I told my minister I felt I had been "called"—in the Baptist church, you hear the "call"—and that I wanted to preach a sermon. And I preached. I don't remember the verse, but it was from First Samuel. My subject was a praying mother, the story about Hannah, who wanted a child. I've never forgotten it—the response. I got up, took the text, gave my subject, and delivered a sermon. The response of the congregation was just unbelievable! I was really overcome by it all.

From that time on, I kept preaching at different churches, Methodist and Baptist churches in the rural areas of Pike County. Churches in Troy would also invite me to come to preach. I continued to do that until I graduated from high school in May 1957. In the meantime I had been ordained by my local church.

That was my first time to leave Alabama for any period of time . . .I knew I'd left something and was going to something new.

My greatest desire at that time was to go to school—to get an education, to study religion and philosophy. Somehow, I knew that this was the direction I must travel in order to become a prepared minister and to be a good religious leader.

I had a fantastic urge to go to Morehouse College. I'd heard of Morehouse, and I knew that Dr. King had gone there. I had my homeroom teacher get a catalogue and an application from Morehouse. But there was no way. I did not know anybody. I didn't have any money. It was just impossible. So this was a dream that was never fulfilled.

My mother had been doing some work for a white lady as a domestic, and one day she brought home a paper. It was something like the *Baptist Home Mission*, a Southern Baptist publication. In this paper, I saw a little notice for American Baptist Theological Seminary (ABT). It was the first time I had heard anything about the school. I'm not sure if it said for blacks or for Negroes or what, but it said, "no tuition, room and board." And I wrote away. I got an application, filled it out, had my transcript sent up, and got accepted.

So in September 1957, I went away to Nashville. That was my first time to leave Alabama for any period of time. I was seventeen years old. I'll never forget that trip, getting on that Greyhound bus; it was my first time to travel alone. Nashville was altogether different from rural Pike County, Alabama. It was just another world. I didn't know what to believe. I knew I'd left something and was going to something new.

They had a work program at ABT, and I got a job in the kitchen washing pots and pans. I was paid something like $45 or $46, and $42.50 was taken out for room and board. The school is jointly owned by the Southern Baptist Convention and the National Baptist Convention. It's primarily the financial burden of the Southern Baptists, a missionary school, in a sense, from the whites to the blacks. It was started in 1924, primarily to keep black Baptists from going to the white seminary in Louisville.

I was pulled into a sort of interracial setting. They had white professors on the staff, and white Baptist ministers from the city would come in for chapel. There would be visiting professors from time to time. It was just an eye-opener to go to Fisk to, say, a Christmas concert, and see the interracial climate. I think my resentment toward the dual system of segregation and racial discrimination—probably the tempo of my resentment—increased at that time. Then traveling from Nashville to Troy and from Troy back to Nashville, we were forced to go to a segregated waiting room, to sit in the back of the bus, and all that.

At that time, Little Rock was going on, September of '57. There were many things happening, and because it was an everyday occurrence, I became very conscious of it. I spent a great deal of time during this period preaching what some people call the social gospel. I just felt that the ministry and religion should be a little more relevant. Some of my classmates would tease me about that.

Even people like James Bevel would tease me. He was a classmate of mine, a semester ahead of me. And Bernard Lafayette, who was a year behind me. We became very good friends, the three of us.[1]

---

[1]Bernard Lafayette and Jim Bevel, participants in the Nashville sit-ins, later went to work for the Southern Christian Leadership Conference (SCLC).

M. L. King Jr.'s Dexter Avenue Baptist Church near the state capitol in Montgomery
Photo by Penny Weaver

Most of the other guys were going to some church out in the country on Sunday mornings to preach because they got a little money. When a minister would invite you to preach, they'd take up a special collection. I didn't do much of that, but Bevel was one of these guys who would always go out and preach somewhere. In the black Baptist church, there's a certain type of minister that is described as a "whooper." Bevel was known as a whooper. It's the tone of voice. Evangelist! Shouting! Some people refer to Aretha Franklin's father C. L. Franklin as a great whooper. These guys can put music in their voice, can turn people on. Bevel went out and did a great deal of this. He was called to a little church in Dayton, Tennessee, and he would invite us to go up, and we would preach for him. And the people would fix a good meal.

During the summer of 1958, I met Dr. King for the first time. It was in Montgomery. I had an interest in withdrawing from ABT. When I look back on it—and I've thought about it from time to time—it was not just for the sake of desegregating Troy State University. I wanted to be closer to my family, my parents, and my younger brothers and sisters. I could stay at home and go to Troy. I got an application and had my high school transcript and my first year of study at ABT sent there. I didn't hear anything, so I sent a letter to Dr. King, and he invited me to come to Montgomery. I took a bus from Troy to Montgomery one Saturday morning. I met with Fred Gray,[2] Dr. King, and Rev. Abernathy and told them of my interest in enrolling at Troy State University. They couldn't believe it. They thought I was crazy! But they were interested. They wanted to pursue the whole idea, and we had a good discussion.

I had written the letter to Troy State on my own without talking it over with my parents. I just did it really, didn't comtemplate it at all, just sent it in and applied. Later, Fred Gray sent a registered letter to Troy State saying that we hadn't heard anything. We never got any return correspondence. Then the question came up of whether a suit should be filed against the State Board of Education, the Governor and the University. At that time, it would have involved my parents signing that suit, and they didn't want to do it. So we had to drop the whole idea.

[2]Fred Gray was the attorney for Mrs. Rosa Parks, whose arrest triggered the Montgomery bus boycott of 1955 and sparked the organization of the Montgomery Improvement Association. Rev. Ralph Abernathy was then the minister of the Ripley Street Baptist Church.

. . .it was like being involved in a Holy Crusade. I really felt that what we were doing was so in keeping with the Christian faith.

I went back to American Baptist in the fall and continued my studies. And then I started attending mass meetings sponsored by the NAACP. In Nashville, there was an organization at that time called the Nashville Christian Leadership Council (NCLC), which was a chapter of SCLC. They started sponsoring some meetings on Sunday night at Kelly's[3] church downtown.

going to lead to something; we got into socio-drama—"If something happened to you, what would you do?"—the whole question of civil disobedience. And we dealt a great deal with the teachings of Jesus, not just the teaching of Ghandi, but also what Jesus had to say about love and nonviolence and the relationship between individuals, both on a personal and group basis, and even the relationship between nations.

I remember we had the first test sit-in in Nashville at two of the large department stores, Cain-Sloan's and Harvey's. It was an interracial, international really, group of students. We just walked in as a group and occupied the stools in one area and went to the restaurant, I think, at Harvey's. They said that we couldn't be served, and we got up and left, just like that. It was to establish the fact that they refused to serve an interracial group, or refused to serve blacks. We did one in November of '59 and one in December.

Bernard Lafayette at lunch counter sit-in, Nashville.
Photo by Jimmy Ellis/The Tennessean

Later, under the direction of Jim Lawson,[4] a divinity student at Vanderbilt, NCLC started nonviolent workshops every Tuesday night. For a long period of time, I was the only student from ABT that attended. It was like a class; we would go and study the philosophy and discipline of nonviolence. There was very little discussion during the early workshops about segregation or racial discrimination or about the possibility of being involved in a sit-in or freedom ride. It was more or less a discussion about the history of nonviolence. I did sense that it was

[3]Kelly Miller Smith is the pastor of the First Baptist Church in downtown Nashville. He was President of the Nashville Christian Leadership Council (NCLC), an affiliate of the SCLC in the early '60s.

[4]Jim Lawson gained national prominence in 1959 when he was expelled from Vanderbilt Divinity School for leading nonviolent training workshops. He later became the pastor of Centenary Methodist Church in Memphis, Tennessee, and played an active role in the 1968 Memphis garbage workers' strike where King was shot.

During the Christmas holidays, Bernard Lafayette and I took a bus home from Nashville. Bernard lives in Tampa, so he took a bus as far as Troy with me. I'll never forget it! We got on the bus in Nashville and got near the front. The driver told us we had to move and we refused. He just rammed his seat back, so we were in the front seat right behind the driver all the way and nothing happened. I think when we got to Birmingham, we decided to move. It was a testing period. I don't know why we did it; it was not part of a plan or anything like that.

When we got back after the holidays, we started attending the nonviolent workshops again. At that time, Bernard started attending on a regular basis. On February first, after the sit-ins in Greensboro, Jim Lawson received a call from the campus minister for one of the black colleges in North Carolina. He said, "What can the students in Nashville do to support the students in North Carolina?" Jim just passed the information on.

That call didn't really come to us in a vacuum; we were already involved in a workshop and preparing eventually for a similar action. So, in a matter of days, we called a mass meeting of students on Fisk University campus, and about 500 students showed up. That's when we outlined the plan. It must have been a Monday night. We said on this Tuesday, or that Thursday—we tried to pick T-day since most of the students had light classes on Tuesdays and Thursdays—we would meet at Kelly's church, First Baptist downtown and we would sit-in. We told them that we'd been going to the nonviolent workshop and went through it with them. The people who had been attending the workshops were to be the leaders, the spokesmen in charge of the different groups. We went down and sat in at Woolworth's and Kresge's and other 5-and-10s and drugstores like Walgreen's that had lunch counters. It was a quiet day for the most part. That went on for a period of time.

Sometimes we'd sit for two or three hours. We'd have our books and we'd just sit quietly, doing our homework. Someone might walk up and hit us or spit on us or do something, but it was very quiet. The Movement during that period, in my estimation, was the finest example, if you want to refer to it, of Christian love. It was highly disciplined. When I look back on that particular period in Nashville, the discipline, the dedication, and the commitment to nonviolence was unbelievable.

Two or three times a week we would go and sit in. And then one particular day—it must have been Leap Year, because I think it was February 29, 1960, a Saturday morning. We met in Kelly's church, and Will Campbell[5] came to the meeting to tell us he had received information that the police officials would have us arrested and would let all type of violence occur. Kelly came to the church and warned there would be violence. But we said we had to go. We were afraid, but we felt that we had to bear witness. So Jim Lawson and some of the others were very sympathetic and felt that if we wanted to go that we should.

It was my responsibility to print some rules, some "do's and don'ts," what people were supposed to do and what they were not supposed to do: sit up straight, don't look back, if someone hits you, smile, things like that. I got some paper . . . you see, I had worked for two years in the kitchen at ABT; my last two years I worked as a janitor cleaning the Administration building so I had access to office supplies. We got a secretary to type it and we used a mimeograph machine. Several of us engaged in a conspiracy to get the paper and get the rules distributed. At the end it said something like, "Remember the teachings of Jesus Christ, Ghandi, and Martin Luther King: May God be with you." We gave them to all those people that Saturday morning.

Woolworth's was where the first violence occurred. A young student at Fisk, Maxine Walker, and an exchange student named Paul LePrad were sitting at the counter at Woolworth's. This young white man came up and hit Paul and knocked him down and hit the young lady. Then all type of violence started. Pulling people, pushing people over the counter, throwing things, grinding out cigarettes on people, pouring ketchup in their hair, that type of thing. Then the cops moved in and started arresting people.

That was my first time, the first time for most of us, to be arrested. I just felt . . . that it was like being involved in a Holy Crusade. I really felt that what we were doing was so in keeping with the Christian faith. You know, we didn't want to go to jail. But it became . . . a moving spirit. Something just sort of came over us and consumed us. And we started singing "We Shall Overcome," and later, while we were in jail we started singing "Paul and Silas, bound in jail, had no money for their bail. . . ." It became a religious ceremony that took place in jail. I remember that very, very well, that first arrest.

Even after we were taken to jail, there was a spirit there, something you witness, I guess, during a Southern Baptist revival. People talk about being born again or their faith being renewed. I think our faith was renewed. Jail in a sense became the way toward conversion, was the act of baptism, was the process of baptism.

Then hundreds of students heard about the arrest. We all went to jail and hundreds of others came downtown and sat in. At the end of the day, they had arrested 98 people. During that Saturday night, lawyers and professors and the president of Fisk and other schools came down to try to get us out of jail, but we refused. We said that we would stay in jail, that we felt we hadn't committed any wrong. They wanted to put up the bond. It was not a tremendous amount per person, but altogether it would have been up to several thousand dollars. Finally

---

[5]Will Campbell was then working with the National Council of Churches in Nashville.

late that night or early that Sunday morning, the judge made a decision to let us out in the custody of the president of Fisk. And we all came out.

We went to trial the following Monday. The judge wanted the trials separately, but the lawyers objected. They wanted us tried as a group. They tried one case, and the guy was fined fifty dollars or thirty days in jail. At that time, we made a conscious decision that we wouldn't pay the fine, that we would go to jail and serve our term. So we all went back to jail. The next day, Jim Bevel took a group of around 60 to the Trailways Bus Station and they all got arrested. So that was more people in jail. That process kept going on for some time.

I think the older ministers in the community—C. T. Vivian, Metz Rollins,[6] and Kelly Miller Smith, saw themselves in an advisory role. They were leaders of the NCLC in charge of setting up the mass meetings. If we needed something, if there were funds needed to pay a fine or get someone out of jail, we could get money from them. For a place, we used Kelly's church and Rev. Alexander Anderson's[7] church, Clark Memorial. They also had contacts. When we needed cars, Kelly would call some of his members to have their car at Fisk or Tennessee State in time to pick up students and bring them to his church. We depended on them for support. They were a resource.

We also got support from the United Church Women and the lady who directed the Tennessee Council on Human Relations, Katherine Jones. A group from the United Church Women would always be on the scene. A lot of times when we were involved in a demonstration in the city, we didn't know that in the store or in the picket line, there were observers from the United Church Women. But they were there, and they were supportive. They came to the courtroom during the trial. They wrote letters and met with the merchants to try to get them to desegregate.

I took a seat in the very front behind the driver. . . . For almost four years I had traveled that way from Montgomery to Birmingham. This time we didn't see anyone.

I once described the early civil rights movement as a religious phenomenon. And I still believe that. I think in order for people to do what they did, and to go into places where it was like going into hell fire, you needed something to go on. It was like guerrilla warfare in some communities, some of the things people did. And I'm not just talking about the students, but the community peo-

ple, indigenous people. It had to be based on some strong conviction, or, I think, religious conviction.

I remember on the Freedom Rides in 1961, when we got to Montgomery . . . personally, I thought it was the end. It was like death; you know, death itself might have been a welcome pleasure. Just to see and witness the type of violence . . . the people that were identified with us were just acting on that strong, abiding element of faith.

In Birmingham, we stayed in the bus station all night with a mob, the Klan, on the outside. On the day we arrived, Bull Connor literally took us off the bus and put us in protective custody in the Birmingham City Jail. We were in the jail Wednesday night, all day Thursday and Thursday night. On Friday morning, around one o'clock he took us out of jail and took us back to the Alabama-Tennessee state line and dropped us off. There were seven of us, an all-black group. He dropped us off and said, "You can make it back to Nashville, there's a bus station around here somewhere." That's what he said. And just left us there! I have never been so frightened in my life.

We located a house where an old black family lived. They must have been in their seventies. We told them who we were and they let us in. They'd heard about the Freedom Rides and they were frightened. They didn't want to do it, but they let us in and we stayed there. The old man got in his old pick-up truck when the stores opened and went and got some food. You see, we had been on a hunger strike and hadn't had anything to eat. He went to two or three different places and got bologna, bread and viennas—all that sort of junk food, and milk and stuff. And we ate.

We talked to Diane Nash[8] in Nashville, and she said that "other packages had been shipped by other means," meaning that students had left Nashville on the way to Birmingham to join the Freedom Ride by private car and by train. We just assumed the telephone lines were always tapped. She sent a car to pick us up, and we returned to Birmingham and went straight to Rev. Shuttlesworth's[9] home to meet the new people. More students from Fisk,

---

[6]C. T. Vivian was minister of a local church in Nashville and active in the Nashville Christian Leadership Council. He later joined the staff of the SCLC. J. Metz Rollins was a staff member of the Division of Race and Society for the Presbyterian Church, and advisor to the local SNCC chapter.

[7]Rev. Alexander Anderson was active in the Nashville Christian Leadership Council.

[8]Diane Nash was one of the most prominent leaders of the Nashville sit-in movement. She later married Jim Bevel and worked on the staff of the SCLC.

[9]Rev. J. Fred Shuttlesworth, a Birmingham minister, was active in the SCLC, and president for many years of the Southern Conference Educational Fund (SCEF).

ABT, and Tennessee State had joined the ride as well as two white students from Peabody. The total number was about 21.

At 5:30 we tried to get a bus from Birmingham to Montgomery, and—I'll never forget it—this driver said, "I only have one life to give, and I'm not going to give it to CORE or the NAACP." This was after the burning of the bus at Anniston and after the beating of the CORE riders on Mother's Day. So we stayed in the bus station. At 8:30 another bus was supposed to leave, and that bus wouldn't go either. We just stayed there all that night. Early the next morning Herb Kaplow, then a reporter for NBC, who's now with ABC, came to tell us he understood Bobby Kennedy had been talking with the Greyhound people and apparently we would be able to get a bus later. So we got on the bus about 8:30 Saturday morning. The arrangement that Kennedy had made was that every fifteen miles or so there would be a state trooper on the highway and a plane would fly over the bus, to take us into Montgomery. An official of Greyhound was supposed to be on the bus also, but I don't actually recall that there was one.

I took a seat in the very front behind the driver along with Jim Zwerg.[10] On the way to Montgomery we saw no sign of the state trooper cars or the plane. It was a strange feeling. For almost four years I had traveled that way from Montgomery to Birmingham. This time, we didn't see anyone. It was the eeriest feeling of my life. When we reached Montgomery, we didn't even see anyone outside the bus station. We started stepping off, and the media people began gathering around. Then just out of the blue, hundreds of people started to converge on the bus station. They started beating the camera people; they literally beat them down. I remember one guy took a huge camera away from a photographer and knocked him down with it.

People started running in different directions. The two white female students tried to get in a cab, and the black driver told them he couldn't take white people and just drove off. They just started running down the street, and John Seigenthaler got between them and the mob. Another part of the mob turned on us, mostly black

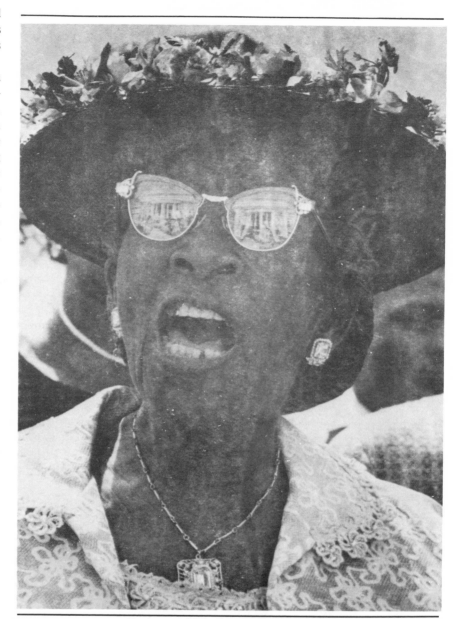

Easter, 1958, State Capitol, Montgomery, Alabama
Photo by Joe Holloway

fellows. We had no choice but to just stand there. I was hit over the head with a crate, one of these wooden soda crates. The last thing I remember was the Attorney General of Alabama, serving me with an injunction prohibiting interracial groups from using public transportation in the state of Alabama while I was still lying on the ground. Yes, I was afraid. I was afraid.

[10]Jim Zwerg was an exchange student at Fisk. When the Freedom Riders reached Montgomery, he was badly beaten and left lying in the street.

The underlying philosophy was the whole idea of redemptive suffering— suffering that in itself might redeem the larger society.

Jim Zwerg was one of the most committed people, and I definitely believe it was not out of any social, "do-good" kind of feeling. It was out of his deep religious conviction. There were others who felt the same; people just felt something was wrong. You know during the workshops in Nashville we never thought or heard that much about what would happen to us personally or individually. And we never really directed our feelings of hostility toward the opposition. I think most of the people that came through those early days saw the opposition and saw ourselves, really, the participants in the Movement, as victims of the system. And we wanted to change the system.

The underlying philosophy was the whole idea of redemptive suffering—suffering that in itself might help to redeem the larger society. We talked in terms of our goal, our dream, being the beloved community, the open society, the society that is at peace with itself, where you forget about race and color and see people as human beings. We dealt a great deal with the question of the means and ends. If we wanted to create the beloved community, then the methods must be those of love and peace. So somehow the end must be caught up in the means. And I think people understood that.

In the black church, ministers have a tendency to compare the plight of black people with the children of Israel. So, I think we saw ourselves as being caught up in some type of holy crusade, with the music and the mass meetings, with nothing on our side but a dream and just daring faith. . . . I tell you the truth, I really felt tht I was part of a crusade. There was something righteous about it.

I really felt that the people who were in the Movement—and this may be short-sighted and biased on my part—were the only truly integrated society and, in a sense, the only church in America. Because you had a community of believers, people who *really believed*. They were committed to a faith.

I was wrong, I think, to feel that way, because you shouldn't become so definitive as to believe that you have an edge on the truth. I think you have to stay open. But, you know, in the process of growing and developing, people go through different experiences.

The Movement—it's strange to say this in 1976—but the Movement later became much more secular. The people that made up the leadership of the Southern sit-in movement during 1960 were ministerial students, or someone who came from a strong religious background. SCLC was founded primarily by ministers in the basement of Ebenezer Baptist Church.

The change toward secularization could have something to do with the Movement becoming an "in thing." It became glamorized. It was no longer a group of disciplined students sitting down in Nashville, or a group of people traveling into the heart of Mississippi on the Free-

John Lewis discusses voter registration with Louisiana sugar cane workers.
Photo by Archie Allen

dom Rides. I think the media had something to do with it; the publicity started attracting many different types of people.

I think the Movement lost something because during the '60s, it affirmed for us, and instilled in us, a sense of hope that change was possible. The whole idea of forgiving—I think we lost some of that. In 1961, we were not just using the nonviolent principle as a tactic; it became a philosophy, a way of life. It was not just the way we treated each other, and not just for public demonstrations. It became a *way*. We have lost some of that "soul"— soul in the way that black people refer to soul—the meaning, the heart, the experiencing.

I think that a great deal had to do with the influx of people from the North, black and white, who had very little relationship, or any real kinship to religious foundations, or to any Southern experience. Most of the people from the South, even those that were not totally committed for religious reasons, had a deep appreciation for the role of religion and the black church. The people who came down, particularly in late '63 and '64, just didn't have any appreciation for it.

There is something very special and very peculiar about the South itself; then there is also something very special and peculiar about black religious life. The church is a special place in a small town or rural community. For a lot of people in the urban centers, it is the heart of the community. It's the only place where people can go sometimes for fellowship and worship with their friends and neighbors. But more than that, it's a place where people can come together and sort of lay everything else aside— maybe it is the *only* place. And they can identify with it, and they can appreciate it.

One reason I think the Movement itself was so successful—and Dr. King as leader, as a symbol—in mobilizing so many people was that it built on strong and solid religious ground. In a sense Dr. King used the black church, and the emotionalism within the black church, as an instrument to move people toward their own freedom. People believed there must be something right about the Movement when its mass meetings were held in the church.

We have lost that sense of ethic, that sense of morality—that you do something because it is right.

I still consider myself a very hopeful and optimistic person in spite of all the bad things that happened since 1960 . . . the assassinations. Sometimes I look back on all those funerals that I went to, people that I knew and loved, the war and all, but I'm still hopeful. You know, Dr. King used to say when you lose hope, it is like being dead. You have to have that element of faith and hope; you have to be based and grounded in something.

I do not hide or try to get away from the fact that I am a licensed, ordained Baptist minister; I am a minister. But on the other hand, I don't see myself going to a pulpit every Sunday morning and preaching; I just don't see that as my role. I feel I can make a greater contribution and do the greatest good by doing what I am doing now. When I go out and tell people to register and vote, I tell people that they should have some control over their lives, that they should organize if they want to get a sewage system, or if they want to get food stamps or want to do something about welfare. Or if they think this man is doing them wrong, they should come together and get someone else.

I see what I am doing now as a continuation of the early Movement, and based on the same principles. One of the things I say to black elected officials and white elected officials is that what we need to do from top to bottom in this country is to inject a sense of morality into a viable politics. I think that is what is missing in the political arena and to some degree, I guess, in what is remaining of the Movement. We have lost that sense of ethic, that sense of morality—that you do something because it is right.

You know, I stopped going to church for a while; I did. Not out of . . . I don't know, I just stopped going for quite a few years. But these days I find myself going back.

I think the churches today are still relevant; I think there is a need for the institution. On the other hand, I think the church, black and white, is far, far behind. The leadership of the church is out of step. I do feel that in this country, particularly in the urban centers, if we continue to get property and build these fantastic buildings, that the day may well come when the next struggle will not be directed toward the secular institutions, but toward the church.

And the church may well deserve that. You have churches with a great deal of wealth; individual churches and religious bodies that own tremendous amounts of land and resources when all around them there is poverty and hunger. The churches are far, far behind.

I think the white church and the black church will remain apart for years to come. The leadership of the black church is perhaps much more socially conscious, much more political, much more involved in the life of the community. They really don't separate the condition around them from the church; for the most part, that is an exception. I think the black church could do more, but I think the black church is much farther down the road than the white church. Black ministers have been leaders; they have been taking the initiative, whether it is in politics, or trying to make the economic conditions better. When you look around the South, at places like Missis-

Photo by Joe Holloway

sippi and south Georgia, and the number of black churches that were bombed and burned down during the early '60s, it is a testimonial. Something was happening there.

In another sense, particularly in the black Baptist church, I think religion is much more personal. It dominates the lives of people. The whole concept of Jesus, as a brother or king, is much more personal. Whether people are working in the kitchen, or the field or whatever, religion takes on a personal quality.

I don't see a great marriage anytime in the near future between the white church and the black church. You know people say eleven o'clock on Sunday morning is the most segregated hour of the week, and it still is. I think that will be true for years and years to come.

Yeh. It's strange. The history of it is really strange.

People's Institute of Applied Religion

by Bill Troy with Claude Williams

[This article is the result of many hours of taped conversations and research in the papers of Claude and Joyce Williams at their home in Alabaster, Alabama. All quotations are by Claude Williams, unless otherwise noted. For additional information about the South during the Depression, especially about the Southern Tenant Farmers Union (STFU), readers are encouraged to see Mark Naison's excellent article on the Williams published in the "No More Moanin" issue of *Southern Exposure* (Winter 1974).]

"Is not this the carpenter, the son of Joseph?" Well, if he was a carpenter, he knew what it was to have horny hands and patched clothing. Because you couldn't do the kind of work he was, felling trees and dragging them to the house to make ox yokes and carts, without tearing your trousers. He was a carpenter. He knew what it was to work long hours with little pay. He was born and reared in a worker's home. He knew what it was to dwell in a shack, because carpenters even today don't build mansions for themselves but for other people!"

That's the voice of Rev. Claude Williams, speaking much as he did thirty-five years ago to groups of sharecroppers in the Arkansas Delta and shopworkers in the war defense plants of Detroit. Standing now in the close quarters of his Alabama trailer-home office, the preacher's voice rings as it did those many years ago, when conferences of workaday preachers and Sunday school teachers would meet for days in churches and union halls to consider the Biblical teaching: "the meek will inherit the earth when they become sassy enough to take it!"

Hanging on the wall before him is one of Claude's unique visual education charts. It is a large affair, three by four feet in dimension. At the top, it bears the legend, "The Galilean and the Common People." In circles and rectangles covering the chart is a succession of modern, simple drawings, each depicting scenes from the life of the Son of Man.

Waving his homemade coat-hanger pointer at the chart, Claude refers to each drawing in turn as he recounts how Moses called the first strike down in Egypt, how Jeremiah spoke out fearlessly in the name of true religion against the rulers and priests of ancient Israel, and how the Son of Man was reared in this tradition by a poor family who belonged to a movement seeking to bring about the Kingdom of God in their own time and place.

This is the kind of talk that went on in the People's Institute of Applied Religion (PIAR), surely one of the most remarkable expressions of religion ever to appear in the South. The PIAR was created in 1940 as an independent means of training the grassroots religious leaders of the cotton belt in the principles of labor unionism. For its principal founders, Claude and Joyce Williams, it represented the unique melding of religious and political convictions that had grown in them over a long period.

Claude and Joyce Williams came by their religion honestly. Both were born into fundamentalist homes, Joyce to a farming family in Missouri and Claude to tenant farmers in West Tennessee. They met and married in the early 1920s at Bethel College, a conservative Tennessee seminary of the Cumberland Presbyterian Church. But their religious views gradually began to change as they pastored their first Presbyterian charge near Nashville. Partly, as in the case of their increasing unease with racial segregation, the change was based on seeing the contradictions in their culture between biblical teaching about justice and actual social practice. At the same time, avid

Photo by Bill Troy

reading led them to discover the refreshing vitality of modern religious social thought represented in Harry Emerson Fosdick's *The Modern Use of the Bible*.

The turning point came in 1927 when Claude enrolled in a series of summer seminars at Vanderbilt University taught by Dr. Alva W. Taylor, a Southerner, member of the Socialist Party and prominent exponent of the social gospel. He recalls that Taylor "had a way of removing the theological debris from the Son of Man under which he's been buried for all these centuries and making him appear human." Claude found it impossible, after this experience, to continue working in a conventional church ministry.

In 1930, the Williams moved to Paris, Arkansas, to serve a small Presbyterian mission church. Located in the center of the state's mining district, Paris offered more opportunities to practice their new religious ideas than they could have ever imagined. Their first real working acquaintance with political action came with their involvement in the miners' efforts to organize a union and join the UMWA. With characteristic energy, they opened the church, their home and their family life to this move-

ment. They participated in strategy discussions, helped raise money, and Claude wrote many of the necessary documents and position papers. Their participation clearly grew out of their religion, and they learned that the warm response of the miners and their families was due, in part, to their interpretation that the union fight was completely consistent with biblical teaching.

The Williams also began in Paris a program of study and learning that became a cornerstone of their long ministry. The Sunday evening "Philosopher's Club," held in their home, was a regular feature of church life. These meetings involved open and wide-ranging discussion of religion as well as the multitude of political and cultural ideas sweeping the country during these Depression years. They encouraged the young people to read, opening their own library for use at the church. Moreover, Claude was much in demand as a speaker throughout the coal fields. He traveled thousands of miles, addressing meetings of miners on behalf of the union, and from these contacts, "socio-Christian forums" grew in several west Arkansas towns. Through all these experiences, Claude was developing his own way of preaching/teaching, emphasizing exhortation and emotion, but likewise encouraging objective analysis and collective action.

Chiefly because of the Williams' work with the miners and the young people of Paris, the church elders eventually brought successful action within the presbytery to have Claude removed from the pulpit. In 1935, they were forced to move to nearby Fort Smith. They quickly became active with the organization of unemployed workers, and Claude was jailed for three months for participating in a demonstration. They moved again, this time to the relative safety of Little Rock, and were soon giving full time to workers' education and organizing with one of the most significant political movements to sweep the Depression South—the Southern Tenant Farmers Union (STFU).

By this time, having endured many difficult experiences and met a number of Marxist activists along the way, their political and religious views had become more radical. Likewise, their views about taking seriously the people's religion were taking concrete form.

They knew from their own backgrounds that working with poor people in the South, both black and white, meant working with people whose view of the world was strongly conditioned by religion. Everything that it means to be good, to live honorably, to find support through life's trials and hope in the future—these are the profound personal and social questions that poor Southerners have answered in religious ways for generations. The Bible is the book that points the way. For many, it was the only book they ever read. The church was the strongest institution in their lives; unlike most other things in life, it was theirs. It was a place where their own forms of community relationships took shape and where their own leaders found legitimacy. The Williams knew well the other-worldly and apolitical dynamics of this religion, but they also learned from experience how important it was to relate to church leaders if the union was to succeed.

As we spoke with the sharecroppers, we were obliged to meet in churches, both black and white. Most of the churches we met in, of course, were black churches. And it developed, especially with the black churches, that the pastor usually was present and chaired the meetings. Unless he said 'Amen' with that certain inflection which got the people to saying 'Amen' and rumbling their feet, we might as well go home.

The first big opportunity to test this view came in 1936 when a number of radical organizations in Little Rock, recognizing Claude's organizing ability, encouraged him to set up a school to train grassroots organizers for the STFU. In essential ways, the New Era School of Social Action and Prophetic Religion prefigured the People's Institute.

In December 1936, we held this first school for the sharecroppers. Nine whites and ten blacks. J. R. Butler (president of the STFU) got the students and I raised the funds. I wrote J. R. Butler from New York that we were gonna have the best school ever conducted in that land of ours 'South of God, decency and democracy.' Well, we did.

We went through every phase of union organizing. It was a ten day school, night and day, solid. We didn't have any charts then, but we discussed the union problems. Then we'd assign someone to go down and organize the people in this county, or this neighborhood. Well, they'd have to study that and then make speeches as though these people were the local people. Then, after we'd done that, we had them go through organizing, setting up a local. Then we went into negotiation, getting a contract. The next to the last night, we had a group of Workers' Alliance people come into the meeting as planters with clubs to break it up. And it was so realistic. One very dynamic woman, whether it was spontaneous to the occasion or whether she just sensed, she jumped right out in the middle of the floor and began to sing: 'We shall not, we shall not be moved. We shall not, we shall not be moved.' . . . Well, they came around.

For the next three years, the Williams were deeply involved in STFU activity. Claude was one of the union's most skillful organizers and a member of the governing board. In 1938, when he became director of Arkansas' famous labor school, Commonwealth College, he made his work with the sharecroppers the field program of the institution. When sectarian conflict within the union's leadership led to his expulsion from the STFU board and his subsequent resignation from Commonwealth, it was natural that Claude would turn to what he did best. The People's Institute of Applied Religion became the vehicle which made use of the Williams' experience in religious workers' education.

By the time the PIAR came into being, the Williams had refined their approach into a more conscious and systematic religious form. The purpose was to work with the natural leadership of the South's poor, always in an interracial setting; to engage them on their own terms, in light of their own experience and their own religious world view; to translate their religious perspective into the need for collective struggle for economic justice; and to develop concrete leadership skills in union organizing. The work was always done on behalf of existing labor organizations.

The three to ten day institute was the chief form of the PIAR's work. Roughly fifty people, equally divided between black and white, men and women, worked through morning, afternoon and evening in intense sessions. "These were people who had some tendency toward leadership," recalls Claude. "They were preachers or preacherettes or Sunday School superintendents or Sunday School teachers." Following the custom among rural churches, each participant often represented a number of communities; at one institute in Evansville, over one hundred churches were represented.

The interracial nature of the institutes was a matter of principle and, in itself, constituted one of the most significant parts of the experience.

It was the first time some of them had even been together in a meeting. Most, if not all of them, had never sat down to a meal together, and most of them thought they never would—especially the whites. The blacks never thought they'd have the opportunity. A black man got up and wept and talked when Winifred Chappell called him 'brother.' He never thought he'd ever live to see the day when a white woman said 'brother' to him.

Even though they depended a great deal on spontaneity and inspiration, the meetings were carefully structured around the people's religious mindset and how it might be approached.

We were realistic, or we tried to be. We discovered that the fact that the people believed the Bible literally could be used to an advantage. For instance, if we read a passage from the Book which related to some issue of which they were aware, although it contradicted what they had interpreted some other passage to mean, they had to also include this. Being so-called fundamentalists, accepting the Bible verbatim, had nothing whatever to do with the person's understanding of the issues that related to bread and meat, raiment, shelter, jobs and civil liberties. Therefore, our approach was not an attempt to supplant their present mindset, but to supplement it with a more horizontal frame of reference. And we found that supplementing and supplanting turned out to be one and the same thing.

We learned we had to contact these people at their consciousness of their need. We recognized that what the social scientist or the social worker saw as the need of the people and what the victim felt were two entirely different things.

Meetings always opened with a song, scripture and prayer, a ritual still practiced in many grassroots political meetings throughout the South. Then:

When we had them together at the opening session, we would say, "Now, we have come here to talk about our problems, the problems we meet every day of our lives. We want to start and let everyone tell us what the problems are that he or she meets, as it relates to food and clothes and shelter and health and freedom."

Well, as long as this person would talk, we'd let him talk. If it took an entire day, we let everyone talk. Well, they were ready to talk, you know, after it got started, talking about the things that was close to them. With the result, after these meetings, they would sit down that evening to a meal together. And

I never heard a murmur, they felt such a oneness.

Following these sharing sessions, either Claude or another workshop leader would begin with the first orientation chart. Claude realized that much of the written material distributed by political organizations was totally inappropriate for the sharecroppers. Those who could read were not prepared to wade through the typical political tract. They needed something visual, something more symbolic than literal, something that would suggest concepts based on the story people were already familiar with—the Bible. So shortly before he left Commonwealth, Claude worked out four basic charts for orienting people to the "positive content" of the gospel. A young artist at Commonwealth named Dan Genin made the drawings.

These charts were used throughout the history of the PIAR, and include "The Galilean and the Common People." Another, called "Religion and the Common People," recounts the origins of religion in superstition, the ways religion has been used by rulers to subject people, and the emergence of people's religion in the Old Testament. A third, entitled "Religion and Progress," illustrates how civil values like equality, freedom and justice support true democracy. A fourth chart, "Anti-Semitism, Racism and Democracy," counters the evils used during the Depression and World War II to create disunity among working people.

Over the years Claude introduced other charts, more diagrammatic then pictoral, but still employing the same simplicity. One, entitled "The New Earth," employs the equation FAITH + VICTORY — WORLD = RIGHTEOUSNESS (WORLD refers to "the present world system"). Another chart, called "Anti-Christs" deals with the forces of evil in the world, especially the Ku Klux Klan. Through these almost simplistic devices, biblical concepts were translated into contemporary content and people were drawn into the learning process.

Usually, each session dealt with one chart, sometimes only sections of a chart, depending on what participants expressed as pressing needs and problems. The presentations were delivered in sermon fashion, full of the emotion and speaking style which people expected from somebody who had a deep conviction to impart. It was through the charts, more than anything else in the institutes, that the supplementing, supplanting process took place, for what people heard were the old familiar events from the Bible, buttressed by chapter and verse, but told in a way they never expected. They exclaimed, "We never heard it on this order!" and at the same time they said, "It makes sense to our minds."

The same spirit of involvement marked other sessions where participants used mimeographed worksheets to study particular problems such as peonage on the plantations, the poll tax and the lack of educational opportunities. Music also played an important part in the Institute's, as it did in the participants' churches. Not

surprisingly, singing became part of the learning experience. In fact, out of the institutes (and the previous training schools in Arkansas) came some of today's best known freedom songs.

One time in this ten day meeting in Memphis, about the third morning someone began to sing:

What is that I see yonder coming,
What is that I see yonder coming,
What is that I see yonder coming,
Get on board, get on board!

As she sung that through, the way she sung it, I could hear the drums of Africa! I said, my God, we've got to do something with that song. When she had finished, I got up. I referred to the songs we had

sung in Arkansas. There's always one verse in the songs that's related to the people. Like (singing):

I'm going down to the river of
Jordan
I'm going down to the river of
Jordan one of these days,
hallelujah!
I'm going to walk on the freedom
highway. . . .
I'm going to eat at the welcome
table. . . .

Well, we changed the "I" to "we" and we sang:

We're going to walk on the

people's highway. . . .
Well, when I sat back down there in
Memphis, this woman got up and began in the same
deliberate cadence:

What is that I see yonder coming,
What is that I see yonder coming,
What is that I see yonder coming,
CIO, CIO!

It is one great big union,
It is one great big union,
It is one great big union. . . .

It has freed many a thousand. . . . Well, I went to
New York and went to Lee Hayes, Pete Seeger and
Millard Lampell and the Almanack Singers. I
repeated this and told them what happened. They
took it to Paul Robeson. Paul Robeson said,
"That's our song. We've got to use it. That's the
basis of 'The Union Train,' been sung now around
the world. And Miss Hattie Walls must be given
credit for it. She's the one who first said it."

The last hour of the institute was something like a
praise meeting, full of singing and prayer and testimony
about what the experience had meant to people.

"We thank you, for we are beginning to see the light."

"Where there's hate, there's separation; where there's
separation, there's weakness. Let's stand together."

"Jesus meant for us to have economic freedom. Let's
not expect God to fill our mouths when we open them."

"We want to thank you for the things we heard that we
did not know. We thank Thee for unity. Break down
every wall of partition. We pray for those in distress in
body and mind. We realize Thy will can be done only in
our bodies. Heavenly Father, take charge of every one of
us."

Then they went home to organize the union.

In its initial years, the Institute worked closely with the
sharecropper movement and developing CIO activities in
the South. A PIAR report for the fall of 1941 describes a
number of institutes held in cotton belt places like the
Missco, Arkansas, federal farm; Longview, Texas; Hayti,
Missouri; Osceola and Carson Lake, Arkansas. The
meetings encountered increasing harassment and threats
of violence from local planters, law enforcement officials
and hired thugs.

At the Missco institute, fifty vigilantes appeared, and
the leadership could not leave the project for fear of their
lives. Because of the intimidation, several institutes were
held on the periphery of the cotton belt where sharecroppers could be transported away from terror. In
March 1941, some fifty cotton belt church folks gathered
in Evansville, Indiana, for an institute, and in late April
another was conducted in St. Louis.

The work of arranging these institutes was carried out
by the Williams and a band of colleagues who joined the
Institute soon after its formation. Some were cotton field
preachers who had worked with the STFU and remained
active after the union joined the CIO's United Cannery,
Agricultural, Packinghouse and Allied Workers of Amer-
ica (UCAPAWA). Chief among them was Rev. Owen H.
Whitfield, a black Missouri preacher, one of the strongest
leaders to emerge from the sharecropper movement.
Whitfield was a co-director of PIAR, and he and his wife
Zella participated in many institutes. Other friends from
STFU days took state responsibilities, including Rev. W.
L. Blackstone in Missouri and Leon Turner in Arkansas.
Claude's brother Dan, himself a preacher and share-
cropper, was active in Missouri and helped arrange an
institute in that state which was broken up by planters.

One of the Institute's most amazing recruits was the
Rev. A. L. Campbell, a white preacher from Arkansas.
Campbell worked on the 60,000-acre Lee Wilson plantation and attended the Evansville institute as a spy for the
Ku Klux Klan. But the message he heard, particularly the
frontal assault on Ku Kluxism, "converted" him, and
thereafter he was one of the Institute's most single-
minded and effective leaders.

Others helped. Don West, who had studied with
Claude under Alva Taylor at Vanderbilt, took responsibility for Georgia. Harry and Grace Koger were also
deeply involved. Harry, a former YMCA executive, was
the regional organizer for UCAPAWA in Memphis. And
Winifred Chappell, a co-worker with Dr. Harry F. Ward
in the Methodist Federation for Social Action, was a
co-founder and co-director of PIAR. She had been a
prominent supporter of the textile strike in Gastonia,
N.C., in 1929, and worked with Claude and Joyce in
Paris, Little Rock, and later in Detroit.

These people formed a network throughout the South,
continually traveling, speaking, organizing meetings, cor-
responding, leading and recruiting people for the union
and the institutes. Each was trained in the institute meth-
odology and the use of the charts; each brought to the task
their own distinctive personalities and interpretations.

They were supported by a network of PIAR chapters
and friends in northern urban centers, including many
well-known progressives from labor and civil-rights
organizations, along with professionals from religion,
education, medicine and even a few businessmen. Claude,
Winifred Chappell and others established and sustained
these committees through frequent travel. The network
provided the financial support necessary for the work in
the South. For Claude and Joyce and the others working
in the nation's poorest region, eating was always a catch-
as-catch-can proposition. Their ability to stay alive and to
underwrite the Institute's activities depended in large
measure on outside support. So, at certain times, did their
legitimacy and their safety. More than once these groups
came to the aid of people, including PIAR staff, who were
in jail or under threat of terror.

In the summer of 1941, the PIAR conducted its most controversial, dangerous and significant meeting in the South. At the time, Memphis was one of the most brutal urban strongholds in America, totally controlled by the violent and racist machine of Boss Ed Crump. When the CIO began to organize in Memphis, Don Henderson of UCAPAWA asked Claude and the Institute to hold a labor school, cautioning that he didn't want "any of that new wine in old bottles stuff." Claude and Joyce, the Kogers and Owen Whitfield, ignoring that instruction, used the charts in all classes, and Whitfield and Koger used them quietly at union meetings. Their work culminated in a ten-day institute that included packinghouse workers from Memphis and sharecroppers from as far away as Texas.

The conference was one of the most spirited and thorough ever conducted by the Institute, and it had more far-reaching effects. Memphis' considerable repressive establishment had been conducting a terror campaign against the CIO for months, and when word of the institute hit the newspapers, the forces of reaction struck swiftly. Harry Koger was jailed for questioning and a few days later Claude was taken to police headquarters and interrogated for two days. The "big union" had come to stay, however. Within months the CIO had dug a foothold into several Memphis industries and within a few years the Crump machine itself would fall. Encouraged to leave town for their own safety, Claude and Joyce once again moved the family and PIAR headquarters, this time to Evansville, Indiana.

During the war years, the Institute remained active throughout the cotton belt. The Williams did not stay in Evansville long, for in early 1942, Claude accepted the invitation of the Presbyterian churches in Detroit to establish a labor ministry there. Detroit was the center of national war production, and new migrants were streaming into the city from the South at an unprecedented rate. Racial tensions ran high, encouraged by an army of reactionary religious demagogues like Gerald L. K. Smith, Father Coughlin and J. Frank Norris. Aided financially by the lords of industry, these "apostles of hatred" preached a divisive message of racial purity and anti-unionism quite familiar to the Williams from their years in the South.

The program they established represented the continuation of the PIAR. With the cooperation of the new United Auto Workers, shop committees of working preachers were set up to use the charts and preach "realistic religion" in the plants at lunchtime. An interracial "Brotherhood Squadron" of speakers and singers appeared in churches. In 1943, Claude authored a scathing expose of the right-wing religious leaders; and Philip Adler, reporter for the *Detroit News*, wrote a series of favorable articles on Claude based on the report. Liberal church forces, along with other professional and civil-rights organizations, were enlisted to help combat the tremendous forces of reaction in the city, and the PIAR leadership played a crucial role in negotiations to end Detroit's second major war-time race riot in June 1943.

As the war ended, the churches who sponsored the Williams' work bowed to the concerted counterattack on Claude by Smith, Norris, Carl McIntyre, and the House Un-American Activities Committee. Charges of heresy were brought against a Presbyterian minister for the first time in over one hundred years. (The inevitable guilty verdict came down in 1954.) The PIAR continued for several more years, but like all progressive forces during the McCarthy years, found the going rough. In a ceremony at St. Paul's Chapel in Brooklyn on July 20, 1948, the PIAR brought its formal history to a close, all members vowing to continue as volunteers of the Way of Righteousness.

Underlying and informing the Williams' work throughout the years has been a concept of religion which at the least, is out of the ordinary. Those who came in contact with the People's Institute of Applied Religion heard its application to the problems of their own time and place. Only a few are familiar with its basic assumptions and the great detail in which the biblical story is spelled out. There is space here only to indicate its outlines.

There are several things that religion is not. It is not a belief in anything supernatural. It is not a belief in a divine force outside human life which directs events. Assuredly, it is not the church or the practice of any organized religion. Nor is it theology, an intellectual discipline which assumes a fundamental distance between God and people. Rather, biblical religion is a way of comprehending reality that "deals solely with the intangible facts of existence and communicates these facts by a symbolic language, by legend, by myth, miracle, parable, and allegory." Religion does not pretend to be science or history. But it does insist that the intangible facts of existence are as real as the tangible, and that the intangible, in fact, gives "warmth and feeling and meaning" to the objective world.

Certain key words are important for understanding the nature of the intangible. One is the word "qualitative," which implies that the nature of reality is personal, that it has to do essentially with human beings and their welfare.

> I believe God is a symbol of the qualitative unity of reality. I don't believe God is a person like we think of a person. But I think personality, communication, thought, things like that are inherent in the universe. I don't believe I'm alone. I believe there is a qualitative essence in the universe of which I am an integral part, and to which I must be loyal to attain my greatest potential. So, I am religious, but I don't believe in supernaturalism as such.

Another descriptive word is "comprehensive." All things are one; life is not defined by any dualism, Greek or otherwise. The physical, rational and emotional in people are distinct from one another, but they are not separate. They comprise a totality, and to treat people as though they can be fragmented into parts violates the intangible reality of life.

course, the way Claude and Joyce understand the Bible has changed a great deal over the years. During the 1930s, a friend gave Claude a copy of Lenin's *State and Revolution,* and he declared it "the most revealing commentary

The NEW EARTH

SCRIPTURE : REV. 21 : 1-8
TEXT : ... A NEW EARTH, WHEREIN DWELLETH RIGHTEOUSNESS - 2 PETER 3:13

F **A** **I** **T** **H**	**V** **I** **C** **T** **O** **R** **Y**	**W** **O** **R** **L** **D**	**R** **I** **G** **H** **T** **E** **O** **U** **S** **N** **E** **S** **S**
F-ELLOWSHIPING WITH ONE ANOTHER (1 JOHN 1:7)	V-ISION - A PEOPLE'S VISION (PROV. 29:18)	W-ARS OF AGGRESSION (LUKE 2:1,2)	R-EIGN OF THE PEOPLE (DAN 7:26,27)
A-DMONISHING ONE ANOTHER (ROM. 15:14)	I-NSIGHT - DISCERNING THE TIMES (LUKE 12:54-56)		I-NTERNATIONAL GOVERNMENT (HEB. 12:25,29)
is + the	C-OURAGE - FROM UNITY IN ACTION (ISA 41:6,7) *that over-*	O-RGANIZED TYRANNY (LUKE 23:11,12)	G-OOD WILL TOWARD ALL MEN (LUKE 2:13,14)
I-NSTRUCTING ONE ANOTHER (2 TIM 3:16,17)	*comes the* T-RUTH - TRUTH THAT FREES (JOHN 8:32)	*and equals* R-ANK HYPOCRISY (MTT 2:8) / A NEW EARTH WHEREIN DWELLETH	H-EAVENLY PLACES ON EARTH (ISA. 35:3-10) T-RUE FREEDOM (LUKE 4:17-19) E-CONOMIC JUSTICE (ISA 65:21-25)
T-RUSTING ONE ANOTHER (JAMES 2:1-4)	O-RGANIZATION - ALL FOR EACH (JOHN 15:1-8)	L-AND MONOPOLY (LUKE 12:16-21)	O-PPORTUNITIES FOR ALL (ACTS 2:17-20) U-NITY OF ALL (ACTS 17:26) S-OCIALISM of JESUS and the PROPHETS (MTT 25:31-46) NEITHER WARS NOR RUMORS OF WAR (MICAH 4:3)
H-ELPING ONE ANOTHER (GAL 6:2-5)	R-ESOURCEFULNESS (JAMES 2:5 / 1 COR 1:26-28) Y-IELDING - EACH TO ALL (MTT 20:25-28)	D-OLLAR DIPLOMACY (JOHN 14:30)	E-VERY MAN SHALL EARN HIS OWN BREAD (2 THES. 3:10) S-ECURITY FOR ALL THE DISABLED (LUKE 14:10-15) S-ERVICE TO ALL THE MOTIVE OF ALL (MTT 23:10-12)

Likewise, people are not separate from one another. They are not isolated individuals but social beings who are inevitably bound to one another. They do not live in a world where the spiritual and the material are separate. The intangible meanings of life are to be found here and now, in our daily activity. The Kingdom of God is a goal to be achieved continually in this world. It is a collective struggle for the good, which is itself comprehensive. The good implies living and working together in a society where everyone has food and clothing and shelter, where everyone is encouraged to learn and imagine and create, and where people care for the natural world around them. For the good to be realized, belief and action can not be separated. In the words of the Son of Man, "Not everyone who says to me, 'Lord, Lord,' shall enter the kingdom of heaven, but he who does the will of my father who is in heaven" (Matt. 7:21).

The source of this understanding is the Bible. Of

on the Bible I had ever seen." As he pondered how the Bible would read in light of this new perspective, he tried an experiment which he later described in a 1947 publication of the PIAR entitled *Religion: Barrier or Bridge to a People's World:*

> In order to bring out in bold relief the class lines of the Bible, take the following simple steps. Write down what any intelligent person knows—that the issues of today demand racial, economic and political justice for all people. Then take the Bible and underline with a red pencil all passages which support these ends. With a black pencil, mark the passages which defeat these ends, by escapism or confusion.
>
> The simplest reader will see Abraham, Moses, the prophets, John the Baptist, the Nazarene, Peter, Stephen, James and others as leaders of the people and at one with them in their flight. He will see Ahab, Jezebel and other robber-murderers; Pha-

roah with his taskmasters, magicians and soothsayers; the landlords with their winter and summer houses; church religion with its false prophets, high priests, priests of the second order; the Baals, Caesars, Herods and Pilates—all these as spoilers of unity, oppressors of the people and enemies of justice.

Here is the foundation of a people's interpretation of the Bible.

Over the years, this "people's interpretation of the Bible" has crystallized into a systematic account of a people's movement that Claude calls "The Way of Righteousness." It is the story of a self-conscious movement of poor and oppressed people beginning with Abraham, a movement that waxed and waned on the basis of political circumstances throughout Old Testament times and always couched its class dynamic in religious terms. Its contours first take dramatic form in the Exodus, when a number of Semitic tribes enslaved by the pharoahs of Egypt unite and rebel. It continues through the time of the kings of Israel, when a prophetic opposition—personified in Amos, Hosea, Jeremiah and Isaiah—protests the oppression of the common people by Israel's corrupt rulers, enduring death and persecution for its efforts. It traces the beginnings of class internationalism in the writings of Isaiah, Elisha and Elijah, and in the story of Jonah.

Then, the account relates how the Way, which for many years after the Prophets had existed underground, goes public again when Rome unites the world's poor in a common condition by declaring a universal tax. Spoken for by the Son of Man and John the Baptist, who were born into families of the Way and trained for leadership, the movement becomes so successful that John is beheaded and the Son of Man barely escapes execution.

After resurfacing at Pentecost under the leadership of Peter and James, the movement prospers and spreads throughout the Roman Empire, despite the efforts of the Pharisee Paul to deflect its revolutionary content into an other-worldly theological individualism which is always deferential to the Roman establishment. Finally, the movement becomes so serious that, three hundred years after the Son of Man, the emperor Constantine becomes a Christian himself, thereby absorbing the movement into the Roman establishment and leaving it for a much later day for the spirit of the Way of Righteousness to re-emerge.

The methods of the underground are drawn in great detail. All activities of the Way are collective. Thus, while Moses or Jeremiah or the Son of Man or Peter may appear in the scripture as spokesmen, behind them is an organized movement working in intricate ways to carry out its goals. The "multitudes" who gather to hear the Son of Man do not appear magically but are the product of hard organizational work. The Way is shrewd enough to cultivate friends in strategic high places, such as Joseph of Arimathea, a member of the ruling Jewish Sanhedrin, and the several centuries of the Roman occupying army mentioned in the New Testament.

The Way is organized secretly, as would be necessary for any underground movement, and is required to speak in indirect and symbolic language. Thus, "houses" (e.g. Mary and Martha) are centers of underground activity and entrance is gained only by password; "angels" are underground messengers; the "wilderness" usually refers to conferences of the underground, where strategies are considered and decided; and "cleansing unclean spirits" actually refers to encounters with people who are dissuaded from liberal reform, nationalism, adventuristic violence and other prevalent ideologies among those who imperfectly oppose Rome.

Those familiar with the "theology of liberation" are aware that the "Way of Righteousness" closely resembles several contemporary theologies which also identify the struggle of poor against rich as the basic theme of the Bible. Unlike some, the Way is not a document written by a professional theologian and published for discussion in the seminaries. Like others, it is something that must be done. And true to its own perspective, it bears the marks of a particular historical experience.

The work of the People's Institute of Applied Religion was based on the important notion that political movements need to meet people with an openness to the positive convictions and yearnings they express within their own frame of reference. The PIAR began by taking this approach to the religious rural poor of the South. In the interaction the Institute learned some important things about the people and their religion, and in its own unique way the Institute offered these lessons to the broader radical movement of the time.

From the whites, they learned that otherworldliness

Photo by Bill Troy

and fierce moralism are essentially a protest against, an escape from, conditions which starve and torment and rob people who have no effective way to resist. From black people, they learned that religion is all these things and more. It is also a way of looking at the world which embraces life's misery yet finds joy in the present and hope in the future, and which is willing to move politically when the realistic opportunity arises. The willingness of both groups to join an interracial movement for economic justice under the most threatening conditions, and to do so within their religious faith, gave witness to the Institute's perceptiveness. It was these people, hundreds of poor black and white believers, who joined with the Williams and the PIAR to write a new chapter in the "Way of Righteousness."

Part Three

Religion in the South
Its Personal Expressions

"All o'er those wide-extended plains
 Shines one eternal day;
There God the Son forever reigns,
 And scatters night away."

"And We'll All Sing Together"

by Rich Kirby

Trying to describe the religious folk music of the Southern mountains is a little like trying to organize the church itself—songs, like people, just will not line up quietly in neat rows. Still, there are patterns in this varied and vital tradition, and searching for them reveals, as well as anything can, the intensity of religious feeling that has always been part of mountain life.

Religious singing in the mountains flourished with the wave of revivals that has swept the region in the last two hundred years. The emotional intensity of these movements combined with the strong musical traditions of the area to produce some of America's most powerful music. It is true folk music—home-made music that people use in their everyday lives to express their deepest feelings.

At the same time, the familiar dynamics of social mobility have acted as a counterweight to this tradition. Typically, churches which begin on the fringes of established religion change as they get more rooted; a generation that goes to carpeted churches and listens to the choir looks back in embarrassment on its predecessors who shouted and danced on bare boards. This process has happened to every religious revival movement in the mountains. But persistent economic hardship has prevented the mountains as a whole from going through this upwardly mobile change. As a result, the reservoir of folk creativity, often left behind by various churches, has waited for the next round. The process continues today.

Roots

Folk traditions in the British Isles go back unbroken to the pre-Christian era. Their heathen origins, however, meant that English songs were repressed by Anglicans, and even more by the Puritans. Of the little religious folk music that survived, only a small portion crossed the waters with the early settlers. The New Puritans continued to scorn music and celebrations altogether, and finally reduced church singing to no more than two dozen tunes. Only in the backwoods could people who wanted to sing do so unhampered by convention or the restrictions of the church. It was here on the New England frontier, outside the cities where music was controlled by the wealthy, the educated and the church, that folk music took its first root in America.

Singing schools, conducted by itinerant masters and held in taverns, quickly grew up to satisfy people's desire to learn religious music. They taught the notes of the scale by an Elizabethan system of "solmization" in which the seven-note scale is rendered FA-SOL-LA-SOL-LA-MI. Singers could learn tunes by these syllables before singing the words.

Then around 1798, two innovators named Little and Smith found a new way of putting music on paper. They took the four syllables FA-SOL-LA-MI and gave each a separate shape on the musical clef:

Rich Kirby lives in Dungannon, Virginia. He has been a student of mountain music since his grandmother sang Old Regular Baptist hymns to him as a boy in Kentucky. These days he sings on records like "New Wood" and "Cotton Mill Blues" (June Appal) and plays with anybody who will stop to pick a while.

Shape-note singing will no doubt rank as America's great contribution to the teaching of music. It simplified the notes and their relationship to each other, allowing the old singing masters to teach music to people who the city-bred musicians considered hopeless. The system quickly won acceptance and its influence continues to the present day, especially in the South.

The music centers in the East were less friendly. They disdained the new works of the self-educated, shape-note song writers, forcing them to develop their own publishing institutions. The new music drew heavily on folk tunes and the democratic spirit of post-Revolution America; the tunes were lively, strong, and popular. Harmony was introduced, making the music all the more unconventional to the Puritan critics. Nevertheless, writing music in shapenotes persisted. Perhaps the best of the little recognized but highly talented shape-note composers was William Billings (1746-1800), a cobbler who, according to the *Sacred Harp*, "was criticized by many musicians and music writers, and while he did not believe so much in rules he wrote some very fine music." Another rugged individual, the Reverend John Leland, was described vividly in the *Sacred Harp*:

> In 1808 he took a preaching tour from his home in Massachusetts to Washington with his Cheshire cheese which made his name national on account of that trip. . . The farmers of Cheshire, of whom he was pastor, conceived the idea of sending the biggest cheese in America to President Jefferson. Mr. Leland offered to go to Washington with an ox-team with it, and preach along the way, which he did. The cheese weighed 1,450 pounds. He died with great hope of rest in the glory world.

Revivals

Despite the established church's distaste for shape-note singing, the music was well developed by the time the Baptists and Methodists began to penetrate the religious vacuum of the frontier. The Presbyterian Church dominated the New World outposts, but it held little appeal for the poorer and less-educated settlers. In sharp contrast to the Calvinists' elitism, the revivalists' Arminian doctrine (salvation open to all by faith) and down-to-earth emotional style struck a responsive chord on the frontier. The democratic impulse that had nourished the rise of religious folk music was now being tapped for an even larger social movement. As one historian writes, "The close connection of the Colonial Government, the Established Church, and the aristocracy of the Tidewater makes it impossible to treat the (revival) movement as solely religious. It was more than that. It was a protest against religious, social and political privilege—and because education was closely associated with the privileged classes, somewhat too against education."[1]

Revivalists, especially Baptists, were heavily persecuted from 1750 to 1775, but they flourished nonetheless. the influence of their doctrines on the frontier was boundless, and by the dawn of the nineteenth century they had unleashed a storm of religious activity in all but the plantation South.

The revival movement culminated in that amazing phenomenon, the camp meeting—a gathering of hundreds or thousands of people in remote areas for days or weeks of continuous religious observances. It was with the camp meeting that religious folk music took root among the masses of the Southern mountaineers. The first camp meeting was held in Logan County, Kentucky, in 1800. For the next 30 years, common people—mostly black and white farmers—attended these incredibly intense gatherings that centered on the struggle within the participant over her/his feelings of sin and salvation. Preachers vividly described heaven and hell. Songs, prayers, groans and shouts from repentant sinners and the energy released by so many people crowded together made the camp meeting an irresistible force. One observer writes, "at no time was the floor less than half-covered. Some lay quiet, unable to move or speak. Some talked but could not move. Some beat the floor with their heels. Some, shrieking in agony, bounded about like fish out of water. Many lay down and rolled over for hours at a time. Others rushed wildly about over the stumps and benches, then plunged, shouting 'Lost! Lost!' into the forest."[2]

The singing at the meeting was nothing less than pure folk music. Baptists and Methodists generally used the hymns written by John and Charles Wesley and Isaac Watts, who set out to write for "the meanest Christians" and therefore used plain English. But on the frontier, people persistently made their own music. Louis Benson, the historian of sacred music, deplored the camp meeting's "illiterate and often vulgar Revival Hymnody":

> The people were ignorant, the preachers were itinerant . . . and the singing largely without books . . . The tunes had to be very familiar or very contagious, the words given out one or two lines at a time if not already known. Under these conditions the development of . . . a rude type of popular song, indifferent to anything in the way of authorized hymnody, seems to have been inevitable.[3]

Benson was accurately, if unwittingly, describing the creation of religious folk music—an evolving body of songs improvised from familiar hymns and the Scriptures,

---

[1] John C. Campbell, *The Southern Highlander and His Homeland* (Lexington: University Press of Kentucky, 1969).

[2] Louis F. Benson, *The English Hymn* (1915), as quoted in George P. Jackson, *White Spirituals in the Southern Uplands* (New York: Dover, 1965), p. 215.

[3] Ibid.

ODE ON SCIENCE

*A shape note hymn written
by Deacon Janaziah, 1798*

The morning sun shines from the east
And spreads his glories to the west
All nations with his beams are blest
Wheree'r the radiant light appears
So science spreads her lucid ray
O'er lands which long in darkness lay
She visits fair Columbia
And sets her sons among the stars
Fair freedom her attendant waits
To bless the portals of her gates
To crown the young and rising states
With laurels of immortal day
The British yoke, the Gallic chain
Was urged upon our necks in vain
All haughty tyrants we disdain
And shout long live America

(Original Sacred Harp, 242)

interspersed with refrains and set to easily singable tunes.

We know about the camp-meeting songs largely because of the shape-note songbooks, which were firmly established in the South by 1810 and shortly afterwards disappeared everywhere else. Collections were introduced as late as 1855, and several are still in print, notably the *Sacred Harp, New Harp of Columbia*, and *The Southern Harmony*. In the years before the Civil War, the books and their accompanying singing schools meant music for large numbers—the same folks, by and large, who went to camp meetings—so the songbook compilers included many camp meeting songs. From these songbooks we can see the vital process that produced a large body of native folk music.

● Familiar words were set to new tunes. For example, the *Sacred Harp* has five tunes for "When I can read my title clear to mansions in the skies," five for "Farewell vain world, I'm going home," and six for

On Jordan's stormy bank I stand
And cast a wishful eye
To Canaan's fair and happy land
Where my possessions lie.

Ballad tunes were used for sacred songs ("Lord Lovel" became "And Am I Born to Die"). So were fiddle tunes, considered "too good to remain in the exclusive employ of the devil." Interestingly, the songbook composers preserved some fiddle melodies in jigtime (6/8) as well as the usual reels (2/4 or 4/4).

● Music was designed to involve many people, not just a few trained specialists. Group singing was more important than a good "performance." In the shape-note books each of the three or four parts is developed like a melody, a practice resulting from what George Pullen Jackson called "southernizing." Southern frontier congregations had no instruments to carry harmony and no choir director to assign parts, so the alto part had to be interesting— or no one would sing it.

This sort of democracy extended to the singing style as well. "Who is going to tell Sister So-and-so not to step on it quite so hard," asked Jackson, "and why, in the name of good sense, should she bear the audience in mind when there is none? This is democratic music making. All singers are peers. And the moment selection and exclusion enter, at that moment this singing of, by, and for the people loses its chief characteristic."[4]

● Complicated texts became more simple and repetitive, thus more suitable for group singing. This additional democratic feature of camp-meeting songs is similar to black spirituals, and in fact, some songs from the period have been preserved among singers of both races. There is some dispute over the direction of this interchange. Jackson pointed out that blacks learned Christianity from whites and probably learned white music also. Folklorist Alan Lomax argues that blacks led in developing "songs of great beauty within the fragmentary compass of the easy-to-sing congregational leader-chorus formula; and it was in this direction that the white folk spiritual has steadily developed."[5] Certainly frontier religion brought the two races closer together socially than any other activity in the old South.

The result of this freewheeling cultural crusade was quite astonishing: hundreds of thousands of people, often illiterate, learned to sight-read music and sing in four-part harmony—an achievement of which store-bought music was and is incapable. From this creative ferment evolved many of the forms of mountain religious music we know today, including the familiar verse-chorus form and the spiritual, like "Bright Morning Stars," that is largely chorus.

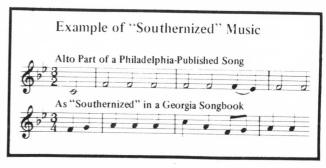

Example of "Southernized" Music

Alto Part of a Philadelphia-Published Song

As "Southernized" in a Georgia Songbook

[4]Jackson, *White Spirituals*.

[5]Alan Lomax, *Folk Songs of North America* (New York: Doubleday, 1960).

Bright Morning Star

Bright morning stars are rising,
Bright morning stars are rising,
Bright morning stars are rising,
Day is a-breakin' in my soul.

Oh, where are our dear fathers,
Oh, where are our dear fathers,
Oh, where are our dear fathers,
Day is a-breakin' in my soul.

They are down in the valley praying,
They are down in the valley praying,
They are down in the valley praying,
Day is a-breakin' in my soul.

Bright morning stars are rising, etc.

Oh, where are our dear mothers,
Oh, where are our dear mothers,
Oh, where are our dear mothers,
Day is a-breakin' in my soul.

They have gone to heaven a-shouting,
They have gone to heaven a-shouting,
They have gone to heaven a-shouting,
Day is a-breakin' in my soul.

Bright morning stars are rising, etc.

Retreat

The tide of religious enthusiasm was clearly shifting by the mid-1800s. As early as 1830, trained musicians had settled in Southern cities and driven the uncouth shape-note singers back into the hills. The more urban Methodists and Baptists had never been too sure about the "excesses" of the camp meeting or the perfectionism it implied. As time went on, there disapproval was less and less subtle. The former underdogs were by now well off, well accepted, and well enough satisfied to be uncomfortable with the crudities of the past. They came to look down on the average mountain church—and its music. For example, the first general Methodist hymnal (1859) systematically ignored camp-meeting songs, taking only 17 of its 357 tunes from the shape-note books, and none of those had camp-meeting origins. Only in the mountains were people able to keep up their own music without undue interference from those who thought it unseemly.

In the years following the Civil War, the mountain churches split and split again—evidence not only of doctrinal difference but of a desire to keep the church local, democratic, family- and community-centered. Isolated from each other and from the outside, communities built up individual song traditions. Some churches used instruments. some did not; different ones used different tunes for the same texts. Often enough churches split over whether to adopt some musical innovation, with one faction choosing to "seek the old paths and walk there-

Photo by Baldwin-Watriss

in." Nevertheless, religious folk music continued to evolve in the mountains, as did fiddle music, old ballads, and the like.

The two traditions that survived the best, that dug deep in the hills and can be found intact today, are shape-note singing and the music of the Old Regular Baptists. Shape-note singing seriously declined after 1870, but its widespread influence continued. Groups using the songbooks still meet in north Alabama, east Tennessee, western North Carolina and north Georgia. More importantly, I believe the experience of so many people singing harmony helped shape a larger tradition of trios and quartets as well as particular features of popular music today. For example, the use in many shape-note songs of a harmony part pitched higher than the melody (completely foreign to conventional church music) still survives in the high harmony heard in so many country churches and bluegrass songs.

The Old Regular Baptist Church preserved a style of singing wholly different from anything else in the mountains. As Calvinist Baptists, their doctrines differed radically from the Arminian revivalists: if salvation is predetermined, revivals are a waste of time. In fact, the church was known for awhile as the "anti-missionary Baptists" (see Ron Short's article elsewhere in this issue). In general, they disapproved of instrumental music and displays of emotion in church, but they shared a number of tunes and texts with the camp-meeting and shape-note singers. The Old Regulars sing now, as they did in the nineteenth century, in complete unison; words are either lined out by a song leader or read from a songbook printed without music. The tunes are slow, solemn, highly ornamented, and quite often in archaic-sounding modes or gapped scales (five tones instead of seven). Other traditions, including the early Puritans, the camp-meeting revivalists, and even today's Old Order Amish, use the lining-out method, but nothing in American music compares to the power of a group of Old Regular Baptists singing their somber tunes. Even when standard hymn texts are used, they are sung to different music. For example:

Photo by Baldwin-Watriss

The details of other developments in religious folk music immediately following the Civil War are largely lost forever. We know that many congregations refused to change at all. Others clung to the musical forms of the past as they sang new evangelical hymns "in the old manner, with marked and arbitrary rhythm and inserted slurring half notes."[6] The awareness of the outside world's hostility toward their forms of worship seems to have increased steadily as Emma Bell Miles recalled in her remarkable book *Spirit of the Cumberlands* (1905):

> God knows what the old ceremonies mean to those who take part in them; but such is the persecution in some places where the curiosity of the town is pressing close in on us that even after a congregation has met together to hold a foot-washing, if any city people are present who are not well-known and trusted,

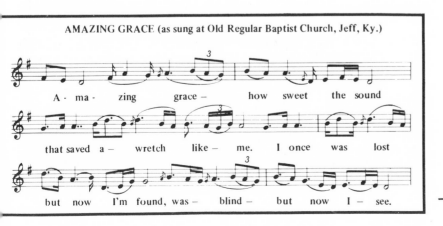

AMAZING GRACE (as sung at Old Regular Baptist Church, Jeff, Ky.)

A - ma - zing grace — how sweet the sound that saved a — wretch like — me. I once was lost but now I'm found, was — blind — but now I - see.

[6]Campbell, *The Southern Highlander.*

the occasion will be quietly turned
into an ordinary preaching.

But neither repression nor inaction from the mainline denominations could keep the religious spirit of the lower classes from bursting forth. In 1867, a National Holiness Movement started (the source of the present Church of the Nazarene) and when it assumed respectability, another holiness movement called the Latter Rain Movement began in east Tennessee in 1892 (which led to various branches of the Church of God). Similarly, revival activity on a local level periodically erupted, fell away, and returned.

Re-entry

The next major period for religion in the mountains began around 1900 when the outside world came crashing back in. Appalachia's rich timber stands, then coal, brought in capital and capitalists. Coincidentally, the national denominations discovered in their own back yard a people so benighted that they required the church's best missionary efforts. The outside church continued to pity or scorn the uneducated, undisciplined, emotional mountaineers, but now it wanted to transform their culture, their entire life style, into something more familiar to mainstream American institutions—a process which, of course, helped the economic exploitation of land and labor.

The music the missionaries brought with them included the products of a commercialization of religious music that began after the Civil War and continues to the present. Newly respectable church members wanted a more refined sort of music which would suit their calmer decorum, and a number of writers began to fill this need, notably P. P. Bliss ("Almost Persuaded," "Hold the Fort"). The style turned into a musical movement when a travelling revivalist named Dwight L. Moody hired Chicago YMCA singer Ira D. Sankey. Sankey's moving tenor added a striking emotional appeal to Moody's preaching and soon the pair were enthralling throngs on two continents, making them the first of the "superstar" evangelists. Sankey himself wrote hundreds of songs, now mostly forgotten, and other writers were not long in following. Publishing houses quickly issued songbooks, recognizing that there is more money in peddling copyrighted originals than in folk songs. Homer Rodeheaver (who sang with Billy Sunday) was the most prominent entrepreneur of what has been called a "religious Tin Pan Alley."

This music was essentially a religious version of Victorian popular music, with flowery tunes (almost always in major keys) and conventional harmonies. Where frontier people had sung of salvation through struggle, the new music talked of salvation through quiet acceptance—an obvious way of encouraging people to reconcile themselves to the emerging industrial society. Optimism was the encouraged mood, and revivals flourished amid thickets of joy bells, heavenly lifeboats and fountains of delight.

There is no record of what happened when this music was introduced to the mountains, but shortly afterwards the mountain gospel song (of the sort recorded by the Carter Family) made its entry. It is a cross between the popular evangelistic music and the older mountain traditions, taking themes and images from the mainstream music and vigor and directness of tune and style from folk music. Most of the popular tunes are owned by one publisher or another; but "Keep On the Sunny Side," "I'll Fly Away," "Will the Circle Be Unbroken," "Somebody Touched Me" and many similar pieces deserve at this point to be called folk songs.

Needless to say, the folk roots of gospel music are not well cared for, certainly not by the publishers. Few songbooks have more than a token of the old music. Most are harmonized for the pianist's convenience, not the singer's interest. The old minor tunes are largely gone, as are the archaic and beautiful five-toned ones. Songs that country-church singers render (in a more or less oral tradition) with a steady driving beat are often written with a singsong, watered-down rhythm. Publishers have issued songbooks and sponsored singing schools to popularize their music, just as they did a century ago—only now the music has more connection to a safe and sedate mainstream than to folk traditions.

The missionary churches left little room for religious emotion or for social action. It is not surprising then that a reaction burst out in the form of the Pentecostal Holiness movement, which swelled in the 1920s and within two decades had, by one estimate, as many adherents as any other brand of Protestantism. Like the emotional

Photo courtesy of Baptist Home Mission Board

revivals of the past, Pentecostalism appealed to the dispossessed in society, whose ranks were swelled by the Depression. Like the previous revivals, the movement released a vast reservoir of energy and emotion. Once again, people danced, sang, spoke in tongues and in other ways reproduced the climate of the camp meetings, though now in more hostile surroundings. One Methodist historian of sects claimed Pentecostals attracted people with "unstable nervous structures . . . the ignorant, in whom the lower brain centers and spinal ganglia are strong." Others have called them apolitical for their rigid doctrinal rejection of the world, but this seems to me to be consistent with a belief that the world as we know it is truly in need of radical change, a belief that has led many country preachers to be excellent organizers for social change.

Like the previous revivals, the Pentecostal movement made full use of the power of music—lively, simple, repetitive, accompanied by guitars, banjos or whatever is handy, and involving the whole group. Alan Lomax noted the following piece from Kentucky, pointing out that it used the very old leader-chorus form of a Negro work song:

Today

At present, religious music in the mountains covers a cultural range equivalent to that of secular music. At one side is the more or less pure folk music of Regular Baptist and Old Harp Singers; on the other the Nashville-style slick gospel groups like the Oak Ridge Quartet, which recently achieved the distinction of being the first gospel act to book into a Las Vegas resort. To get some idea of this territory one has only to turn on the radio Sunday morning. Start early—stations rarely give rural churches prime time—and consider the fact that this is the only time you can ever turn to the media for live folk-style music. Religious music is subject to the same forces as all mountain music, including commercialization, emphasis on polish and performance, and the general invasion of city culture into the country—and as Dr. Jackson said so long ago, "city people do not sing." Still, churches have been able to shelter more handmade mountain music than any other institution. To hear it is to renew and affirm the journey mountain people have traveled in the last 200 years.

O DAVID! (collected by Alan Lomax in eastern Ky.)

That Holding Out Spirit

by Guy and Candy Carawan
photography by Robert Yellin

Johns Island, six miles from Charleston off the South Carolina coast, is a low-lying swamp-covered sea island; until the '30s it was accessible only by boat. On it live the descendents of plantation slaves who, in their isolation from the mainland, preserved more fully than in most rural black communities the richness of their Afro-American folk traditions. The earliest forms of black Christian worship in which prayer, testimony, sermon, possession, music, and dance were intertwined (as they were in Africa) have remained alive on Johns Island. Moving Star Hall has played an important role in this survival.

A number of such meeting houses used to exist throughout the sea islands. But when we moved to Johns Island in the early 1960s, only Moving Star Hall was still thriving. Throughout the 1960s it served as a central factor in the community and religious life of a portion of the black population of Johns Island. Besides housing weekly interdenominational class meetings (most people coming to Moving Star Hall also belonged to a regular church on the island) there was a burial-and-tend-the-sick society and a fraternal order.

Today the tradition of meeting at Moving Star Hall is dying out. Only a few gatherings are held in the hall each year. The all-night watch meetings of Christmas and New Years and most of the other religious services take place at the regular denominational churches on the island.

Photo by Thorsten Horton

Here am I again once more,
Heavenly Father.
The worm of the dust
Ready to bow this hour of the
morning
On my bruised and bending knee.
Thank you, My Father, for your
guardin' angel,
That guard me all night long
Until morning light appear.
And before he went from his watch,
He touch my eyes this morning
with a finger of love,
And my eye become open
And behold a brand new Monday
morning.

Oh God, if you so please
Give us that holding out spirit,
That You may own us all
When we done trod across the
many street of Charleston.
Oh God, what I say for our
neighbors,
And the neighbors' children around
in this vicinity,
Oh please, Our Father,
Make them more patient,
more acknowledge,
May we love each and one another.
Help us to help each other.
                    —Mr. James Mackey

I remember when Moving Star Hall was built, 'round about 1913, '14. Father help build the hall. Mother, too. We all throw money until we gets enough to buy the land. All pay seven dollars for the lumber. All join and make that hall.

—Mrs. Isabel Simmons

In the meeting, Brother Joe Deas, he are the oldest person in there, we takes him for the leading man. Brother Deas takes the text, when is preaching night, and the boys supposed to preach from that text he give you. You can go preach any- where you want to preach, but you come right back to that same text. Any individual, soon as the man finish preach, if you want to raise a song, you raise it. And another way, anytime we call someone up to preach, if anybody want to sing for you, can sing you up there. Then one can sing you down. Anybody.

—Mr. John Smalls

That's so much the most thing I could do—shout. I'll tell you, with the spirit of God, you don't care what pain you got. You forget about that when you shout. When I going out, I feel so painful I scarcely don't go. But I say to myself, just as well if I go now, 'cause will come a day when the limbs fail me.

—Mr. James Mackey

Now some of us, because we can read a little bit more, forget about the place we came from and some of the songs which help us go on. When older folks sang those songs—"Been in the Storm So Long," "Nobody Knows the Trouble I've Seen"—it helped them realize they're trusting in God and reaching for a better day. We certainly wouldn't want the children to get away from it. We should cherish it, we should preserve it and keep it.

Now if we hide those sweet songs and try to get away from what we came from, what will we tell our children about the achievement we have made and the distance we have come?

—Mr. Esau Jenkins

We all as kids went to Moving Star Hall. As far as I was concerned, I just had to be there. We used to enjoy the singing and the shouting. And at a certain period of the night, all the youngsters in there had to go up front and kneel down and everybody prayed. . . . All of a sudden it just start dying off. For one thing most of the young people started going away. Like me, I went in the Army. I was about fifteen. Once the kids start going to different places, and we start to be more enlightened, then we start getting away from this old type of thing. . . . This is good, but it doesn't help your eating. Why waste time with something that you aren't gonna get anything out of at all? You gonna be looking forward to when you die, and man, you hungry now.

—Mr. William Saunders

Granny Reed
A Testimony

interview by Paul Gillespie and
Keith Head

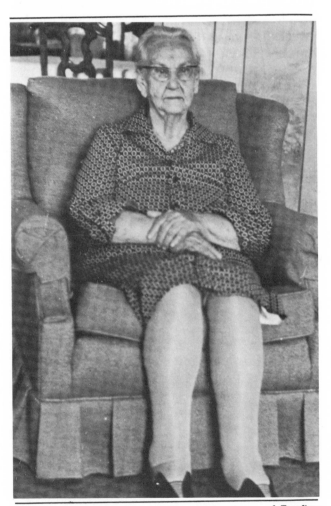

Photo courtesy of Foxfire

[I have been acquainted with Granny Reed, as she is best known, for quite a while. I remember, as a young child going

with my family to the Assemblies of God camp meeting at Cullasaja, North Carolina. There in the old sawdust-floored tabernacle nestled near the slow, lazy Cullasaja River, the rafters would seem to swell as the people offered their prayers, praises, and the "songs of Zion" unto God. At some point during the service, "testimonies" would be given. Voluntarily, people would stand and publicly tell what God had done for them. Then Granny Reed would get slowly to her feet and as all eyes focused on her, she'd begin, "Children, I've been walking with the Lord many a year now . . ." When she finished, there were few dry eyes and even fewer sad hearts in the congregation.

Granny Reed is ninety years old. For a long time she was a Baptist, but now she is a proud member of the Church of God in western North Carolina. The Church of God is one of several churches in the Pentecostal movement. Each believes in the gift of the Holy Spirit as another definite Work of Grace, with "speaking in tongues" as the initial evidence of this gift (Acts 2:1-4). Generally, the Pentecostal churches differ only in minor points of doctrine or church organization.

Those who have come to know Granny Reed love her simply because of the love she shows toward them. I have never seen her without being greeted with a warm hug, and hearing her say, "God bless you." Granny Reed is a testimony and a credit for both the Church of God and Christianity.

—Keith Head]

This interview with Granny Reed is excerpted from a publication by *Foxfire Magazine* on religious experiences in the mountains, edited by Keith Head and Paul Gillespie. Keith Head was a member of the *Foxfire* staff while a student at Rabun Gap Nacoochee School in north Georgia. Paul Gillespie is also a *Foxfire* alumnus. He rejoined the *Foxfire* staff in 1975 after graduation from the University of Virginia. Granny Reed's testimony appeared in *Foxfire* number 7 (Spring 1982), © 1976, 1982 by Foxfire Fund, Rabun Gap GA, and is used by permission.

Born Again

I have been a Christian about seventy-eight years. I'm ninety now. I was converted when I was twelve years old. It's been a long time. Then it wasn't like it is now. We didn't know anything about the deep things of God. We just knew the born-again experience. And we really did have a born-again experience in those days.

I never had thought about being a sinner. I never had thought about it. I was going along a little barefooted girl. We always went barefooted until we were in the teens in those days. I was going along and kicking up sand and playing, you know.

My daddy said "huh" like that. When he said that, I knew he wanted to say something. I said "What is it, Dad?"

He said, "You're old enough to know what you're going to church for, instead of playing along like that."

I stopped and I thought, "Well, does Daddy think I'm a sinner?" I began to study about it. I thought, "Well, him and Momma pray for me every night and I'm a child of God surely." I stood there and waited until he got in front of me and I dropped in behind him and started on toward the church.

I cried till I thought I couldn't cry. I thought, "Oh, dear God, I'm a sinner and I'll be left here. Mother and Daddy goes to heaven and I'll be left." It troubled me to death. These days, children don't pay any attention to things like that. But, oh, it broke my heart. I went on into church. I had a little cousin; her daddy was my mother's brother and he was a preacher. He was preaching. I went in and scrooched down beside of her and said, "Zadie, if you was to die, would you go to hell?" Me and her was the same age.

She said, "I don't know, Rosie. Papaw prays for us every night and I never thought nothing about it."

I said, "Daddy thinks we're sinners. He thinks we're old enough to know what to do."

She said, "I guess we are. We're twelve years old."

We sat there a while and I said, "I'm going to the altar when they call. I ain't gonna risk it another night, for Jesus might come tonight."

She said, "They'll make fun of us and us barefooted."

I said, "I don't care. I'd rather be made fun of than to go to hell."

She said, "If you go, I will."

So whenever they had the altar call, we went and just knelt and cried. We didn't know how to pray or nothing. In a little while, they broke up (the meeting) and we didn't get saved. Oh, how bad I was troubled. I went to the church door and I said, "Uncle Issac, do you care if me and Zadie don't go home for dinner?"

They had two services a day. They never did have a service of a night in those days. It was just two services a day and you went home for lunch. I said, "Do you care if we stay and not go home? I don't want any dinner."

He laid both of his hands on our heads and said, "God bless you, children. Stay if you want to."

So when they all got out of sight, me and Zadie (we was right by the river at the old Brush Creek Church) went up the river to an old sheltering rock and we walked in between them rocks. I looked at her and said, "Zadie, do you know how to pray?"

She said, "No, I don't. Papaw does the praying."

I said, "I don't know how. For Daddy and Mother both prays. And I don't."

We stood and looked at each other for a while and she said, "Well, we could say 'God, be merciful to us a sinner' for we're sinners."

We knelt and prayed and cried. We didn't know what to say except "God, be merciful to us sinners." We cried and cried and when they came back to the church, we ran down to the river and washed our faces and pushed our hair and went on into the church. I never heard anything the preacher said, I was so anxious to get to the altar to get saved before dark, because I didn't want to risk it after dark. Jesus might come. I might die, and oh, I couldn't stand it. I never heard anything said. And the minute they called the altar call, we went. We went and we prayed and we prayed. I was praying so hard and Zadie was too. After a while she jumped up and came flying to me and said, "Oh, I'm saved, and God's going to save you."

Well, I thought I was the vilest sinner on earth. He's saved Zadie and he ain't saved me. That made me worse than ever. I liked to cried my heart out. I said, "God, if you don't save me now, I'm going to die. I've done everything I know how to do and I don't know anything else to do." When I said that, an awful feeling came over me. I was mashed down low and lower. I couldn't hear them singing or nothin. I felt like I was going through the floor. All at once, it begun to come up like that. And when it come up, there I was standing in the floor. Everything was as bright as sunshine. I jumped just as high as I could. I jumped and grabbed Uncle Issac and hugged him. My daddy was just parting the people trying to get to me. Well, I thought they was the prettiest people I'd ever seen in all my life. Never after that did I doubt my experience. I know I was born again.

Well, I was determined to live in His steps. All my life I've wanted to live in His steps. And when anyone asks me to go to a show or a ballgame or place of music, I would just say, "Now would Jesus go there if He was here?" No, He wouldn't be there. He'd be somewhere else, praying or reading or doing some good to people. I never have been to a ballgame or a theatre in my life. I've just tried to follow in the steps of Jesus.

The Light of Holiness

As quick as the light of Holiness came into this country, I was there. The Lord spoke to me and told me to go or I wouldn't have gone, because I didn't know what kind of people they was and I was afraid of them. But you know, I was almost dead. I was sick. I was awfully bad off. I had an abscess in my side and I'd been operated on, but it didn't do any good. I was going to die. I knew I was. I had my family, two boys and a little girl. I said, "Lord, I hate to die so early and leave my family. My little girl needs me so bad, she's so sick all the time."

You know, whenever I told the Lord that, I just laid there a little while and he spoke to me in an audible voice and said, "Go down to the Holiness tent meeting and I'll heal you."

I didn't know it was the voice of the Lord. It scared me so bad. I looked all over the room. He'd never spoke to me in an audible voice before. I looked everywhere and there was no one around. I lay there just a-trembling.

I stayed till the next morning, laid there studying about it. Next morning, I said, "That didn't sound like a wicked voice. It must have been the Lord."

But why would He ask me to go to that place—a Holiness place? They're wicked people (for I thought they were). I'd been taught that! All at once it came again, "Go down to the Holiness tent meeting and I'll heal you."

I said, "Lord, I ain't able." I couldn't raise up without fainting. I was awful bad off.

He said, "I'll make you able." And that was the last I heard.

I thought to myself, "If that's Jesus, I'll put my feet down on the floor and try it and see and if I don't faint, I'll know that it's Him." Well, I got out on the side of the bed and I turned myself this and that a-way. I didn't feel like I was going to faint, and I said, "Now, Lord, if it's you that's leading me in this way, let me walk in the living room there and sit by the fire." I got up and walked, but I was stiff and sore. I walked in there and sat down.

My mother-in-law, Mother Reed, was waiting on me in there. She looked in and saw me and said, "How come you ain't in bed? Who brought you in here?" She knew I couldn't walk.

I said, "The Lord." When I said that, she thought I was out of my head. She run out and called my husband. He come in and I told him about the Lord speaking to me.

He led me right on in and he said, "Well, go to the Holiness church. We'll go down there if He promised to heal you."

And I said, "Yes, we'll go." I was still afraid to, nearly, but I went. That's where I got into the light of Holiness; it's been about fifty years. I never got healed until I got the baptism of the Holy Ghost for I didn't ask to be. [The preacher] just had his healing services on Friday night. After I went down there on Friday, I thought I was going to get healed that day. They had cards to give out and the ones that had cards went up to give them to him and stood in line. I didn't have one and I didn't go. Oh, I was disappointed so bad. When he got through praying for the sick, I could just feel the power of God go through my body, and I'd feel down there to see if I was healed, and I'd say, "No, I'm not healed. It's still there—that sore place." I studied about it.

When he got through, he said, "Everybody that's sick and afflicted, hold up your hand." Well, I held up my hand real high. I was afraid to let it down; afraid he'd miss seeing me. He came to me and handed me a little card and bowed and went back.

Well, I had to go home with that. I didn't know nothing else to do. When I got home I read that card. "Are you saved? Have you been baptized with the Holy Ghost? How long have you been sick? Do you believe God can heal you? Will you read your Bible and pray daily?"

I said to my husband, "I don't know how to answer this card. I can answer every one but there's a distinction here between 'Have you been saved?' and 'Have you been baptized with the Holy Ghost?' There's something else to it some way. I reckon I have been baptized in the Holy Ghost. I was baptized in the Father, Son, and the Holy Ghost."

He said, "No, Rosie. There's something else to it. I'll tell you what I'll do. I'll take you down there Monday morning and let you stay with your Aunt Minnie (she lived right there by the tent) till you find out something about it before next Friday." Next Friday was the healing night.

Sunday morning I was so heartsick about everything, I couldn't eat a bit. I said, "I don't want nothing to eat." I went on to my aunt's and told her not to fix anything for me to eat. I wanted to know something about the Lord before I eat anything more. I just got convicted to death! I never eat a bite for three days and nights. The first night of the revival he preached about the baptism of the Holy Ghost and I've never in my life had my eyes opened so. It just struck me that I'd die or have that gift.

I said, "Lord, here I am. Been a Christian all these years and thought I was walking in the steps of Jesus and I ain't even halfway started!" I felt awful about it. I went on fasting and praying and on Tuesday night—that was three days and nights that I had fasted—I went in there and told the Lord that now I was ready for the baptism and I said, "Now you give it to me. I'm setting way back here in the tent and nobody won't know that I'm wanting it."

Well, it came down just like a shower of rain. It was like a funnel in the tent just r-o-o-a-a-r-r-i-i-n-n-g. I fell over on the bench and my lips felt like they were an inch thick. I said, "I won't disturb." And when I said that, it just left me like that. Then I sat there a little while and I said, "Lord, did I imagine all of that?" I never had such feelings in all my life. I said, "You didn't get mad at Gideon for putting out a fleece twice. If I ask You to send it one more time, then I'll know it's You." And it come again.

Right then the preacher was saying to everyone that wanted the baptism to go into the prayer room. Well, I said to the entire congregation, "Come on, children, this is of God. I done asked Him."

I went in there. There wasn't no room at the benches.

Photo by Rob Amberg

They was all lined up. I just knelt down right in the middle of the floor and received it.

Walking By Myself

Oh, yes, Honey. They turned me out of the church and wouldn't have a thing to do with me. My own people wouldn't ask me home with them. First time I went to my own church, I thought I'd be the greatest help to them in the world, and they just turned their backs on me. They wouldn't dare listen at me or ask me home or nothing. [Before] they'd always thought I was the only one at church. They was so good to me.

I went up through the old field. I was walking by myself, all alone. My daddy was against me; everybody was against me. I went on to the top of the mountain and looked back over the mountain at the settlement. I got on top of the mountain and I said, "Lord, if nobody in this earth speaks to me anymore, my daddy nor nobody, I'll walk these hills alone with You. I'll never turn back." I'd cried all the way up the mountain. I was heartbroken because they had treated me so dirty, and I hadn't got to where I didn't have a lot of feelings, then.

When I said that, the glory of the Lord came down on me and just wrapped around me a sheet of love. Oh, how

happy it made me. I shouted all the way down. I never cried anymore about my church. He took it away. But they turned me out.

They didn't know any better. My poor old daddy said I'd sure land up in the asylum—I'd gone plumb crazy. Yeah, he thought he'd have to send me to the asylum.

But my mother just accepted it every bit and got the baptism in my house. Oh, she was like me, she wanted all the Lord had for her. My daddy was good, but he was scared to death; he thought it was some kind of strange doctrine. But before he died, he said he saw the light. He said he knowed it was right.

I was brought up in a good Christian home. They had their family prayer, and they made us go to church and never thought of nothing but doing right. I never heard my mother nor my dad say a dirty word in my life nor never seen nothing wrong out of them. They was good people. My daddy thought that the only religion in the world was the Baptist. He just thought that was it. But mother could see a little further in the distance.

I said one day, "Mother, what does it take to be holy? I don't do nothing wrong." I thought the Holiness people didn't eat meat back then. So I said, "I don't care about meat. I can do without that. Why can't I be holy?"

Mother said, "Honey, there's something to it I don't understand, but if we keep reading and praying and trusting God, one of these days we'll find out what Holiness is." She knew we should be holy. But my daddy thought it was holy enough to be Baptists.

[The Holiness] didn't indulge in the worldly things of life. They didn't think it was right, and I don't yet. I don't think we can be two people. I think we either have to belong to God or not at all. I think we have to turn loose of the things of the world that's got any foolishness in it at all, because the Bible says that all that is not good is bad. If you don't find any good in something, there isn't any use to partake of it.

Divine Healing

There was a little girl, and sandbones had eaten her backbone out to where she was in a steel brace, and she hadn't put her feet on the floor to stand up for seventeen months. She was sitting in a wheelchair with her steel brace on.

They drove the car up to the tent and raised up the tent close to where the preacher was preaching where she could listen at him preach on divine healing. Well, the preacher was boarding at their house, and he went on home that night. When they came back and started to carry her out of the car, the preacher said, "Just let her alone. She's going to walk to the house tonight."

And he went around and laid his hand on her and prayed a few words—he didn't ever pray but just a few words—and she leaped out of that car and ran to the house! She run in and she ran upstairs and jerked that steel brace off and put on her clothes. She went into every one of the bedrooms of her brothers and woke them up and told them what God had done for her. She's still alive yet!

Oh, I don't know of the healings that took place up there. They brought one woman from the hospital that they'd given up to die, and the preacher went out to the car and prayed for her and she was healed perfectly. There's been lots of healings since.

I've prayed for people and they was healed time and time again. But it seems like these days that it's harder to get through to victory. I don't know why. I went to a little baby that was dying of diphtheria and its little head was swelled up and its eyes was rolled back in its head. They was going to take it to the hospital, and they had to wait for the train to run before they got there. They thought the baby was going to die before the train got there, so they called for me. I never had seen the people. I ran down there and I asked the Lord as I went on, did He want me to pray for it secret or out loud. I said, "If You want me to pray in secret, You cause the woman to ask me to lay my hands on it. I know You're going to heal it, Lord, but I want to know how to pray about it."

So when I went in, she was holding it. The baby was about two years old and you couldn't see nothing but the whites of its eyes and it was gasping, trying to breathe—couldn't breathe hardly at all.

And the mother said, "Lay your hand on its little neck and see how hard it is. It's like a rock." And I knew then so I just lay my hand on its neck and began to rub and say, "Thank you, Jesus" in my heart. Every drop of that swelling just oozed out and the fever left. That little thing popped its eyes open and looked at me and laughed. It jumped down out of its mother's lap and run into the kitchen, got a stick of stove wood, and it came back pecking on the stove and looking at me and laughing. It hadn't seen me before but it was tickled to death. It knew something had happened! It was well from that day on.

The man come in and he said, "What in the world happened?" The baby was just playing and laughing and running around me.

Mrs. Blair said, "Miss Reed just laid her hand on its neck and it got well in a few minutes!"

And he said, "Well, there ain't no use to go to the hospital, is there?"

I said, "No, your baby's all right, Mr. Blair. It's all right."

I never told them what happened and next morning, I felt condemned about it. I didn't know what to do so I went back and asked her if she knew what made the baby well. And she said, "You prayed for it."

I said, "Yes, Jesus healed it." Then I told her how God did work through people.

The Trip to Mother's Funeral

Beverly A. Asbury

Called from a meeting in the Divinity School
I walked down the hall at mid-day
To take an emergency phone call.
Flashing through my mind was the expectation of a University Voice—
Perhaps the death of a student early in the year.
Or a School Voice about my children and some mishap.
One's experiences, anxieties, and fears coincide, converge
While calmness and panic compete.

The Voice was on "hold" on the phone in the receptionist's area—
Exposed, public, a traffic island
   allowing no privacy for hearing the Voice
   whatever news was to come from it.
"Bev, this is Ed."
"Ed?"—my friend in New York, my mind raced.
Why would he be calling me as an emergency?
A wrong inference drawn from the name.
I hadn't recognized the sound of the Voice
Now saying "Mother died this morning."
So estranged and separated were we it had not occurred to me
That the voice was my brother's.

Mother had died. A couple of hours earlier.
On her way out to lunch at a friend's home.
This had been a good day for her.
Her arteriosclerosis had subsided.
Her mind had been clear, clearer than usual.
Her gray hair was set in a bluish tint,
Dressed and happy on a rainy day

Mr. Asbury is university chaplain and director of religious affairs, Vanderbilt University. "The Trip to Mother's Funeral" originally appeared in *Religion In Life* 44:4 (Winter 1975), © 1975 by Abingdon Press, and is used by permission.

She walked out the door
    with her husband of forty-nine years
    watching her through the window
As she went to enter the car with four other old ladies
    her lifelong friends
    who endured her bad times
    and shared her good ones.
She put a hand to a Buick's doorhandle
    and gently eased backward
    in a slow-motion collapse
    onto the wet sidewalk
"Dead," as they would say, "before she touched the ground."

"Dad wants you to call him."
"I'll see you sometime tonight in Elberton,"
    the small Georgia town
    we both had left in our teens, a good while ago.
"Thanks, Ed. I'll call Dad right away."
And I realized again where I was
    and that I was crying, upset
    although I had known that this had had to come.
All the traffic around me
    was aware of me
    as I was becoming of them.
"My mother just died," I explained
    against my better judgment.
I didn't want to talk
And I didn't want my words to bring forth
    as I feared it would
All the sympathy of "divines"
    who didn't know me well enough
    truly to sympathize.
Then all the questions which replace sympathy
    arising out of the guilty expectation
    that one *should* sympathize verbally—
"How old was she?" "Had she been ill?"
    and all that.
    You can imagine.
What difference do the answers make anyway? Really?
    I wanted to be alone.
    I had to be alone.
I worked my way out of the traffic,
Adroitly parrying questions with the expected unrevealing answers,
As an expert driver works himself off the highway
    and onto the ramp and into open space.
Free now to feel and explore the feelings alone.

"My mother has died," I explained anew.
But the people in my meeting related more satisfactorily
    than the divines.
Here I got only one pat religious reassurance.
They let me be.
    And I went away to be.
    Away from sugary piety and verbal assurances.

They called Dad to the phone
    to talk with his oldest son.

We cried and talked a bit, awkwardly
I heard again of what he had seen
Of how he felt when Mother died.
Then he turned to other things, tenderly.
To me as "the minister in the family"
    and not as son alone
To see when I would arrive
    If a funeral tomorrow would be "too soon."
    If a graveside service alone
      would be acceptable to me.
    If keeping the casket closed
      at the funeral home
    And greeting people at our home
      would be agreeable.
No matter about differences on things racial
    and some things personal.
Here our values, expectations, outlooks
    coincided, were the same.
    A good feeling, really.
"Son, when you get here, wake me up
    no matter what time it is."
    I knew that I would.

Friends told in Nashville.
Arrangements made to be away.
Duties shuffled onto others.

Finally, an early evening flight to Atlanta
    the first one with an open seat.
An Avis Plymouth rented for the weekend
And one hundred miles of wet, lonely road
    ahead on this trip.
Driving through the South's city of glamour
    onto the interstate East
A sign beckoned to a familiar town
    on a state highway off the beaten track,
More dangerous on this stormy night probably.
But it followed along paths of childhood nostalgia
Driving with her to Atlanta shopping
During Depression days when an extra dime
    was my "allowance" for the city;
Down past Winder and Senator Russell's old home
    through Athens, past my alma mater
    onto that last familiar stretch of road
    associated with early life
    and the mothering that got me
      through it.

The lights were on in the century-old home
    on Heard Street
    named for one of Alex's ancestors.
Parking in the back and entering from the kitchen
    the house itself seemed dead at midnight.
Ed slept fully clothed on the couch in the sitting room.
He woke, and we spoke briefly.
He told me to see Dad, upstairs in bed.
And he went to bed in Mother's room downstairs.

No time now for a personal exchange,
But it felt OK because these estranged brothers
    seemed to affirm unspoken bonds.
When a mother has died, are sibling rivalries
    dead at last?

Dad awoke to hug me and cry.
In bed with him was Sally, Ed's daughter,
A very favorite granddaughter,
    this niece of mine
    who was a poignant reminder to me
    that I now had no wife
    and that my children had not come
        to "Ma's" funeral.
The death of Mother had brought me home
    for the first time
    since the final death of my marriage,
    a death she had so strongly resisted.
Grief added to grief and all so real
Dad's grief spoke to a son's,
    and each shared the same griefs,
    the other as one's own.

He assured himself and me again
That she had died as she had wanted to die—
Quickly, instantaneously,
    not according to her dread
    of being a mindless invalid
    after so active and verbal a life.
"A timely death," he will always say, I'm sure,
    but measured by her sense of time
    not by ours,
    for we would choose to have her still.
Sure, seventy-two is longer than some
    but not as long as others.
    Age is so relative a thing
    and life can be precious, whatever one's age.

Dad went back to bed.
All the plans had been made.
I went downstairs and poured some Ezra Brooks on ice.
Ed's wife gave me a kiss of lipstick,
    the model of a *Southern Living* woman—
    properly dressed and smelling nice
    on her way to join her husband in Mother's bed.
I sat and drank and fell asleep alone.

"Morning has broken as the first morning . . ."
People already are bustling about, early.
Aunt Janie is in charge, a job she does well.

Food is everywhere; that's expected.
Breakfast is sumptuous; the South has risen again.
It's a family reunion; accents galore.
We all know why we're there,
    but nobody mentions it.
And before eating is done
    visitors are arriving to speak.

Southern training reasserts itself.
   "Why we haven't even dressed yet"—
meaning we men haven't got our ties on yet.

People whom I haven't seen in years
   even on visits,
People I'm surprisingly glad to see.
Even in mobile America I do have roots
   and relations.

The morning's procession has begun
And litany's refrain rings in my ears:
"Bev, we're so glad to see you,
   except, of course, under the circumstances."
"So sorry about your mother. . .,
   but she had lived a good life."
And the antiphons in return,
"Thank you. It's really fine to see you."
"Yes, Mother *died* as she wished."
   The only mention of the seemingly dreaded word
   as if it were to break a rule to say it—
   before the conversations ignored the occasion entirely.

By mid-morning the unreality was staggering
The repetition numbing.
The lack of emotions, mine and theirs, frightening.
It was as if Mother were simply away
And we were socializing, waiting for her return
With the small sandwiches and smaller talk
   of a Saturday morning bridge party with the ladies.
And the ladies, there they were, in the front hall,
   politely vying with each other in the direction of traffic.
What was real was the familiar funeral process.
Mother's death was not yet real to *me*.

Seeking Dad out in the living room and hardly having privacy
   I whispered, "Do you mind if I go see Mother's body?"
Without hesitation, "No, of course not, do you mind if I
   don't go with you? I don't think . . . remember
   I saw her yesterday . . ."
Agreed. I understood.
Against instinct as I passed my brother
I asked if he wanted to go with me.
"Are you crazy? No, I never want to see a body.
   Certainly not hers.
   I don't want to remember her that way."
We had passed each other in the dark again.
No more questions were asked.
No explanations were offered.
"We really are different," I say to myself.
"The morbid brother, the kook," I guess he's thinking about me.

A bit shaken but undeterred,
   I drive up Heard Street to the funeral home.
The name of the man, long unseen, wings back.
"Horace, I'd like to see Mother's body.
Will you open the casket for me?"
With no false airs he takes me inside the once lovely old home

serving as a mortuary,
Opens the modest box Dad had rightly chosen,
Exposes the blue-tinted gray hair to the light
And eases out of the room, pulling curtains
     behind him to give me privacy.
Personal courtesy—or professional consideration—
     nice, I don't care which.

There she is, dead indeed.
Slightly puffy, waxen Mother.
I cry a moment and then speak.
"Hello, old lady. I hope you rest in peace.
All the fighting is over.
We had our problems. But we settled them.
And we had some good times too.
You were a strong woman, a fine mother.
I thank you for my life and soul.
God willing, I'll see you in the Kingdom."

Crying now, really for the first time
Experiencing grief as if at the moment of death
I drive around until I've felt the feelings
And then I return quietly to the procession of people
Into the green house down the street.
The ritual hadn't changed there.
But now I had, *inside*.

A few minutes later, still before noon,
At the front door stood an old Negro man.
From the living room in a moment's flash
I watched the old ladies' faces
     wondering what to do.
In their day no black man would have come
     to the front door of a white home
     in small-town South.
But this wasn't their house to rule
     as it wasn't any longer *their* South.
Before they could utter a word
     Dad saw the face at the door:
     "Luther, Luther Harper, come right in."
Dad made his way to greet this man
With whom he had worked, who had worked for him
     and sometimes for Mother, for over twenty years.
"Come in, Luther."
     As the old ladies tried to direct him
     to the sitting room
     a less formal place
     to put a black man,
Dad took Luther by the arm
     and let him in to sit
     and talk in the living room.
Well, I may have been the family "niggerlover"
As my brother always called me to his friends and to my face,
But my Dad, for all his prejudice, acted rightly
     toward a friend
     who came because he cared
     and not because he had labored.
Things were beginning to look up.
     That's a fact.

The preacher came by.
No, I didn't want a part in the service.
His plans sounded "fine."
    I really didn't want to bother.
    There was no way to do it my way anyway.

Dinner—my first funeral dinner at home
    people's way of being kind
    providing a Southern smorgasbord
    and a respite in the people procession.
    Siesta still observed.

    Dressed. The time at hand for the service,
    The family gathered.
    Cousins. Cousins. Cousins. Cousins.
    From all over Georgia.
    South Carolina.
    Some close cousins.
    Some successful.
    Some sad.
    Some mediocre.
    Some lost souls among them.
    Some embarrassed over my divorce.
    Young and old, according to some scheme
    I knew not and cared nothing about
Were placed in cars to go to the cemetery
    on this gray, warm, drizzly day.

A large group was there, gathered all around the grave.
Red Georgia clay dug from the family plot
    covered with a rug of artificial green grass
Flowers on the casket last open for my viewing.
We took our seats in the "family section"
    under the awning
And the Methodist minister, standing at the "head"
    read the service I knew by heart.
Straight, simple, and unsatisfying to me
Calculated to repress my grief.
Sally shed the only tears at Word's end
But the poverty of it all cried in my guts.
No action, no movement, no feeling—
    as unreal as an absent body.

As we rose to leave, I knew I could not go
    after all
    without acting my part, my feeling in this funeral.
I plucked some real grass
And a clod of red earth
Dropping them in the grave
Intoning to myself alone:
    "Earth to earth
    from this earth, back to this earth
    from you of this earth, I came
    go back to it, as I hope to in time to come, in peace."
I was half-aware that my act had been seen
    or half-seen
But no one spoke or asked then,
    nor did I as we drove through the town square.

When we arrived back at home
    so short a time after we had left
    and with a new procession of kinfolk beginning
I knew within what I really wanted to do.
"Dad, I just can't come in now.
I can't greet people for a while.
I'm going to take a ride," lying a bit.
    Fearing obstruction from stating the truth.
Alone I returned to the deserted cemetery.
The grave plot attended now
    by four black gravediggers
    the red clay uncovered to the sky
    the casket already lowered
    and a fiberglass vault top about to go on
    as required by "perpetual care,"
    the cemetery of the future.

Conscious of still being dressed I stepped past
    the pile of red clay
    saw the vault locked in place.
And the men commenced to shovel.
I took a handle and threw a spadefull in.
Another, another, another.
"Burying one's dead, one's own dead. Burying one's dead."
Working out one's grief, burying one's dead.
A custom long-lost in polite society
    burying one's dead!
    Suddenly I was conscious of working alone.
    How long had I been oblivious of hostile stares?
    The black men were staring me to a stop
    of burying my dead.
    I had offered no explanation.
    Had I been mistaken as checking up on them?
    Was I violating union rules?
    (Union rules in small town Georgia!?)
"I'm sorry. This is my mother. I'm only going to stay a minute.
    I wanted to help bury my dead. I hope you don't mind."
Not a word was said.
Slowly work resumed.
I left soon to join Dad
    sitting on the back screened porch
    for an afternoon drink away from visiting folk
    a privacy still respected.
    And again no questions were asked
    and no words spoken
    of any of this.
It wouldn't have been understood anyway, I suspect.
So the day drew on with family visits
    eating, playing with nieces
    and cousins' children.

Sunday broke forth with sunshine.
After breakfast we visited the grave
So different from the day before
Everyone viewing the grave for the first time
    except, secretly, me.
To church, as usual

and it was church-as-usual
Everything-as-usual except my private exceptions
   of which there was one to go.
One final trip. To which everyone was invited.
After Sunday dinner, a drive into the country
to Mother's lovely old homeplace
   now restored by a fortunate family
And on to old Antioch Church and its graveyard.
   Ten miles from town
   Cotton country gone to pine and cattle
   Deserted by black and white sharecroppers
   Who worked for the likes of my ancestors
     buried here.

A walk among eighteenth- and nineteenth-century markers.
   An occasional Confederate Cross.
Great-grandparents. Grandparents.
   Lost infants I'd never heard of.
Dad put his arm around me.
"This was a good idea, son.
It makes me feel better.
I just realized that your mother lived to be older
   than anyone in her family.
That makes it easier to give her up.
We had her a longer time than anyone had the others in her family."

The funeral trip was over.
Every trip had been made
   save those inward ones of the soul.
After another night and appropriate and loving words
   of parting
I'd take the Interstate to Atlanta
   for the plane to Nashville.
The road was now wide open.
Other trips lay ahead.
As they do for us all.

Part Four

Religion in the South
Its Diversity

Being Southern Baptist on the Northern Fringe

by Horace Newcomb

There is a time of late afternoon that is special for me, a time when all things fall together. Lines collapse. The edges of objects fade into each other. Smells and sounds mingle together. It is often a time for nostalgia though certainly not of the cheap, destructive sort. It is a time when memory chains are set off by something random and things follow one another in the logic of soft but accurate arguments. It is an important time for me, one when I reassure myself that things are good, that the children will be home soon or are enjoying their play a few houses down the street, that the people around me are not malicious, but are working out their lives in special and kindly ways even when they are, like me, confused.

Lately, I find myself whistling old hymn tunes during this time; not in a self-conscious, show-offy way, as I sometimes do when flaunting my Southern differences before slightly patronizing "general American" audiences. Rather I have found the tunes to be meaningful and real, powerful additions making the time itself still more important. These are the same tunes that are "folk songs" to a younger generation whose experiences have been limited in ways different from mine. They hum and sway as their favorite singers render "Showers of Blessing" and "What A Friend We Have In Jesus" and "Throw Out The Lifeline," believing that the tunes and words emerged from the depths of a cultural unconscious. They know nothing of such old friends as P. P. Bliss, Fanny J. Crosby, or B. B. McKinney, the people who wrote songs out of need and conviction.

When you know something by heart, you know it so well that it sings itself, without thought or examination. I often sing verse after verse of the old songs in this manner without a hymn book. And though my memory is now poor from disuse, there was a time when I could easily list the books of the Bible in order and recite lengthy passages of scripture. I could locate, on command, any verse of scripture in a matter of seconds in an exercise known as the Sword Drill ("... the sword of the Spirit, which is the word of God" Ephesians 6:17).

Accepted doctrine, approved dogma, and supportive apologetics were abundant, surrounding and comforting. They were couched in the highly structured ritual of informality that defines behavior in Southern Baptist life. The four Sunday services, two study and two worship; the Wednesday night "prayer meetings" consisting mostly of brief devotional talks; the Daily Bible Reading program which plotted the course of shared study and assured everyone of reading the Bible through every five years. All these things made it easily possible to know the proper words "by heart" without having to think much about their meaning or their application to daily life, which is *not* to say that they were not applied. Because almost everyone knew the same doctrines, the same words, the same rituals and hymns, "proper" behavior could be carried out in familiar and relaxing contexts, rarely questioned, seldom changed.

Such a system functions well and protects the people within it as long as it is not critically questioned. But like many other young people, I was unwilling to take it without question; my questions led to anger and I left.

There is another meaning to knowing something "by

Horace Newcomb is a graduate of Mississippi College and the University of Chicago. He teaches American Studies at the University of Maryland, Baltimore County, and became a fellow of the National Humanities Institute at the University of Chicago. He is the author of *TV—The Most Popular Art* (Doubleday/Anchor) and edited *Television—The Critical View* (Oxford University Press).

Photo courtesy of Baptist Home Mission Board

heart," a meaning that might be phrased more accurately as knowing "with the heart," for it speaks to the process by which we know something deeply and surely, know it as right in a sense that transcends cultural and social rightness. I have begun to go to church again on Wednesday nights. In my present congregation, we do not call it "prayer meeting," though it would not bother me if we did. We speak of it as our "family night," and that, too, is a good name. A small group of young families attends, but most of the people are older. I look out at them some evenings, a sea of gray heads, some of them feeble, some twinkling, some in roisterous laughter, and see that they really are part of my family. I am glad that I can share this night with them and that my children can sense the importance of being here. I want to be a part of this group.

One of the things I want to share is the fact, the knowledge, that they have had great troubles and trials and peace and joy, and that they now know (if they have not always known) a great, powerful portion of their lives "by heart." I am knowing it, too, as best I can. I've made my way back to the Southern Baptist Church, a journey I once thought I could never make in good conscience. Strangely enough, I've about decided it is the only way I could come back, that it offers me a path that demands good hard thought and work and "heart" tasks, and is worth the effort.

That I, or anyone like me, should return to the church is really not difficult to understand. You do not easily root out of your life a set of behaviors that has filled as many hours, consumed energy on such a scale, and roused emotions to the degree that religion has for me. I cannot remember not going to church. I was accompanied there by my parents who were quite active in it on all levels. Later, it was the place where I met most of my friends and where activities were planned for us that covered the spectrum of our social activity and taught us proper social behavior.

The church provided a huge portion of my education that went far beyond religion in the narrow sense and into ancient history, politics, ethics and even sociology. I have always been convinced, too, that my ease in dealing with imaginative literature stems from daily reading of the King James Version of the Bible. I have been directly involved in the processes of literary interpretation since the age of six. That words have deeper meaning, that groups of words lead to unusual conclusions is a mystery to many of my students, but never to me. When the lawyer asked Jesus, "Who is my neighbor?" and He replied with a parable, that was only the first step. In lesson after lesson, sermon upon sermon, that parable was interpreted, applied, explicated, and examined for me and by me.

Beyond this extended intellectual activity, the church educated me in matters of sex, social custom, parental relationships, attitudes toward civil authority and countless other areas. Sometimes the answers were swift,

abrupt, and explicit: "Don't Do It." In other cases, there was a fearful sort of ambiguity: "Every Date Is A Potential Mate." "Love Your Neighbor" was especially tricky because of racial questions. A similar difficulty could be wandered into by taking too literally the text that "Man looketh on the outward appearance, while the Lord looketh upon the heart." In spite of this, we always dressed up for church.

It is essential to understand that this teaching was not catechistic. There was no list of rules to memorize and recite other than the Ten Commandments and their New Testament versions. There were no classes in which we formally demonstrated mastery in a specific body of man-made rules or interpretations that were agreed upon in council. Rather we were instructed to turn to the Bible as our single source for proper action and were admonished to behave as Jesus would behave in a similar circumstance. Our image of Jesus, if not austere and remote, was surely properly Southern Baptist.

The suggestion that one look to the Bible for practical instruction is not, I think, a bad one. It is a rich, tough book. The difficulty arises in the knotty area of interpretation. While admitting that the Bible states that women are not supposed to cut their hair, or men to trim their beards, or groups to use musical instruments in church, Baptists have ways out of such problems. Other groups have ways in and out of their own doctrinal mazes, and, as everyone knows, Protestantism is a giant maze of mazes that leads easily into controversy and rancor. Differing interpretations could cause problems if it were not for the fact that almost everyone in the deep South is Baptist.

As a result, Baptists define the cultural norms. It would, of course, be inaccurate to identify Southern Baptist belief and behavior with Southernness. I do not think, however, that it is too far off the mark to say that Baptists are at the very center of the culture. It is with that realization that many of us have broken in anger our ties with this powerful, enveloping, life-consuming institution, for such an identification makes it impossible for the church to call out the major weaknesses, the sins, of the culture.

Often the break has come because of racism. For many years the Southern Baptist Convention (SBC), like the ballast in a ship, has steadied the course of Southern racism, sometimes with specific doctrinal "evidence" of racial distinctions but more often by perpetuating and making comfortable the dominant values. Those few individuals and congregations who have chosen to oppose racism as their Christian duty have often been condemned and ostracized for their views. They became theologically suspect and were labelled "liberal," that basic slur which shifts easily from socio-political to theological application.

The church's stand on racism is part of a larger opinion that sees "social" issues as beyond the appropriate realm of a religious group. Intent on the cultivation of personal salvation as expressed in the moment of individual conversion, much Baptist doctrine is meant to protect the church from the impurity of social gospel issues. Selective application of the doctrine, however, permits large numbers of ministers to descend on state capitols to lobby against liberalized liquor laws. By contrast, to condemn the Viet Nam war would have been wildly out of bounds, for it would have countered the cultural context in which the church has its being.

Others have broken with the church because of its emotionalism. Its emphasis on individual commitment is used to justify highly charged manipulative techniques. The old traditions of revivalism, exhortative preaching, browbeating, and guilt-tripping are all too often brought to bear on the very young. Church rolls are filled with small children because it is quite clear to them that they are expected to make their commitments between the ages of six and twelve.

I, for example, was seven or eight years old when I made my "public profession of faith." I walked down the aisle during a Sunday night service, quite sure that God had told me to do so. (Indeed, I'm still pretty sure that's what happened. At least it was not overly premeditated and was the result of a deep emotional response on my part.) When I took the outstretched hand of our pastor, who was a good friend, he asked me if I felt that Jesus had forgiven me for all my sins. Now that's a strange question for an eight year old, even when he knows the answer. I knew that I was supposed to say "yes," though I doubt that my sense of sin was up to the standards of that particular preacher. He once found me playing ball with his son in the sanctuary of our church, took the ball from us and said that it would have to be burned. We felt bad about the whole thing, but what it really indicates is that the Southern Baptist line emphasizing the necessity of a child-like faith is not the same as being an adult and *choosing* a child-like faith. The latter is an act that demands great intellectual and theological sophistication.

Closely allied to this criticism is the view that the SBC is generally anti-intellectual, that it denies much that we know about biblical history, about the nature of biblical texts, and so on. But it is not merely in the realm of scholarship that the intellect is missing. Probing sermons, especially those read from notes, are suspect, and heaven help the minister who expresses his own doubts. Too often, emotionalism becomes a disturbing substitute for the kind of deeper exploration which might actually lead to deeper Christian growth.

A third allied criticism is that the Baptist Church lacks proper respect for the aesthetic qualities of worship. Gatherings are generally informal and the buzz of friendly conversation preceding the church service annoys those who wish for a quieter, more respectful atmosphere. The old hymns with their reliance on the imagery of crucifixion have come to be known as the "slaughter-house hymns," and the more sensitive worshippers object to being asked whether or not they have been "washed in the blood of the lamb."

Underlying these critical observations is a more nagging concern for the overarching pride and self-righteousness of the whole enterprise. There is, in the Convention, little sense of penitence. Indeed, the answer goes, why should there be. Southern Baptists have been, as they would say, richly blessed. Their numbers continue to grow. Their programs flourish and move to new regions. As individuals, they are among the more prominent citizens in their communities, and they share common roots with their cousins in the farms and pasturelands of the South. The Lord has allowed them to prosper, to create a system of wealth and religious power that continues to be internally defined and that has changed little in over a hundred years.

This pride, it seems to the critic, is sinful. So the critic, especially the young one, becomes the rebel and then the outcast. The critic leaves the church and with it a great portion of his or her personal history. A gap is left in the mind. It may be replaced with political fervor for social justice, with the intellectualism that was found to be missing, with an aesthetic religious experience in a "more formal" church, with an easy humanism, or with a fervent plunge into the cults of humanistic psychology. But it cannot remain empty. Too much psychic stress pulls at the edges. In some cases, like my own, it is filled with a journey back, with an exploration of what it has meant to be Baptist at other times and places, with a reinterpretation of the old symbols. In my experience the journey back does not mean an end to criticism. If anything it means a far more vigilant attempt to make the system responsible. On arrival in the old territory I find there is much worth preserving and a potential for exceptional strength in a time of cultural flabbiness. It is not at all difficult for me to identify myself now as a Southern Baptist, but it still requires explanation.

The explanation must begin with the particular congregation of which I am now a part. Any Southern Baptist will certainly understand the importance of that observation, and for non-Southern Baptists it provides the best beginning for explanation. Formally, doctrinally, there is no ecclesiastical hierarchy in the Southern Baptist Convention. No one, no agency, no group, no administrator can tell an individual Southern Baptist church what to do. In practice, of course, there is not a great deal of difference among churches. They look the same, and if asked to define their beliefs, they will sound much the same. It is important for them to affirm liberty while strongly insisting that one can't believe "just anything" and still be Southern Baptist. Basic doctrines such as the Virgin Birth, the Fatherhood of God, and the fact of the Trinity are accepted easily while exploration of the highly complex nature of such doctrines is not encouraged.

Moreover, the Southern Baptist Convention, the democratic political governing organization, wields a great deal of power and influence in the life of every affiliated congregation. Meeting annually as a group of messengers from each congregation, upwards of 12,000 individuals take care of the issues for the rest of the millions of individuals at home. Most believe that the Convention is the best way to do business. Though there are continual minor controversies over shades of liberalism and conservatism, most individual members favor the maintenance of conservative positions and are quick to criticize the more liberal agencies such as the Christian Life Commission which is charged with comment and education in the realm of social ministries.

Paradoxically, all this voting and dividing and governing has great influence in the life of the individual congregation, and no influence. The money contributed at home is spent by boards whose actions gain their final approval at Convention meetings. The Convention passes resolutions on every issue from abortion to homosexuality to votes of thanks to the host city. Yet any individual can say "this is not what I believe about abortion or homosexuality and besides I think that Norfolk was a lousy place to have the meeting." The problem, obviously, is that the individual's voice, ultimately, has little to do with the "big image" of the Southern Baptist Convention. Nevertheless it has a great deal to do with the home congregation, which is also run as a participatory democracy.

A good example of this local autonomy is my own church. Much has been said about the lack of aesthetic sophistication in Southern Baptist Churches, the missing ritual that serves to focus our devotions, tune our minds and direct appropriate actions. Yet, our preacher wears a pulpit robe, an act that would be unacceptable in many churches. An acolyte, also robed, lights candles before each service in our church sanctuary. The choir processes formally into the church, through the congregation and into the choir loft. They sing complex music, the classics of the church, ancient and contemporary. In keeping with their excellence, paid soloists head each choir section, a practice directly counter to the Baptist tradition of volunteerism in such matters. The hymns sung by the congregation are often hymns from the Anglican tradition. The minister preaches with a stated awareness of current theological questions, often referring to contemporary theologians and popular non-sectarian apologists.

In short, to many Southern Baptists we would be too fancy, too formal, too much the up-town church to satisfy their stereotyped version of what it is to be Baptist. It would be assumed, incorrectly, that we are a "cold" church, for that goes hand-in-hand with the "formal" tag. It might also be assumed, correctly, that the church is wealthy and intellectually oriented. But in no way would these differences enable others to say that we are *not* Southern Baptists, for this is merely the way in which we choose to worship. We are tolerated by many and praised by some.

Still, the matter of music and clerical robes are surface issues. Perhaps a more indicative example would be the baptism ritual. Baptism by total immersion is one of the most important of the "Baptist distinctives" separating the church from other denominations. Indeed, this image of persons being lowered beneath the surface of water in a baptismal pool or a rural stream is surely the one which non-Baptists, particularly in the deep South, are most conscious of. I was recently asked by a former Tennessee Episcopalian, "Do you still dunk 'em?"

While Southern Baptists do not believe that the ritual of baptism, in this form or any other, contributes one whit to an individual's salvation, they are convinced that this is the "correct" manner in which the ritual should be observed. It is especially crucial that the symbolism of total immersion—death, burial, resurrection—be applied to persons of other traditions who affiliate with Southern Baptist congregations. This implies, of course, that one is not saved until one joins the proper tradition, a translation which most Baptists would feel very uneasy with, but which is under the surface nevertheless.

Many people in my congregation are uncomfortable with this requirement. They say that it is presumptuous, that it is doctrinaire in the worst sense, and that it opens us to the accusation of sinful pride. On a number of occasions there have been moves to change the requirement. Most recently, the church went through a lengthy process of study and self-examination. The minister prepared a series of learned lectures on the history of baptismal rites. Discussion and study continued over a period of a year, turning up some interesting facts. The early church, for example, was guided more by expediency than by doctrine or by the meanings of words. Original languages clearly imply total immersion, yet early churches resorted to pouring or sprinkling when necessary. And so the practice has changed and been changed throuogut the history of the church. Even Baptists have been inconsistent in the form of the ritual, and have not always baptized by immersion.

The deeply frightening thing was its easy acceptance of the culture, so that the rules of the culture became the rules of the church.

Armed with all this knowledge, all the discussion and prayer on the part of individuals and groups, and all the leadership from men, women and spiritual sources, this congregation, noted for its intellectual image and liberal attitudes, voted. It voted, by narrow margin, to retain the requirement of immersion for all new members, regardless of their previous confession of faith.

There are several points to this example. Most obvious to someone not involved is the fact that the congregation affirmed the more conservative position. That fact is indeed important, for it measures the depth of an attitude toward tradition, toward the distinctive historical factor of being Baptist. It was doubly important for this highly diverse group.

Not so obvious is the importance of considering the issue in the first place. There is some possibility that the congregation, had it relaxed the requirement, would have found itself severed from the fellowship of its local Baptist Association, a group consisting of all local churches affiliated with the SBC. That would have meant little, other than strained personal feelings, for it is quite unlikely that the Southern Baptist Convention would have taken any action on that scale. It has not done so over other issues nor on this one in the few churches that have changed their baptismal requirements. It *cannot* do so under the strict terms of what Baptists believe because the belief in the autonomy of the local congregation is ultimately stronger than the belief in baptismal form.

Of greatest importance, however, is the fact that the congregation sensed that this discussion was right and that it should proceed. Those members who knew at the beginning that their views would not change realized that for others this was a matter of conscience. Consequently, the discussion, even when heated, was never rancorous. When it was over, there were disappointments, but no bitter recriminations, no betrayed friendships. Persons on opposite sides of the issue had remained faithful to the larger meanings of open discussion and democratic procedures. For those of us who were "defeated," there was a greater sense of victory, for we were assured that religious liberty had been maintained. No dogmatic, authoritarian rule had been enforced, nor had there been felt any need for separation. We had had our say and could be content with the results. No doubt we would try again later.

The congregation was free. I had known it before, had sensed the attitude that made me comfortable. I had heard the sermons that were so different from the ones I had grown up with and felt for the first time that the Southern Baptist church was not somehow inherently restricted from wrestling with the meanings of texts that I had wrestled with privately. I had met individuals who felt as I did regarding social issues. I had learned that here one was expected to express doubt in order to gain strength, rather than hide it in embarrassment and fear of punishment. Still, after the discussion on the baptism question, I knew that I had come home, and that I had discovered something much deeper than I had anticipated. A richer vein existed in this tradition than I had known about.

My journey had been not only a quest for what was valid in the tradition, but also a search for the answers to the theological questions that confront any professing Christian. I had worked out what it meant to me to believe in Jesus in a personal way, and concluded that in His example we have the best record of perfect human freedom defined by an awareness of a transcendent God. Through this example we learn how to accept life and those who live it. We are free to live as we please, so long as we do not harm others, and so long as we work to liberate those who have been and are being harmed and oppressed by evil in the world.

The terrible and vital tension that exists in that sort of free responsibility is the heart of Christianity for me. With that realization, I discovered what I had so feared and rebelled against in the Southern Baptist tradition, and I learned as well what it was in that tradition that I found so necessary, so demanding and so liberating.

The deeply frightening thing about the church for me was its easy acceptance of the culture that surrounded it so that the rules of the culture, so tightly defined and so corrupt in many places, became the rules of the church. Scripture came to be interpreted through eyes of the culture rather than as commentary on that culture. Never did I know the church to rise up in wrath and condemn the culture that fed it. We had defended war and racism and violent confrontation with legal authorities. We had prohibited human development and had crippled with guilt those young people who were trying to discover who they were sexually, intellectually and socially. We were bound rather than free. We were the authorities, the law that Jesus came to fulfill and end. We were the Pharisees, the whitewashed sepulchers. There was deadness about us because we were so closely allied to the world in such insidious ways. Sam S. Hill, Jr., a scholar who has studied the Southern Baptists puts it best.

> Potential conflict is aroused by the fact that the Christian church demands a total loyalty, while the South as a cultural system presents itself as a nurturing and teaching agency lacking in self-critical powers. In very different ways both Christianity and Southerners lay exclusive claim upon the white people of the region. . .they are participants in two primary frameworks of meaning, two cultural systems. Their lives are governed by two culture-ethics, God who is society and God who is the subject of existential experience within the Christian community. Both provide context, identity, community, and moral constraint.[1]

If the discovery of this relationship served to explain some of the death that so many of us had experienced as Southern Baptists, it nevertheless indicated another

---

[1]"The South's Two Cultures," in *Religion and the Solid South*, ed. Hill, et. al. (Nashville: Abingdon Press, 1972), pp. 46-47.

direction. Once again the faith itself provided the symbol. For deep within the tradition that is entombed in Southern culture, there is the life of belief and meaning, a new life that united Baptist and Christian names in a union of real strength. The discussion and debate on baptism had led us into the heart of what it was to be Baptist. We rediscovered a history and a tradition for ourselves. We spoke again of what it meant to believe profoundly in the "free church." We were able to read the words of another Southern Baptist historian with pride.

> As a distinct denomination, Baptists first began in seventeenth-century England. Label the religious parties of that period and here is what you come up with: Anglicans (English Episcopalians) are the "conservatives"; Puritans are the "liberals"; Quakers, Congregationalists, and Baptists are the "radicals"! Think of that! Baptists were not among the conservatives, wanting to maintain the status quo. They were not even among the avantgard liberals who wanted to tamper with the status quo and change it a little. They were among the radicals who wanted to reverse the religious establishment. That, reader friend, is a heady heritage! One that many Baptists have never learned. Or else it is one they learned and conveniently forgot. Either way, it is a tragic misuse of history.[2]

This sort of historical realization, and the strength it brings, can lead to a diminution of the pride so often found in Southern Baptist churches. It is a strength that allows us not only to criticize the denomination itself, but to separate it from the un-Christian aspects of the culture that support it. If the church can stand apart from the culture, then it can get on with the business of calling the world to judgment in the name of the Lord. This task is impossible as long as the world and the church remain identical; but it is essential for Christianity to be truly radical, to cut to the roots of evil, to transform the world with transformed men and women. Christians can speak with authority once again and do so in the best, but often hidden, Baptist tradition.

Perhaps the perspective from the Northern fringe allows me to make this sort of synthesis. We are in a minority here, even in a border state, and things look different. Still, I hope it is not merely an individual matter or even a matter of this particular church. I hear that there are other churches like this one I have discovered and that not all of them are outside the deep South. Perhaps this feeling that we must look more closely at the contradictions that seem so prevalent in our lives is shared by increasing numbers of Southern Baptists. Like ours, they may find themselves embroiled in controversy from time to time. Yet I suspect that one hears little talk of "split" congregations, for there is strength in recognizing free responsibility to one another that is not found in appeals to authoritarian leadership or in easy acceptance of the "old ways."

Strangely, for me, this discovery of new perspective has had an ironic twist. Now that I can affirm the name and have found a deep worth in being Baptist, I find that I would like to hold on to more of the cultural tradition as well. The identification of culture and theology might not be healthy for theology, but it is probably very good for culture. It legitimizes certain factors and enables them to maintain validity in a time of great shift and change and uncertainty. It anchors experience. The Southern churches, for all their problems, offer individuals, and most importantly, offer families, a center of life. People support one another there. They care about the sick and dying. They love the children of their neighbors in specific ways rather than with a soft concern for the "world." They grieve when personal problems arise in other homes.

Personally this means that I have, in some ways, become one of the conservatives in my congregation. I constantly remind myself of Brother Will Campbell's words: "Whenever a church moves out of a brush arbor it loses something." Translated into my experience, this means that I call for us to spend more time together in church, perhaps even reinstitute the Sunday evening services. I sometimes long for the old hymns during our "high church" worship. I even wish, at times, for a stronger emotional sense in our appeals for personal commitment rather than the carefully controlled sequences in which the sermons are separated from the decisions made by individuals with offering collection and special music. Having suffered from one sort of imbalance—lacking in intellect—I do not wish for any simple reversal that slights or abandons the emotional life of Christian fellowship.

In all of this, I feel old urges rising, urges to call out for change and reform. But when I feel impatient now I know two important things. First, I know that my brothers and sisters here will listen with love and care to the suggestions that I or anyone else wishes to make, though they might not go along with us in the end. There will be no charges of heresy, no denunciations of character. Secondly, I know that my family and friends can look forward to those nights when we go and have dinner with the older people and share thoughts and songs and prayers. We will share our lives. There I find myself part of a community of truly common belief that transcends the forms in which we express ourselves. Being Christian is more important than anything else in my life, certainly more important than being Baptist. But being Baptist makes it possible to be most Christian. It is a personal matter rather than a theological one now. It puts part of my life back into place and fills an empty space that nagged for too many years.

Those evenings of shared experience, the days of controversy and resolution, the peace of worship all contribute new resonances to that quiet time of day. That time

---

[2]Walter B. Shurden, *Not a Silent People* (Nashville: Broadman Press, 1972), p. 12.

has now become a richer metaphor for me. It expresses best what I understand by a scriptural phrase, "the fullness of time." It is in that time that the Lord chooses to do things in the lives of men and women who can then do things in the world. I am more and more comfortable with that phrase. No less impatient in my need for reform, I have learned to be far more patient with people. I am not alone. Leaving the church, then, is not an alternative. I must simply wait for a while.

The Old Regular Baptist Church

by Ron Short

Photo by David Massey

When I was nineteen years old, I joined the Air Force, mainly because my one year of college had been less than satisfying and I had absolutely no idea of what else to do. The education that I gained during the next four years changed my attitudes about a great many things. In truth, it was my first extended encounter with the world outside

Ron Short grew up in the Old Regular Baptist Church in southwest Virginia. He is on the staff of the Highlander Research and Education Center and is editor of *Highlander Reports.*

the mountains of Appalachia. I found quickly that my life had been very different from my fellow airmen.

It was the first time I was ever offended by the use of the word "hillbilly." At least I was not alone. A friend from high school had joined with me, and even though they probably didn't deserve it, two other young men were labeled hillbillies because they were from Arkansas.

When you join the Air Force, they issue identification tags that you are expected to keep on your person at all times until you leave the service. I thought the process of obtaining "dog tags" would be the easiest thing I had thus far encountered during my brief military career. A young sergeant sat behind a metal stamping machine, a complicated version of the bus station model. I handed him a piece of paper with my name, newly-assigned serial number, blood type and religious preference—the latter two are required in case you are wounded and need blood, a minister, or both. We had no trouble until we got to religious preference.

"Old Regular Baptist."

"What's this?"

"Sir?"

"What the hell is this Old Regular Baptist?"

"It's the church I go to, sir."

"Where the hell are you from, boy?"

"Southwest Virginia."

"Oh, West Virginia."

"No sir, Virginia, the southwestern part."

"If you're from Virginia, then say you're from Virginia and if you're a Baptist, then say you're a Baptist. Don't give me all this crap about southwest and Old Regular. Are you a Baptist or not?"

"Yes sir, I guess I am."

I rationalized the encounter by feeling sorry for a man who had to spend his days sitting behind a machine stamping out little metal tags. Still, I was disturbed by his attitude, and was immediately defensive. The Old Regular Baptist Church was the only church I had ever known.

After several weeks, it was decided that we would all go to church on Sunday. It was, in fact, part of our training schedule; we were divided by denomination and marched off to church. By that time, I had been further defined out of the general category of Baptist and into the much broader category of Protestant. Even my Arkansas friends knew when to stand and when to sit, when to repeat lines or when to be silent. I bobbed up and down, mumbled words and followed as closely as possible the actions of everyone else. The closest I came to prayer was my fervent wish for the service to end.

It was a confusing time for me. One of the more disturbing aspects of the experience, however, hinged on an area that was somewhat of a surprise. Although I had always attended church, I had never considered myself a religious person. Only once before had I seriously questioned my feelings about the matter. While lying in bed with a pillow tucked up under my side to relieve the pain of a brand new

appendectomy, I had been easily cornered by an evangelical preacher who wanted to know if I were a Christian. When I answered an honest "no," according to my own definition, he immediately promised I was bound for hell. Since I thought I was going to die anyway, I did some thinking about my religious convictions. Two days later, however, these thoughts had subsided with the pain.

Now I was discovering that this minister was not the only one who had no way of knowing what I meant by being a Christian.

Wintertime in the mountains,
And the snow is fallin' down;
Daddy's loadin' the pickup truck,
To haul the "bakker" into town;
There'll be new shoes for me and Sara,
And for Momma a new gown;
Peppermint sticks and orange slices,
When Christmas rolls around.

Chorus

We believed in the family,
And the Old Regular Baptist Church;
And we believed in John L. for a while,
Till things couldn't get much worse;
They tell me times was harder then,
And I remember that for a while;
But, I remember the way my Daddy laughed,
And the way my Momma smiled.

My Daddy would come home from workin' in the mines,
With his shirt frozen to his arms;
And ever'time my Momma would cry,
He'd laugh and say, "It won't do me no harm;
You know a man's got to work for a livin' today,
And come spring I want to build a new barn;
But a man can't raise a family no more,
On a rocky hillside farm."

Chorus

July meetin' on a hillside,
For family that's passed away;
The preacher talks of their lives,
And prays for a brighter day;
Brothers and Sisters shoutin',
Oh Lord, how they could sing;
Raisin' their voices to the sky,
They made the mountains ring.

©1975 Ron Short

The Old Regular Baptist Church was once the center of Appalachian community life. Stressing the need to establish unity and cooperation among its own members and to act as a working example of harmony, its influence extended into the broader community. Today, the church still clings tenaciously to its religious traditions and to its own view of the spirit of Christianity and the Word of God. Yet in an age of massive cultural and technological advancement, it is often viewed as a unique sect of backwoods Christians with neither the mentality nor the spirit to survive. But to me, this church, which embodies the spirit of unity, cooperation, harmony and fellowship, is the very essence of Christianity.

The denomination traces its history back to the internal splits between the Arminians, the Calvinists, and Revivalists. There is no national organization and no one designated spokesman. Each church is separate and independent. Churches in a several county area form their own association and annually elect one elder as moderator, the religious and spiritual leader of the entire association.

Tracing Back the Old Regular Baptist Church

1. The Apostle John was with Christ on the Mount where the church was established.

2. Polycarp was baptized by John on the 25th of December, 95 A.D.

3. Polycarp organized the Partus Church at the foot of the Tiber, 150 A.D. and Tortullon was a member of that body.

4. Tortullon from the Partus Church organized the Turan Church at Turan, Italy, 237 A.D.

5. Telesman, a member of the Partus Church, organized the Pontifossi Church at the foot of the Alps in France, 398 A.D.

6. Adromicus came from the Pontifossi Church and organized the Darethea Church in Asia Minor, 671 A.D.

7. Archer Flavin from the Darethea Church organized the Timto Church, 738 A.D.

8. Balcola, from the Timto Church in Asia Minor, organized the Lima Piedmont Church, 812 A.D.

9. Aaron Arlington was ordained in 940 A.D. by the Lima Piedmont Church.

10. Aaron Arlington organized the Hillcliff Church, 987 A.D.

11. The Hillcliff Church, located in Wales, shows in its records that members of the Church came to America and later became members of the Philadelphia Association.

12. Dr. John Clark, from the Church of Wales, came to America with four others and organized the first Baptist Church in this country at Newport, Rhode Island, 1638 A.D.

13. The Church of Rhode Island helped organize the first Baptist Association, the Philadelphia Association, in 1707.

14. The Philadelphia Association organized the Katockton Association in Virginia in 1766.

15. The Katockton Association organized the Hosten Association in North Carolina in 1783.

16. The Hosten Association organized the South Elkhorn Association in Kentucky in 1784.

17. The South Elkhorn Association organized the South Kentucky Association in 1787, which became the South District and North District of United Baptist in 1801.

18. The North District organized the Burning Springs Association in 1813.

Continued on page 104

Continued from page 103

19. The Burning Springs Association organized the New Salem Association in 1825 and the Paint Union in 1837. These too were called United Baptist.

20. The New Salem Association, mother church of The Old Regular Baptists, organized the Mate's Creek Association in 1849 and the Union Association in 1859. The Union Association played a crucial role in the final evolution of the Old Regular Church.

21. The Old Regular Churches today trace their development from the New Salem and Union Associations. The Doctrine that was established in 1894 is maintained relatively intact today with very few changes in the "old style" of worship.

Although I had always attended the Old Regular Baptist Church, I was never a member. Only those people who have been baptized are considered members; the rest of the community is the congregation. Church seats are arranged accordingly. Covering nearly a third of the floor space is a raised platform for preachers and members. The congregation sits behind and below them on long bench seats arranged in typical church fashion. Women and men sit separately.

The Old Regulars' belief in the great magnitude and responsibility of being a church member and the importance of the individual's decision to receive God into his total life outweighs their desire to swell the ranks of the church. There is no pressure from church members to stimulate others in the community to join. There are no revivals and no membership drives; no undue influence is brought on family and friends. My great grandfather, J. C. Swindall, was moderator of the Union Association of southwest Virginia and east Kentucky for 42 years, yet only three of his nine children joined the church and they did so only after they were married with families of their own.

After each meeting, the closing minister opens the church for new members. Any person who has reached the "age of accountability," usually 14 or 15, may come forward and express their desire to join the church. Usually the prospective member will relate how he or she has come to this decision. It is obvious that the deliberation has been careful and long and, in many cases, related to a personal religious experience.

Any dissent from a church member can keep the prospective member from being received into the church. However, the person who raised the question must be prepared to defend his reservations with church doctrine. There is usually no question of acceptance, and a time and place is set for baptism.

The Old Regulars baptize by total immersion, usually in a stream or river near a church. One of the more interesting by-products of stripmining in Appalachia is the difficulty the church now has in finding unpolluted streams or rivers for their baptisms.

Baptism is one immersion in the name of the Father, the Son and the Holy Ghost. As the new member wades from the water into the arms of family and other church members, he is greeted by glorious shouting and singing.

Members retain lifetime membership in the church where they are baptized, but may transfer without rebaptism to a new church with a letter of recognition from the old. Any member of another denomination must be rebaptized into the Old Regular. "Backsliders," as my granny called them, can re-establish church membership if they show proper signs of repentance for their wayward actions and upon examination can convince the other members of their desire to return to church.

Church services follow closely the schedules of the old days when preachers were scarce in a community, and services were held on alternate weekends.

The furnishings of the church are bare necessities. The front wall usually contains pictures of beloved elders who have contributed their life to the church; inspirational pictures and wall plaques may hang there as well. There is a communal water bucket and dipper. Children often wander from the lap of a relative on the stand to the parent who sits with the congregation and anyone may come and go at will during the service. This is in no way considered a breach of etiquette. Only the very new churches have indoor toilets and many still do not have central heating. Air conditioners are almost non-existent, so many local business men still pass out fans with a picture of Jesus on one side and an advertisement on the other.

Each church has an Elder who serves as Moderator and primary preacher, although any preacher in full fellowship may preach also. Elders in the Church are treated with great respect. They are not trained and educated for the ministry, but are "called," their abilities derived from the power of God.

New elders must be baptized church members and must receive sanction from other preachers within his church to take on the role. After a trial period to test speaking ability and knowledge of the Scriptures, which may last from a few months to a year, a special presbytery of church members is appointed to further question the candidate. If all members of the group are in agreement, an elder then "lays" hands upon the Brother and ordains him. Elders receive no pay and, unless they are retired, work at a regular job, assuming all costs of their ministerial duties.

Although some have inferred that the preachers' sermons are random rambling loosely based on the Bible, specific biblical texts are chosen and carried through to conclusion. Since several preachers may preach on any given day and the order is determined just prior to the beginning of service, an idea may be abandoned if another minister delivers his sermon on that text. Sermons are not written and the Old Regular minister must rely heavily on his knowledge of the Bible and "a double portion of the Sweet Spirit" to get him through. It is not uncommon for a preacher who flounders to be "sung down" by the members. They may also be sung down if they tend toward long-windedness, for Old Regular services are uncommonly long even in normal circumstances.

There is no way to relate the emotional impact of Old Regular Baptist singing. There is no music but the voice. The songs are "lined," sung by one person and then repeated by the group. This practice comes from a time when there was a shortage of songbooks and from the fact that the melodies, which do not follow standard notation, have depended on the oral tradition for their continuation. The melodies are closely "modal" and are hard to follow using the standard scale of music. Without drastic changes they cannot be translated for musical accompaniment. Although there are now abundant songbooks, they contain only words, no music.

The songs maintain the "long meter" tradition with great emphasis on feeling rather than rhythm. To some, the sound is melancholy and mournful; for others, it is a glimpse into the very soul of man. Some people, in their uneasiness, try to deal with it by laughing or total silence, but no one can ignore it.

It is common for people who like to sing to exchange songs they learned in church, and I am often asked to sing some of mine. Though I understand their interest, I cannot bring myself to do it. In many cases, the words are familiar because the Old Regulars simply adopt any song they like. The delivery, however, is a different matter. The first time I heard "Amazing Grace" outside of church, I believed it to be a popularized rendition of an Old Regu-

Photo from Photographic Archives / Alice Lloyd College

lar Baptist hymn. It is deeply satisfying to sing these songs, but at the same time, it calls for deep reflection in order to approach their true quality.

In their practice of the sacraments, the Old Regular Baptists interpret literally the words of the Bible. The bread is unleavened, usually baked by the wife of the deacon. The wine may be real or it may be grape juice. Women partake of the bread and wine separately from the men. Each takes a small bite and a swallow of wine and passes it to the next person until all have shared.

As the singing continues, the deacons and usually their wives prepare basins of water and towels for the foot

Photo by Rob Amberg

washing. One by one the Brethren and Sisters kneel and wash each other's feet, drying them with a towel which hangs from the waist. Here, vanity is cast aside, and their faces reflect the great joy in the humbleness of this act.

Memorial services are scheduled on a yearly basis. In my memory this date has never changed. I know that wherever I am, on the third Saturday and Sunday of July, memorial services for my great-grandfather and other members of my family and community will be held.

Memorial services were the first church services I ever attended. My mother and father took me to the graveyard where we sat in an open shed built of skinned poles and a tin roof. The structure was built on the slope of a hillside and the seats, made of rough boards nailed to small poles, rose gradually with the hill, so that everyone could look down upon the platform in front which serves as a stand for the preachers and members. Many structures such as this are still used yearly in Appalachia.

Memorial services are a time of great excitement and joy as well as remembrance. For some, it serves as an annual reunion. Hospitality and community spirit run high; cooking may go on for weeks prior to the meeting.

Saturday is a warm-up day, with services at the church. On Sunday, everyone gathers on the hillside, dressed in

their finest, be it a new pair of overalls or black patent slippers. As the last prayer ends, the somber air is instantly transformed with shouts of "Ever'body who'll go home with me is welcome." People from the community, especially families of the deceased, are expected to ask everyone in sight.

I had a great-uncle whose name was Columbus, though everyone called him "Burrhead." It was said that he sold moonshine, and memorial time was about the only time he attended church. His wife had been dead for many years and he lived a bare existence. Yet each year his voice was first and loudest, "Ever'body who'll go home with me is welcome." Everyone knew that it was doubtful he had anything prepared, but everyone also knew he would share whatever he had.

I remember a conversation my Dad had with him which was repeated almost yearly by someone. "Why don't you come on down to the house and eat with us. You can save your food and eat it next week. It'll keep."

"Well, I believe you've talked me right into it," he said with a laugh.

Though there have been drastic changes in the life styles of many Appalachian communities, the Church still plays an important role in the attitudes of the people. In their efforts to exemplify the teachings of Christ, members and Elders lend strength and assurance to those around them. Their deep personal commitment is felt but never intrudes.

As long as I can remember, there have been black preachers and members in the Old Regulars. I think it is important to point out that while this country has labored under the burden of continued racial strife, this Church has maintained the equality of people as a natural part of the Christian ethic, not as defined by the legal limits of a person's civil rights.

The Old Regulars also believe that the church must exist with total harmony among members. Each person must carefully search his heart and mind and there must be full harmony for the services to begin. Any dissent must be voiced with the full recognition that the unity of the church is broken, the most grievous state which can exist; but to stifle a question one feels should be asked is just as harmful.

Even today, there is a cooperative spirit among people in the communities of Appalachia that has its roots deep in the historical development of the region and, I believe, in the development of the Church.

As long as there are people who have taken part in the Old Regular Baptist experience, it will never die. I will most surely carry a part of it with me for as long as I live. With the great Appalachian out-migration, the church has now spread from the hills of east Kentucky and southwest Virginia to the cities of the North. Like me, many younger people are confronted with the dilemma of being part of two worlds. I call on my mountain roots for strength and security, but I live in a society that demands a more complex attitude for survival. I am still surprised at the effect the Old Regular Baptist church has on my attitudes, and the intensity with which I recall the things I saw and heard at church services. The memories may be clouded with childhood innocence, but my intellectual attitude cannot break my emotional ties. A part of me refuses to be totally swept up by a culture that has long forgotten the values that I have taken for granted most of my life.

Photo by David Massey

Growing Up Catholic

by Pam Durban

Aiken, South Carolina, has a long tradition of combining strange cultural forces. Esteemed as a health resort by virtue of its dry, pine-scented air, by the late 1800s, it had become a winter season gathering place for the very rich. The W. R. Graces and the Ambrose Clarks, the Goodyears and the Vanderbilts maintained palatial "cottages" there. Every year they arrived with their stables of polo ponies and thoroughbred riding horses and train loads of servants to encamp for six weeks of gala partying, riding to hounds and competing with each other in horse shows before drifting on to Palm Beach or back to Long Island. Most of these "winter people" were Roman Catholic.

There was also a small and thriving population of local Catholics, black and white. I was one of these and my father, following a long tradition of Catholicism in his family, raised us as devout Catholics with, I believe, the best of intentions. The construction of the Savannah River nuclear power plant in 1950 deposited more Catholic Northerners in the town.

The Catholic community was large enough to support a parish church with the size and sweep of a small cathedral. St. Mary Help of Christians church was set on spacious grounds which it shared with a delicate chapel, a national wonder among church architects. St. Mary's boasted Byzantine gilt ceilings, wooden pews with brass plates for family name cards, several large marble statues of saints and a formidable marble altar. The Monsignor of the parish, the son of a wealthy Northern family, rode to hounds with the winter people and was included in all their social events.

There were few poor Catholics. The very poor attended a smaller mission church in "the valley," Horse Creek valley, a textile mill community not far from Aiken.

St. Mary's parish supported a Catholic grade school and a high school attended by local Catholics and boarding students. The Dominican order of nuns who taught in the grade school lived in a winter resort home on some acreage.

Black Catholics rarely came to Mass at St. Mary's church; none attended St. Mary's school. St. Jerome's church and school had been built especially for them and an order of black nuns taught there. I remember one time when a group of concerned white mothers held a hurried conference with the St. Mary's principal because they had heard she was going to invite students from St. Jerome's for a get-together. They never came.

I don't think it crossed my mind then how curious it was for there to be an entirely separate group of black Catholics. We didn't think about race: concern for racial equality paled beside our utter absorption in the church.

In those days, being Catholic in Aiken meant that I had few friends outside the church. Opportunities for interaction were few, and the mutual mistrust between "us" and "them," between Catholic and Protestant, was deep. The mother of my best non-Catholic friend discouraged religious conversation between us and forbade her to go with me where there were more than two Catholics gathered together. Likewise, I did not attend activities sponsored by another church. My mother was Presbyterian but had signed papers before she married, vowing to raise her children as Catholics. Her religion prompted occasional, deep torment in me since I believed with a child's devoutness that "outside the Catholic church there is no salvation."

Our lives were further segregated from our peers because we spent so much time at church. We went to Mass every Friday and Sunday; during Lent, we went

Pam Durban is on the staff of *The Patch* in Atlanta, Georgia, and has written for the *Great Speckled Bird* and the *Atlanta Gazette*. She recently edited a collection of interviews and recipes called *Cabbagetown Women, Cabbagetown Food*.

every day and were expected to receive Holy Communion. If we didn't, a nun would take us aside after Mass and ask leading questions about the state of grace in our souls. The true test of friendship between girls (the only acceptable friendships) was the frequency with which you knelt together and received communion. We confessed frequently, starting at the age of seven.

Beginning in first grade, we studied our catechism fervently, first period every morning. It must have sounded odd to hear small children discussing transubstantiation and consubstantiation understanding the definition as well as the nuances of each term. Even now, I am amazed and somewhat frightened that I can reel off cathechism responses almost automatically though I haven't been to church in years. The Dominican nuns were a teaching order and their zealous dogmatism was matched by their unflagging intellectualism. When I entered public school in ninth grade, I was intellectually quicker but emotionally more infantile than my classmates. I was extremely naive, a perspective I carried through years of dirty jokes and to the bitter end of my first love affair. He was a Baptist and we separated, finally, when I balked, horrified, at his suggestion that we commit the serious sin of French kissing.

My sense of propriety was shared by my Catholic friends and in all of us it was balanced, fortunately, by our flair for the dramatic. We got this ability to intensify any situation, I believe, from years of being steeped in the exotic medieval rituals which punctuated the liturgical year.

Christmas Eve midnight Mass was the climax of the church year; St. Mary's church really pulled out the stops at Christmas. The church glowed with hundreds of candles flickering against a background of fresh greens and banked poinsettias. The Knights of Columbus, a men's fraternal order, formed a double line from the door of the church to the altar. Dressed in black capes and tall plumed hats, they drew their swords simultaneously to form a silver arch under which the Monsignor walked. Accompanying him were a dozen altar boys swinging decorative incense pots; one carried the gold chalice for communion on a purple velvet pillow.

Everyone, Catholic and Protestant, it seemed, came to midnight Mass for this amazing pageant. Many were drunk. People fainted and left suddenly, and the woozy smell of gin rose with the incense. It was also one of the few times I saw black Catholics at church.

I suppose the biggest, most obvious, difference between me and my non-Catholic contemporaries was the high visibility of our religious fervor. We wore school uniforms year round, miserable shirts, jumpers and skirts of a distasteful color approaching turquoise blue (the Virgin Mary's color) and so flimsy that the winter wind cut right through. We wore medals of devotion to our patron saints around our necks or pinned to our identical gray sweaters. At the beginning of each Lenten season we could be seen with ashes marking our foreheads. We refused meat on Fridays. Girls went to extremes, shunning sleeveless shirts, low-cut shoes, pull-over sweaters or non-devotional jewelry as affronts to virgin modesty. Movies were checked against the approved list posted beside the confession booth. We murmured our prayers and sang long, atonal chants. We were noticeably subdued during the forty days of Lent while we did penance and meditated on the crucifixion. I usually gave up ice cream and candy for Lent and ate candy and ice cream on Easter Sunday until I got sick.

If this had been my only life, I would by now be certifiably insane. But I had another life outside the church, a life just as extreme in its own way, which gave me valuable balance. I was deeply pious, but my time outside the church was spent running wild through the woods just behind my house. Every afternoon and weekend I would disappear into these woods, alone or with friends, and play great fantasy games with my herds of wild horses.

Chanukah,
Camp Hill, Alabama

by Janet Rechtman

Photo by Marie Morris and John Speaks

The Jewish kids played in the pasture, a sister and brother in an Alabama town. Soon the sun would set and Chanukah begin. The dry field grass scratched her legs when, Indian wrestling, she rolled on the ground to break a fall. The incredible blue sky, sunless, chilled the sweat that sank salt into new wounds.

The wrestling became a spat and he left victorious. The girl played on alone, a new game. She pretended the holiday was not her own. She was neuter, no, a Christian, a Gulliver pinned by Jew hammers, Jew strings, and Jew nails, changed for a night to a Jew.

Her parents explained that it wasn't so bad. She had eight days of Christmas, not a sickly one. Eight times the joy! Eight times the gifts! Except she was ten, and she would only have one gift this year. And eight times the void on the other nights.

"Why is this night different from all others?" She didn't know what to say to the boy who came through the field with a cow. Bovine both, she was terrified. What if he asked another unanswerable question? Like "How come you're not saved?" She lacked the gifts to make herself understood and ran away mutely, leaving him laughing at the shit on her shoes.

Better stay near the house now. The sky was red.

Jane Rechtman is a poet and writer from Atlanta, Georgia. She occasionally writes for the *Atlanta Gazette.*

Her little sisters played store in the back yard. They still had eight days—she'd seen the tiny oven that was the first of this year's potlatch. On the back stoop she watched them imitate a mother and friend: they did not ask her to join in. Impatient she found a stick and cleaned her shoes.

Sundown was close. Where should she be when they called?

She ran to the front yard, to the pecan tree with the rounded crotch that was her favorite perch when she was little. Tonight she was grown up, though. A more dignified spot was required. In the orchard down by the wild plums perhaps—but she'd eaten the fruit already and she'd only get dirty on the red clay bank.

She was running to the grape arbor when she heard the call.

Eldest, she lit first, a pink shamas and a green spiralled taper, and read prayers from the paper that came with the candles. The two lights flickered in the silver menorah. She wanted to touch the flame, but was afraid.

"Boruch atoy adonay." She wondered at the ancient violence and longed for the prince of peace, for the easy tunes of Christmas instead of the tortured cadence she now sang. "Rock of ages let our song, vast thy saving power. Thou amidst the raging foe wast our sheltering tower."

They brought out the gifts, unwrapped as always. The first of eight for the others, one alone for her. A doll. Her friends had dolls and she'd wanted one too—but not like this, a lady doll with embarrassing breasts, red lips and bouffant hair. She hated it, but acted pleased so no one would say she was childish.

Seven nights she brought the doll woman out, the badge of her growing up. Seven days she hid it in her room. On the eighth morning her brother found it and drew nipples on its breasts and a moustache of pubic hair between its legs.

That afternoon she went out to see what her friends had under their Christmas trees: skates, baby dolls, chemistry sets, BB guns, footballs and bikes. They were all laughing as they played, joking about how hard it was to be good all year.

The girl ran home crying. She cried because of the doll. She cried because she was captive, imprisoned where she did not belong. She cried because her parents had lied when they said there was no Santa Claus.

The Lectureship

by Don Haymes

CONSIDER ALL OPPONENTS AS FRIENDS & GUESTS
GOOD SPORTSMANSHIP—A SCHOOL'S GREATEST PRIDE
NEVER HISS OR BOO A PLAYER OR OFFICIAL
APPLAUD OPPONENTS GOOD PLAYS
PLAY BY THE RULES TO WIN WITH FAIRNESS
WIN WITHOUT BOASTING—LOSE WITHOUT EXCUSES
COMPETE AS YOU WOULD HAVE OTHERS COMPETE WITH YOU
—Sign in Bader Memorial Gym, Freed-Hardeman College

Tennessee 100 threads its way through the gently rolling landscape of west Tennessee toward Henderson, eighty-four miles and ninety-five minutes from Memphis. One may drive Interstate 40 to Jackson, and then take US 45 into Henderson, but Interstate travel is not what it used to be, and Tennessee 100 is smooth, two-lane blacktop, flawlessly maintained, dotted with picnic benches, lined with farms and forests. On a chill, dreary February morning, it is almost deserted. As the visitor nears his destination, he would find it no surprise to encounter a Model A or a '36 Chevy at the crest of a hill; it is that kind of road, and the psychical distance to Henderson is greater than the physical. Tennessee 100 is the better way to go.

The psychical distance to Henderson is greater than the physical.

To enter Henderson (pop. 3,500) is to come upon a page from the American past—not the past of Paul Revere or the pioneers, but of Booth Tarkington's *Penrod*

or Sinclair Lewis's *Main Street*, moved south; the past when Americans lived in small towns and believed in God, and in an honest day's work, and in the president of the United States. It is late morning by the time the visitor slips down the narrow main street, past cafes and clothing stores, a bank, a cinema, a small supermarket, a courthouse, a service station, coming, at last, to a fork in the road, and Freed-Hardeman College.

In Henderson, Freed-Hardeman is not hard to find. Founded in 1908 by A. G. Freed and N. B. Hardeman, after another school had foundered in the division between the Disciples of Christ and the Churches of Christ, the college and its 1,400 students dominate the town in the way—in the public mind—the University of California holds sway in Berkeley. In fact, the influence of Freed-Hardeman extends far beyond the borders of Henderson and of Tennessee: its graduates are to be found on every Christian (meaning Church of Christ)

Don Haymes's essay appeared in two issues of *Integrity*—7:10 (April 1976): 154-58, and 7:11 (May 1976): 167-73—and is reprinted here by permission.

college faculty and at not a few "secular" institutions, as well as in pulpits and mission posts throughout the world. They are, by and large, industrious and inexhaustible, plain-spoken and fiercely combative. They are taught to "contend earnestly for the faith"—a rigidly formulated compound of biblical interpretation and oral tradition—and they are prepared for the task with a rigor and precision that would awe an Aquinas. They are the Jesuits of the Church of Christ: "hard shell" Campbellites. To the uninitiated, they may appear harsh, mean-spirited, obsessed; but they see themselves as soldiers of the Lord of Hosts, and it is the misfortune of men trained to combat to be ever on guard, ever on the offensive.[1]

It is the misfortune of men trained to combat to be ever on guard, ever on the offensive.

Turning into a driveway, the visitor finds the campus packed with cars, parked every-which-way on every available patch of pavement. Nearly 6,000 people have made the pilgrimage to Henderson this week, from all over America and across the seas, for the Fortieth Annual Freed-Hardeman College Bible Lectureship. It is this event which has brought the visitor to Henderson for the first time, to see and hear for himself. With great fortune, the visitor finds a newly-vacated parking space and, at 11 a.m., makes his way into Bader Memorial Gymnasium.

At this hour, the last lecture of the morning is winding down; in his melodious Scottish brogue—hinting of the ancestry of the dialect of most of his listeners—Andrew Gardiner is discussing "The Restoration Movement in the British Isles." There is standing-room-only in the gym. Highly-polished wooden bleachers extend from all four walls, and folding chairs cover the floor space in front of the speaker's platform. Lectures and classes have begun in this building at 7:30 a.m. The students in the bleachers are well-scrubbed and earnest; their hair is more closely cropped, on both men and women, than that of most of their peers in other places. There are, however, a few neatly trimmed beards and a large number of "Afros." Most of the students are watching the speaker closely, and a few are using tape-recorders; most of them appear attentive but passive.

Andrew Gardiner concludes his remarks—"modernism," he says, has been the greatest problem in the British Isles—and turns the platform over to E. Claude Gardner, the president of Freed-Hardeman College. "This is not a conference," Mr. Gardner warns the

audience. "We are not here to legislate anything. . . . God's book has already fixed these things. We are here to study it and to learn."

The crowd disperses rapidly; lectures may satisfy the soul, but now it is the stomach's turn. Seeing a few familiar faces, the visitor shakes hands here and there, exchanges a few pleasantries with strangers, and wanders uphill to the Lectureship Exhibit Tent, a fixture of most such gatherings among the Churches of Christ. This one is only medium-sized, small compared to the two tents used in Abilene, Texas, and is a garish affair in red, white and blue stripes. A few mission posts are represented, as are schools of preaching, camps, and homes for orphans and the old. There are many kinds of wares for sale, from (anti-) *Abortion Handbooks* to *Bus Ministry Coloring Books* to biographies and Bible commentaries to recordings of sermons to "Roman Crucifixion Nails" handsomely boxed.

Leaving the tent, the visitor walks to the basement of the Student Center, where women from churches in the area have provided a meal of fried chicken, rice, peas, rolls, and dessert for $1.89. The visitor manages to bypass, with abundant regret, the rich-looking slices of home-made pies and cakes, and finds a vacant seat at one of the tables. Preachers' wives and their children are much in evidence here. "We've been to every lecture this week," says one lady, trying to corral her well-mannered but restless daughters, age seven and five. These women appear more relaxed and at ease than others the visitor has seen at other recent gatherings. Beyond doubt, they and their children are disciplined and patient, and they do not appear to be "up-tight" about their place in the world. An older woman at the table has engaged a preacher she knows in an earnest conversation about the views of another preacher encountered by a friend of hers in Denver. The food is simple, down-home, and good.

These women do not appear to be up-tight about their place in the world.

---

[1] And yet there are others in whom some chemistry of the spirit works a subtle change, even in the stereotyper's mold; they emerge somehow less rigid, more open to choice and chance; their world begins in Henderson, but it does not end there. Many more of these folk exist than the other image might suggest: there is Heber Taylor, who has won two Fulbright Scholarships in Journalism; Robert Meyers, of *Voices of Concern* fame; Mack Langford, who was on the staff of Crozer Theological Seminary (now defunct); Leroy Garrett of *Restoration Review*; and the editor of *Integrity*, Hoy G. Ledbetter.

It is time to return to the gym, where workmen have straightened the rows of folding chairs, cleaned the shiny surfaces of the bleachers, and removed the detritus of the morning. The floor is covered with heavy butcher-paper, to protect it from the chairs and the crowds. A closed-circuit television camera broadcasts the lectures in this building to three other locations, including the auditorium of the Henderson Church of Christ. During the rest of the year, a student explains, the equipment is used to perfect the oratorical style of student preachers; the student's sermon is video-taped, then played back for a critique by the professor and other members of the class. "They work on gestures, facial expressions, everything," the student says. "And it really works. Somebody can criticize your work, but there's nothing like seeing it for yourself. You get the message a lot faster." The visitor can only marvel.

Promptly at 12:50 p.m. (the programs run on time in Henderson), the doors to the gymnasium close, and a young song leader calls for Number 212, "Wonderful Words of Life." After a prayer, Danny Cottrell, a Freed-Hardeman professor, mounts the platform to deliver a lecture entitled "Christ Has Made Us Free: Motivation for Mission Work."

Mr. Cottrell begins by stressing that his approach to the subject will be through the Bible. "The Bible is God's inspired, infallible, inerrant . . . authoritative word. . . . And when I talk about inspiration, I am talking about *verbal* inspiration."

"Modernism," Mr. Cottrell says, "is simply not conducive to mission work." He charges that "eighty per cent of the work being done is social work," not gospel preaching. After listing and explaining in detail some of the names of the Son of God given in the Bible—Jesus, Christ, the Word, only begotten son, beloved son, Lamb of God, mediator, high priest, Lord, Master—he concludes that "if we have the exalted view of Jesus that the Bible has, we will have no trouble getting mission work done."

Mr. Cottrell then traces a relationship between Jesus' role as "Redeemer" and the doctrines of Reconciliation and Atonement, which he explains as "at-one-ment." God's aim is to free man by redeeming him—"buying him back"—and reconciling him—"bringing him back"—to himself. "Christ is the agent, God the subject, man the object."

From Jesus, Mr. Cottrell turns to the Church. "Missionary thrust," he says, "is an important index of its vitality." He thinks that the mission zeal which arose after World War II "has waned," in part due to "modernism" and the "efforts of some to establish a new image," as well as "internal strife," which is "a bodily sickness."

"But modernism cannot bear all the blame," he adds, striving toward a conclusion. "Materialism and secularism" have meant less money for missions. "When money is taken from the mission field to build bigger buildings, put soft cushions on pews, and repave the parking lots, then our priorities are all mixed up." Not only is money a problem, but "we can't find people to go . . . who will leave the comfort of Saturday afternoon at McDonalds. . . . Are we that much in love with the Big Mac?"

Outside, a persistent drizzle has turned into a downpour. The visitor retrieves his overcoat from his car, and hustles through the campus and down the street to the Henderson church building. Twelve people, two of them black Freed-Hardeman students, have gathered for a class on "Restoration History Among Blacks," taught by a young black minister named David Meek, who also serves Freed-Hardeman as an "Admissions and Financial Aid Counselor."

White preachers followed Keeble and baptized hundreds who would not submit to the rite at the hands of a black man.

Mr. Meek's approach is to offer brief lives of various preachers, many of them unknown among whites, and trace their influence. Today, he is listing disciples of G. P. Bowser, some of whom are still alive: Alonzo Jones, M. F. Holt, R. N. Hogan, G. E. Stewart ("The Blind Wonder"), the brothers S. L. and A. L. Cassius, and John Hannon. He concludes this list with a brief overview of the career of the late Marshall Keeble, "the sum total of Campbell, Womack, and Bowser." A turning point in Keeble's career came in Henderson, when a black farmer named Crooms obtained permission to use the Oak Grove school house for a Keeble meeting. Beginning the third Sunday in July 1918, Keeble preached for three weeks and baptized eighty-four people. He went on to baptize 40,000, both black and white, and establish 400 churches. White preachers followed Keeble, Mr. Meek says, and baptized hundreds who would not submit to the rite at the hands of a black man.

After summarizing the careers of four of Keeble's disciples—Luke Miller, John R. Bonner, O. L. Acre, A. C. Holt—Mr. Meek looks to the future. "We've got to get together," he says, "as God intends for his people to get together. . . . 'Let there be no divisions among you.' . . . There's a gap between our preaching and our practice. We need to close the practice gap."

"We already passed up one of our greatest opportunities," Mr. Meek continues, "in the Freedom Movement of the sixties. We could have stood up then, we could have said that's what we've always believed, that all men are equal in Christ. . . . But brethren said, 'Don't get involved—that's political.' Yet when John F. Kennedy was running for President, they were preaching against him in the pulpit, because he was a Catholic. It's amazing to me, how we can get involved in some political ideas, and not others."

Someone raises the question of "intermarriage." Mr. Meek smiles. "I guess everyone on this campus knows how I feel on that subject," he says. "Two white people get married, they'll have problems. Two black people get married, they'll have problems. So will a black person and a white who get married. Race relations is a matter of faith. There are problems, but the Gospel is the same."

"It was hard for me when I first came here," says a white Freed-Hardeman student. "I'm from Pittsburgh, and I never went to school with any blacks, I was never in an integrated situation like we have here. I just never met any *nice* black people until I came to Freed-Hardeman."

One of the black students rises, struggling for the right words; for him, perhaps, nice *white* people have been few and far between. "I was not a Christian when I came here," he says. "I'm not the same person I was. . . . I'm glad I came here."

There is good conversation after the class; one young man, a Freed-Hardeman graduate, rides a circuit for five black congregations he has helped plant in rural Georgia. By the time the visitor gets back inside the church building, C. W. Bradley, a minister in Henderson, is wrapping up his class on "Unity." Pentecostalism, gifts, and claims of miracles in the Churches of Christ have been a great concern to him: "I never thought I'd see the day come that our own people in the Church would be claiming these things." He offers 1 Corinthians 13 as a guide to "essential attitudes for unity in a congregation." In conclusion, he says that "Most of our splits arise . . . over personality and power struggles, over who's going to rule. . . . Until we're humble enough to get ahead of self, we'll not work together in unity."

Mr. Woods has confined his practice of law to the Church.

The rain has stopped, and there is a great rush back to the gymnasium for what is, to many, the main event of every day at the Freed-Hardeman Lectures: the Open Forum. Again there is standing-room-only, the visitor is fortunate to find a seat in the bleachers, by two older friendly black preachers. People are still coming in, peering anxiously about for a seat, as the song leader calls for Number 25, "Worthy Art Thou."

The Open Forum began as the exclusive domain of Nicholas Brodie Hardeman, who brought to it his considerable skills as an orator and debater, and in it honed his own, pragmatic version of "Ockham's Razor":[2] "If you can't answer any Bible question on a post card, and have room to tell about your family and ask about theirs, then you're not a Gospel preacher." He created an atmosphere in the Forum part "Problem Page," part Roman Circus, part Day of Judgment. He could be as pleasant or as pugnacious as a questioner or question seemed to demand. Taking on all comers, Hardeman gave, year after year, a virtuoso performance.

Guy N. Woods is a worthy heir to the Hardeman tradition. At sixty-eight, he is short, balding, and owl-eyed, not a physically imposing presence, but he possesses a diamond-hard intelligence, lightning-fast mental reflexes, and an unerring instinct for the jugular. He is the author of twelve books and uncounted articles, and is booked in advance for 200 "gospel meetings." On the platform now, soft-voiced and solemn, he thanks his hosts for the various courtesies of the week, and sails directly into a question posed about a speech of the previous evening. He argues for varying degrees of punishment and reward in the life to come, parsing the texts—"Watch the comparative adjective"—with all the skill of a corporation lawyer dissecting a contract. (The analogy is useful, for Mr. Woods studied law and is a member of the Tennessee bar, although he has confined his practice of law to the church.) Another question: Is the office of elder part of the age of miracles which has passed away? "If this were true, then preachers would have passed away."

Laughter. But there is a tension in the air—something is about to happen. . . .

Earlier, someone had told the visitor: "Some real young people were asking questions here the other day. I was surprised they had the courage to do it." A youth rises in the bleachers, and necks crane for a good view. Is it possible for man to know there is God without having read the Bible? Mr. Woods assumes an expression of patience and longsuffering—yes, he has been dealing with this one all week.

"You have to have the Bible to find out who God is," Mr. Woods says. "Some people try to say that I want a leap in the dark. It's nothing of the kind. A leap with the Bible is a leap into the light. . . . You can't find God without the Bible. If somebody can do it, give us the proof."

---

[2]*Entia non sunt multiplicanda praeter necessitatem*; "entities are not to be multiplied beyond need." William of Ockham (ca. 1280-1350) used this "razor" to revolutionize philosophical theology in the fourteenth century and prepare the ground for the Reformation, presaging John Locke's empiricism and Schopenhauer's philosophy of the will.

In another part of the bleachers, another young man rises, Bible in hand. He refers to Psalm 19:1—"The heavens declare the glory of God; and the firmament sheweth his handywork"—and then reads Romans 1:19-20:

> Because that which may be known of God is manifest in them; for God hath shewed it unto them.
> For the invisible things of him from the creation of the world are clearly seen, being understood by the things that are made, even his eternal power and Godhead; so that they are without excuse. . . . (KJV).

The argument is that nature and the created universe abound with evidences which prove the existence of God, by the application of a certain kind of reason. The young man is earnest, pressing his argument; if there is disagreement, then there *must* be heresy. Mr. Woods sends him a post card: "How much can you learn about the design of baptism by looking at the moon?"

There is murmuring in the bleachers: "Aw, come on . . . what's he trying to do? . . . He's missing the whole point. . . ." The young man continues to press, "Well if Dr. Warren held your position, Brother Woods, then he wouldn't stand a chance when he goes into this debate with that atheist . . . that man won't accept anything but logical proofs. . . ."

The rhetorical cat is out of the bag, and running amok. These young men are disciples of Dr. Thomas B. Warren, who was formerly the chairman of the Bible department at Freed-Hardeman and is now Professor of Philosophy of Religion and Apologetics at Harding Graduate School of Religion in Memphis. His approaching debate with British philosopher Antony Flew, scheduled to take place at North Texas State University in Denton, 20-23 September 1976, is their immediate object of concern. For years, Dr. Warren has been constructing a ponderous, often murky and dense, system of philosophical presuppositions with which to defend the existence of God and the infallibility and inerrancy of his view of Scripture. His students are widely regarded as among the most abrasive and thoroughly prepared of the younger crop of Church of Christ preachers. And here, with or without their master's blessing, they are pitting Warren's epistemology against Woods' exegesis (or eisegesis).

For his part, Mr. Woods is toying with his young, would-be tormentors—not unlike a fleet-footed beast of prey taunting a litter of lion cubs in the African Savannah—all the while continuing to wear his expression of put-upon patience. For the older folk in the audience, it is a pretty funny show; for the young partisans, it is increasingly frustrating.

"Why, if you relied on nature, you'd be nothing but a savage," Mr. Woods is saying. "The people who live closest to nature are the furthest from God . . . they see him as a vengeful, wrathful being. . . . I use reason. I've had more debates than any man living in the Church. But I don't start with reason. . . . I'm glad my faith in God does not depend on a system of logic."

Someone interjects that man can, by reason, see the attributes and characteristics of God, again referring to Psalm 19:1. Mr. Woods is holding up his wrist watch. "This watch is a creation of man," he says, "but how many men made this watch? One or a dozen?"

"These views are extremely dangerous," Mr. Woods says sternly.

One youth rises in the bleachers and proceeds to recapitulate the argument. Mr. Woods cuts him off and invites him to come down to share the platform. He accepts, and there is a collective intake of breath—"Look at that . . . golly . . . he's got courage!"—as he makes his way through the bodies in the bleachers and down the aisle. Once on the platform, he is edgy, and his voice rises: "If human reasoning is faulty, how can we know the Bible is true?" He refers again to the upcoming debate between Warren and Flew. Mr. Woods exudes total calm, and allows the young man to run his course with only occasional interjections; the youth is on the defensive. "All we're trying to say," he says, finally, "is that man is *responsible* for knowing there is a God." As he leaves the platform, there is a burst of applause from the bleachers behind the platform; Mr. Woods turns, and fixes the offending students with a withering stare. They fall silent. Mr. Woods, apparently, does not hold with applauding "opponents"; perhaps he would deny that the "opponent" made a "good play."

"These views are extremely dangerous," Mr. Woods says sternly, to the consternation of the young men in the bleachers. "This is how the evolutionist justifies evolution." There are groans in the bleachers. "Of course, I don't believe that these young men would support evolution. But the evolutionist attempts to sustain his view of the creation of the world by human reasoning." He is summing up now, ready to move on. "What value would it be to know there is a God, without a revelation from him?"

A question from the floor: Does the Hebrew word—*almah*—in Isaiah 7:14 mean "young woman" or "virgin"? Mr. Woods warms quickly to this topic; the tension in the room is, for the moment, abated. "The older versions and lexicons recognized that *almah* meant 'virgin.' . . . It is not correct to follow liberal scholars in these matters. . . . It is dangerous to advocate this. . . . If this is right, Matthew was wrong."

This leads Mr. Woods to a denunciation of the Revised Standard Version and, by implication, the discipline of textual criticism: "The RSV scholars attempted to correct the text. Any effort on the part of men to correct the text is out of place."

Ira Y. Rice, Jr.—of *Axe on the Root* fame is on his feet in the first row in front of the platform, demanding to be heard. He has, he says, documented proof that a Freed-Hardeman teacher is using and recommending the RSV. Mr. Woods is stern but defensive, his voice low and nearly inaudible; this charge is not a matter for this forum, he says, and he is sure that the officers of the college will deal with the problem, if there is one. Two senior Freed-Hardeman faculty members rise to rebut Mr. Rice; they say the charge is completely untrue. "I don't mind the use of other versions in study," Mr. Woods continues. "I refer to them just as I'd refer to a commentary." Mr. Rice is silenced.[3]

> *Mr. Rice claims*
> *to have documented proof that*
> *a teacher is using and*
> *recommending the RSV.*

There is a last question about translations: what about the New American Standard Bible, a recent revision of the American Standard Version? Mr. Woods is in a hurry, and this question cannot be answered on a post card; he is discomfited and apologetic: "I'd prefer not to comment on that in the very brief time we have left. . . . I will say this: I don't know what anyone would want with anything except the American Standard Version. . . . I've been studying the Greek text every morning for thirty years, and the ASV is closer than any other. . . . I'll debate that any time. . . . A person that stumbles over obsolete words will have trouble studying any translation."

The gym empties slowly; several knots of conversation are drawn together throughout the building, rehashing arguments or renewing acquaintances. Already, workmen have begun a new round of cleaning and straightening in preparation for tonight's activities. Outside, above the damp chill, the sky is darkening. In the tent, many of the exhibitors are packing materials for the trip home. Ira Rice interrupts his boxing of unsold copies of *Axe on the Root* to assure a pair of well-wishers that he does indeed *have the proof.* The visitor exchanges pleasantries with an old acquaintance who, with her husband, ran summer camps for many years in the Northeast. They now operate a camp and retreat center near Jasper, Alabama, and are selling recordings of the late Gus Nichols to help finance new facilities.

The college library, which the visitor had hoped to explore, is closed. In the student center, the ladies of Freed-Hardeman are selling only sandwiches and desserts; the regular cafeteria line is long. The visitor sets out down the main street, in search of food more compatible with his diet. It is 5 p.m. and nearly dark; the restaurants and most of the stores are closed. The cinema marquee advertises *Tommy*, the rock opera, and *Rain of the Devil*. The visitor turns back; he has just passed the bank when a big station wagon pulls to the curb and a door opens. "Aren't you Don Haymes?" a voice calls. Peering into the gloom, the visitor can see a small, wiry figure, eyes gleaming behind thick lenses under a furrowed brow.

"I'm Glenn L. Wallace, of Visalia, California." The handshake is firm. "You and I had some correspondence once, some time ago."

"Yes, sir, we did." It has been ten years. "How's your health?"

Mr. Wallace has been afflicted by heart attacks and several bouts of surgery. "Oh, *I'm* fine. The Lord watches out for me." The people in the front seat are becoming impatient. "Well, I just wanted to meet you. Good-bye." The door closes, and the station wagon moves away, west out Tennessee 100; it is a long way to the California sun.

The supermarket is still open; the visitor quickly buys some cottage cheese and a banana, and carries his purchase back to the student center, where he buys a paper cup of iced tea and a plastic spoon, for a dime. He is discovered by the mother of an old friend, who has come down from Crockett County to help out the Freed-Hardeman ladies. She brings around a succession of friendly kinfolk, in-laws and out-laws. There is more good conversation with a man who is passing the time, waiting for his wife; he preaches in a nearby town, and looks ten years younger than his age, thirty-eight. There is an exchange of cards, and mutual invitations.

> *The black experience*
> *of religion in America is*
> *overwhelmingly fundamentalist.*

---

[3]Apparently, the object of Mr. Rice's ire is Rubel Shelly, who moved from Memphis to the Freed-Hardeman faculty last fall. Intelligent and articulate, Mr. Shelly out of the pulpit could easily be mistaken for a young physician or research scientist; in the pulpit, he is a smoother and more mild-mannered version of his mentor, Thomas B. Warren. A year ago, in a debate with a Presbyterian, he is said to have referred to the RSV as a "standard translation."

Tonight's program will not begin for another half-hour, but already the gymnasium is crowded. This is "Youth and Parents Night" at the Lectures, and the Freed-Hardeman admissions staff has gone out into the highways and by-ways of rural west Tennessee, Georgia, Alabama, and Mississippi, spreading the word in the churches. This is their crowd, and much of it is black. Freed-Hardeman enrollment has doubled since 1968; a substantial percentage of that growth has been, and continues to be, black. This development represents a significant break with the past, and is as interesting for what it says of the present and portends for the future.

How did the young and tender branches of racial equality come to be grafted, here in this place, to the ancient trunk and roots of fundamentalist theology? How did two so divergent strands of the American experience come to be entwined here? The visitor wonders as he waits, watching the swelling throng fill this building past capacity.

It was the Unitarians of Boston, not the Bible believers of Nashville, who saw the evil and horror of one man owning another, and campaigned for the abolition of slavery in America. That is the *white* experience of religion and race. But the black experience of religion in America is overwhelmingly fundamentalist, grounded in the pages of the Bible, wedded to trust in the literal truth of every word. These were men and women who had learned, through bitter trial and unceasing humiliation, that the promises of *men* could not be trusted—that what Abraham Lincoln could give, his successors could take away. Only the promises of the God-man of the Bible—"release to the captives," rest in heaven for the obedient—could offer the possibility of fulfillment; God's Law could not be amended or circumvented by the white man. And while white racists in and out of the churches encouraged these beliefs, hoping that blacks would think of the pie waiting in the sky rather than of the chicken that was not waiting in the pot; while they often paid and used black preachers of the Gospel as agents of *control* of the black community; they at the same time sowed the seeds of their own doom. The black church became the supreme instrument of education in the black community, and the Bible the textbook. And in the fullness of time Martin Luther King would, with the fire of his personality, weld the images and promises of the Bible he learned at his father's knee to the tactics of Mahatma Gandhi he learned in the library of Crozer Seminary, and so create the modern Civil Rights Movement.

Fundamentalism did not flourish in the hostile climes of the northern, secular cities, and King's movement was supplanted there by hardened, more materialistic, inevitably violent forms and leadership, reflecting the culture in which they grew. But in the rural backwaters of the South, in farming communities and small towns, a literal understanding of the Bible remained the dominant belief of black and white alike. In this culture, the preaching of Marshall Keeble crossed the color line before Martin

Luther King was born; never mind the ropes in the aisles separating the races, the privileged racist leaders who exploited Keeble's preaching and guffawed at him as a cartoon—both black and white heard and believed. And while the black folk flocking into his gymnasium tonight may honor Martin Luther King for his achievements in their behalf, they reserve reverence for Marshall Keeble. "There has been no man like Marshall Keeble," David Meek has said, earlier this day, "except Christ or Paul."

> *These black folk may honor Martin Luther King for his achievements on their behalf, but they reserve reverence for Marshall Keeble.*

There are no ropes in the aisles tonight to separate those who would hear Jack Evans, and Mr. Evans himself embodies some other signs of change and hope. Educated at the now-defunct Nashville Christian Institute, a tiny, segregated crumb from the relatively rich table of the white church, Mr. Evans now possesses an honorary doctorate from Harding College—where until the fall of 1963 he could not have studied for a degree of any kind, and where the former president of the school taught a generation of incoming freshmen that "the nigra race is descended from the Curse of Ham." Mr. Evans has been, for several years, the president of Southwestern Christian College, now the largest institution operated by black members of the Churches of Christ.

Before Mr. Evans speaks, Freed-Hardeman's A Cappella Singers will perform. They present a stiff, formal appearance for this occasion, the men dressed in black-on-white tuxedos and white-on-white ruffled shirts, the women in simple, long black dresses and long white gloves. But no black student appears with this chorus tonight. They open with familiar hymns: an almost lilting rendition of "When I Survey the Wondrous Cross," a melancholy, subdued "How Sweet, How Heavenly Is the Sight." There are ten pieces on the program; it is good material; sung with energy and a touch of confusion. Several parents have brought cameras, and make extensive searches for just the right angle; flashcubes pop. The performance closes with a sombre "This Little Light of Mine" and a strained "Just a Closer Walk with Thee," featuring the director, John Bob Hall, in a solo. The audience is told that this group will be available for European mission campaigns during the summer months. They leave the platform to a standing ovation.

David Meek is on the platform now, leading "How

Shall the Young Secure Their Hearts?" and, after a prayer, "Time Is Filled with Swift Transition." Then Reeder Oldham, the director of admissions, comes forward to praise his staff for bringing in massive increases in enrollment—"twenty per cent over last year"—and for their role in assembling tonight's crowd. He wants to encourage every parent and prospective student to consider the advantages of Freed-Hardeman.

And now it is time to introduce the speaker, who comes, says Reeder Oldham, "from a great tradition"—a disciple of Marshall Keeble; attended Nashville Christian Institute, Southwestern Christian College, Eastern New Mexico University, and the University of Texas. He is presented, finally, as "a great gospel preacher, a great educator, a great brother in Christ."

Jack Evans is an electrifying speaker, whose oratorical gifts and flaming rhetoric recall the pulpit eloquence of an earlier era. Ideas and images flow from his tongue like the rushing of mighty waters over a broken dam. A young man is standing before the platform, interpreting for the deaf; earlier, Mr. Evans says, "he came up to me and said, 'This is going to be a rematch.' He was interpreting for me over at Harding a while back, and some of the things I say *can't be* interpreted." The young man will work hard tonight.

Jack Evans' oratorical gifts recall the pulpit eloquence of an earlier era.

"In the process of time, all men tire of bondage and desire freedom," Mr. Evans proclaims. He tells of an American Revolutionary soldier, who after the war decided that since he was free, he would do as he pleased. But he made the mistake of attacking a man twice his size, who knocked him down and then tried to discover why he had been attacked. "I'm free," said the soldier. "Yes," said the larger man, "but your freedom ends where my nose begins."

"And," says Mr. Evans, "our freedom ends where God's Word begins."

"Many of us are like the old preacher who said, 'If that ain't in the Bible, it ought to be.' . . . God says, 'Give yourself totally to me, if you want to be free.' . . . *Always do it God's way.* . . . Sometimes God makes you go the long way."

He recalls a discussion with another man about celebrating the American Bicentennial: "He said to me, 'We weren't free 200 years ago.' I said to him, 'I wasn't here 200 years ago.' I'm celebrating the *ideal* of America. . . . No man is free until all men are free."

About racial prejudices, he says: "If we perpetuate this madness, we're hell-bound." He recalls the infamous "three-fifths compromise" in which each black slave was counted as only three-fifths of a person for the purpose of determining legislative apportionment. He recounts his recent debate with a professional racist, published in book form as *The Curing of Ham*. "You can cure ham with sugar or with smoke, and when he left, that man was smokin'."

"When your're dead and gone, nobody will know what color you are. Pretty soon, you're only a little mound of dust in a shirt and tie. . . . I've never seen a sermon against racism in any of our gospel papers. . . . The liberals like to use this issue, but I saw a racist statement in *Mission*—I don't mind telling you who wrote it, it was Norman Parks—and I wrote a letter to Forum. *Mission* wouldn't print it. They're 'open' except when one of their own makes a racist statement. So much for being open."[4]

"Don't *tell* me you love me, just *do* it. . . . Some people today are like Rip Van Winkle. He slept through the Revolution, and when he got up he yelled, 'God save the King!'—but the King was dead. We've got some Rips in the Church. . . . You young people out there, don't get involved in all this hatred, don't perpetuate it, it's a thing of the past. . . . You parents, you older people, don't pass on a racist attitude to your children."

Jack Evans is concluding now; all the anecdotes and the images are flowing toward his invitation and challenge: "You want to be 'better' than I am, *live better!* . . . You can't teach what you don't know; you can't lead where you don't go. . . . Jesus Christ the Emancipator has set us free!"

David Meek begins the hymn of invitation, and the rafters ring with its pleading:

God is calling the Prodigal, come without delay!

Hear, O hear him calling, calling now for thee. . . .

It is as if time has come to a stop; waves of emotion radiate through the crowd. Over and over the hymn is

---

[4] Mr. Evans took exception to a footnote in an article by Dr. Parks on p. 14 of the April 1975 issue of *Mission*. The offending line reads: "The role of women in contemporary black Churches of Christ, in which women as a rule are superior to their male counterparts, throws light on this matter." In his letter to *Mission,* Mr. Evans calls this statement "mythical, unsupported by facts, and racist to the core. Dr. Parks is interested, inferentially, only in 'liberating' white women in Churches of Christ, since he attempts to use as a contrast the status of black women in 'contemporary black Churches of Christ.' It is ironic that one who is attempting to 'liberate' is himself 'in bondage' to racist generalizations and stereotypes." Dr. Ron Durham, the editor of *Mission,* says that "Jack Evans' letter was not publishable because in my opinion it contained a patently false charge, wrong facts, and a demeaning tone. It would not be openness but irresponsible journalism to knowingly publish this kind of material."

sung—the visitor, absorbed in the process, loses count of the times. From all over the building young people, white and black, are streaming to the front of the platform. There are tears in many older eyes, but it is the young who have heard this message and, whether moved by guilt or hope, they have believed: "Jesus Christ the Emancipator has set us free!" *They* are the future.

Finally, there are more than two dozen requests for forgiveness and the prayers of the community. Four young people—three black, one white—stand together on the platform to confess the name of Jesus in preparation for baptism.

And then, it is over. Moving toward the platform, to see Jack Evans, the visitor overhears a woman standing nearby: "Couldn't be any place better, unless it's heaven."

Awash in the hope of heaven and the knowledge of the world, in the failures of the past and the promises of the future, in all the contradictions and certainties of Freed-Hardeman, the visitor cannot find it in his heart to disagree.

Part Five

Religion in the South
Its Institutions

> *"Filled with delight, my raptured soul*
> *Would here no longer stay!*
> *Though Jordan's waves around me roll,*
> *Fearless I'd launch away."*

"A Mighty Fortress . . ."
Protestant Power
and Wealth

by Jim Sessions

"A cesspool of Baptists, a miasma of Methodism, snake-charmers, phony real-estate operators and syphilitic evangelists," was H. L. Mencken's characterization of the South. Although notoriously unsympathetic to the region, he at least named "the big two" and touched unkindly upon a central fact of Southern religiousness: its monolithic, pervasive and complicated Protestantism.

The South was non-religious, if not downright irreligious, during the colonial period. The Presbyterians settled in first, but Baptists and Methodists soon surged dramatically ahead through great camp meetings and revivals. Today, the Baptist-Methodist syndrome overshadows all other religious families in its numerical strength. Nearly half of Southern Protestants are Baptists, and Baptists, Methodists and Presbyterians taken together account for four in five Southern Protestants, and nearly three quarters of all Southerners.

This Southern mainline hegemony, in which the Disciples of Christ should also be included, is apparent in a state-by-state survey. In eight states, the Baptist percentage of the total reported religious membership exceeds fifty percent. In five states the proportion falls in the forty to fifty percent range. Methodists in three states make up one-third of the reported white Protestant membership. In six states the combined Methodist and Baptist membership runs upward of eighty percent of the reported total. In five additional states (Alabama, Arkansas, Georgia, Mississippi and Tennessee), if the Disciples and Presbyterians are figured in, the percentages are around ninety percent.

Thus, the fact that "religion in the South has been largely a Protestant affair" virtually requires that our investigation be focused on the predominant Protestant bodies—the Southern Baptist, the United Methodists, and the Presbyterian Church, US—the foremost institutional embodiments of what is really a more encompassing regional church called "White Southern Protestantism."

Southern folklore has it that "a Methodist is a Baptist who wears shoes; a Presbyterian is a Methodist who has gone to college; and an Episcopalian is a Presbyterian who lives off his investments." In the following pages, we hope to examine that bit of doggerel with a focus on the mainline white Protestant denominations of the South: their size, wealth, and just a notion of their influence.

While the following information accounts for a lot of people and assets, it obviously leaves out great numbers of believers. A lack of centralized reporting systems makes it difficult to get an accurate picture of either black denominations or white sectarian churches. We do know that sixty-three percent of black Christians belong to the Baptist denominational family, and twenty-three percent are in the Methodist family; this accounts for almost four-fifths of church-affiliated blacks in the United States. Edwin Gaustad, the demographer of religion, guesses that white Southern sects number about the same as America's Jewish population and more than all the Episcopalians in the country. Other approximations place two prominent sects, the Southern Churches of Christ and the Assemblies of God, at two and two-fifths million members *each*. Many of the small churches—Holiness, Pentecostals, and others—are strictly congregational with no organization beyond the local church, so data is difficult if not impossible to get. Consequently, there are large numbers of believers who happen to be both Anglo-Saxon and white, but who would never be described in terms of WASP power

CHURCH MEMBERSHIP IN THE SOUTHERN STATES, 1971

State	Southern Baptist Conv.	Roman Catholic	United Methodist	Presbyterian Church US	Episcopal	Christian & Church of God	Christian Church (Discip.)	Lutheran Church in Amer.	United Presby. USA	Missouri Synod, Lutheran	Church of God (Tenn.)	Church of the Nazarene	Baptist Mission. Assoc.	Free-Will Baptist	Amer. Baptist Conv.	Cumberland Presby.	Pentecostal Holin.
Alabama	*30.6* / 1,054,917	*2.5* / 85,991	*8.0* / 274,531	*1.3* / 45,551	*0.9* / 32,303	*0.1* / 2,270	*0.3* / 10,008	*0.1* / 3,882	*0.3* / 9,452	*0.4* / 12,701	*0.8* / 27,214	*0.3* / 11,152	*0.1* / 3,067	*0.7* / 24,700	—	*0.3* / 8,836	*0.1* / 2,354
Arkansas	*22.6* / 435,183	*2.9* / 55,025	*9.6* / 184,724	*1.2* / 24,026	*0.8* / 15,762	*0.3* / 5,558	*0.7* / 13,350	*0.1* / 1,193	*0.4* / 7,776	*0.5* / 10,184	*0.2* / 4,000	*0.8* / 15,137	*3.1* / 59,024	*1.2* / 22,555	—	*0.3* / 5,741	490
Florida	*11.9* / 806,088	*13.5* / 917,439	*5.7* / 385,051	*1.7* / 116,705	*2.2* / 150,542	*0.4* / 25,461	*0.3* / 22,333	*0.6* / 43,510	*0.8* / 53,696	*0.7* / 49,950	*0.5* / 34,702	*0.4* / 25,952	—	*0.1* / 7,381	—	—	*0.1* / 5,030
Georgia	*27.8* / 1,276,081	*2.3* / 103,609	*8.5* / 390,240	*2.1* / 94,946	*1.2* / 54,187	*0.7* / 30,090	*0.4* / 16,405	*0.4* / 17,198	*0.1* / 3,444	*0.2* / 7,198	*0.9* / 43,161	*0.3* / 11,630	2,073	*0.3* / 14,806	273	1,092	*0.1* / 3,183
Kentucky	*25.5* / 826,739	*10.5* / 339,375	*6.7* / 214,322	*0.8* / 27,052	*0.7* / 23,213	*2.2* / 69,711	*2.2* / 72,276	*0.3* / 10,341	*0.9* / 27,720	*0.1* / 4,827	*0.4* / 12,267	*0.7* / 24,070	167	*0.5* / 15,572	602	540	169
Louisiana	*16.6* / 602,687	*35.2* / 1,280,536	*3.4* / 125,581	*1.1* / 39,538	*1.1* / 41,348	*0.1* / 3,364	*0.2* / 5,852	*0.1* / 2,014	482	*0.6* / 22,401	*0.5* / 4,063	*0.1* / 4,823	*0.3* / 9,212	—	—	—	25
Mississippi	*30.7* / 679,574	*3.7* / 83,043	*9.7* / 214,603	*2.0* / 44,888	*0.8* / 17,858	*0.2* / 3,783	*0.3* / 6,580	*0.1* / 1,249	*0.1* / 1,791	*0.3* / 3,473	*0.5* / 10,564	*0.3* / 6,034	*1.4* / 30,197	*0.3* / 6,324	107	16,233	682
North Carolina	*24.8* / 1,260,919	*1.4* / 69,133	*10.5* / 534,607	*3.9* / 197,669	*1.3* / 65,665	*0.4* / 22,733	*0.9* / 46,310	*1.5* / 77,656	*0.3* / 15,461	*0.3* / 15,704	*0.6* / 32,140	*0.2* / 7,795	200	*0.6* / 29,714	*0.1* / 5,174	881	*0.5* / 23,334
Oklahoma	*26.3* / 674,280	*3.9* / 100,663	*11.6* / 296,806	*0.2* / 6,001	*0.9* / 23,340	*1.3* / 33,270	*2.4* / 61,376	*0.2* / 3,992	*1.9* / 49,153	*0.9* / 22,790	*0.1* / 3,698	*1.4* / 35,762	*0.3* / 6,448	*0.9* / 23,919	1,270	1,960	*0.4* / 9,911
South Carolina	*28.4* / 734,709	*1.8* / 46,642	*9.9* / 256,888	*3.6* / 92,443	*1.8* / 47,586	*0.1* / 2,208	*0.2* / 4,960	*2.0* / 52,186	*0.3* / 8,839	*0.1* / 1,608	*1.1* / 27,638	*0.4* / 9,131	—	*0.4* / 11,463	—	—	*0.7* / 17,036
Tennessee	*27.9* / 1,095,956	*2.4* / 92,577	*9.9* / 387,529	*2.0* / 77,140	*1.0* / 39,284	*0.7* / 27,104	*0.6* / 21,756	*0.3* / 11,067	*0.6* / 21,936	*0.3* / 10,154	*0.7* / 29,189	*0.1* / 22,946	1,892	*0.6* / 25,340	—	*1.2* / 46,452	1,270
Texas	*21.1* / 2,362,851	*18.0* / 2,012,355	*7.6* / 855,733	*1.3* / 147,194	*1.6* / 175,694	*0.2* / 21,411	*1.1* / 117,597	*1.0* / 32,268	*0.5* / 60,698	*1.0* / 109,616	*0.1* / 11,526	*0.3* / 35,982	*0.9* / 104,751	*0.2* / 4,950	1,853	*0.1* / 8,080	2,400
Virginia	*13.8* / 642,930	*5.3* / 244,678	*10.7* / 497,027	*3.1* / 144,057	*2.9* / 136,755	*0.7* / 33,646	*1.0* / 48,679	*0.7* / 46,075	*0.4* / 16,442	*0.3* / 12,780	*0.3* / 12,591	*0.3* / 11,735	742	*0.2* / 10,007	*0.1* / 6,491	—	*0.2* / 11,607
West Virginia	*1.3* / 22,792	*5.7* / 98,808	*12.5* / 218,312	*2.1* / 36,489	*1.1* / 19,620	*0.8* / 14,690	*1.0* / 16,954	*0.7* / 12,320	*0.1* / 18,354	569	*0.8* / 13,124	*1.4* / 25,073	—	*0.6* / 10,066	*8.3* / 142,963	—	*0.1* / 2,115
TOTALS	12,469,706	5,524,894	4,835,954	1,093,699	843,157	757,673	462,376	314,951	295,244	283,455	265,877	247,222	217,773	206,797	158,733	91,781	79,606

Numbers in italics are percentage of the state's total population that belong to a given denomination. Numbers in regular type are total number of members of the denomination in the state.

COMPARISON OF GROWTH OF CHURCH DENOMINATIONS

CHURCH	1940	1950	1960	1970	1974
Christian Church (Disciples)	1,658,966	1,767,964	1,801,821	1,424,479	1,312,326
Church of God (Cleveland, Tn)	63,216	121,706	170,261	272,278	328,892
Church of the Nazarene	165,532	226,684	307,629	383,284	430,128
Cumberland Presbyterian	73,357	81,806	88,452	92,095	93,948
Presbyterian, US	532,135	678,206	902,849	958,195	896,203
Southern Baptist Convention	4,949,174	7,079,889	9,731,591	11,628,032	12,513,378
United Methodist	8,043,454	9,653,178	10,641,310	10,671,774	10,063,046

CHURCH	Churches 1926	1970	Members 1926	1970
Assemblies of God	671	8,570	47,950	626,660
Church of God in Christ	733	4,500	30,263	425,500
Church of God (Cleveland, Tn)	644	3,834	23,247	243,532
Cumberland Presbyterian	1,225	1,827	63,477	92,368
Pentecostal Holiness	252	1,355	8,099	66,790
Pentecostal Assemblies of World	126	550	7,850	45,000
Free-Will Baptists	762	2,200	54,996	200,000

Source: "Religious Bodies," US Bureau of the Census; Yearbook of American Churches; Churches and Church Membership in the US;

Photo by Carter Tomassi

structures. Southern white sectarianism is not a reporting system, much less an accommodated Americanism.

Though still considerably out of the mainstream, these conservative, fundamentalist denominations have been growing at a rate which exceeds the expansion of middle-class denominations or the general population as a whole. In the last twenty years the number of adults who preferred or claimed membership in one or another of the Baptist denominations (Primitive, Southern, Missionary, Hardshell, etc.) increased by more than twenty-five million. Those who identified themselves with the Assemblies of God grew fivefold, from two hundred thousand to one million. The Churches of God in Christ doubled from four hundred thousand to eight hundred thousand; the Church of the Nazarene increased by two thirds, from three hundred thousand to a half million. Pentecostal Assemblies grew by two hundred thousand, an increase of

in Washington, D.C.; Oral Roberts University is playing big league basketball, and millions of dollars of real estate around Florida's Cape Kennedy is being transformed into a college, conference center and amusement park by Christian anti-communist Carl McIntire.

There are also centers of Catholic strength in the South, some of great duration. Far from dropping out of regional religious figures, Catholics nose out Methodists for second place in total membership. Membership, however, is heavily concentrated in certain places, often with French, Chicano or Cuban histories. The five-and-a-half million Catholics are mainly in Florida (thirteen-and-a-half percent of total population), Louisiana (thirty-five-and-a-half percent) and Texas (eighteen percent). They are not all newcomers. In 1906, Catholics made up sixty-one percent of church membership in Louisiana. By 1971, that membership had only dropped a bare two percent.

Photo by Phil Vaille

one-third. During the same period of time, the mainline denominations held steady or declined.

William McLoughlin estimates that sixty "fringe-sect" groups in the US, including Pentecostal and Holiness, have grown in membership by 500 to 700 percent over the last twenty years. While mainline church programs, colleges, membership and periodicals have faltered, conservative-fundamentalist activities and organizations have been flourishing. Billy Graham continues to head the "most admired" list. Religious publishing firms can't keep up with demand. A "Christian Embassy" has opened

Twenty-one parishes (counties) in Louisiana are over half Catholic, with that percentage reaching ninety-one percent in Lafourche Parish. In several Texas counties, like Zapata and Edinburg, eighty-five percent of the total population is Catholic. There are also several Kentucky counties that have a quarter to a third Catholic population.

As in the rest of the US, the Jewish population in the South is heavily urban. Atlanta, Dallas, Miami, Memphis, Houston, Richmond and Birmingham are such centers. The total Jewish population in the South is sparse.

PER CAPITA CONTRIBUTIONS OF SELECTED CHURCHES (full members)

Denomination	Membership	Full Membership	Total Contributions	Per Capita of Total Contributions	Per Capita of Congregational Contribut.	Per Capita of Benevolences
Christian Church (Disciples)	1,312,326	854,844	$140,252,869	$164.07	$139.72	$24.35
Church of the Nazarene	430,128	430,128	120,568,181	280.31	243.59	36.72
Cumberland Presbyterian	93,948	55,577	10,707,206	192.65	173.08	19.57
Episcopal Church	2,907,293	2,069,793	305,628,925	147.66	121.49	26.17
Free-Will Baptist	215,000	215,000	34,347,000	159.75	144.19	15.56
Presbyterian Church, US	896,203	896,203	174,875,885	195.13	156.45	38.68
Southern Baptist Convention	12,513,378	12,513,378	1,342,479,619	107.29	89.77	17.52
United Methodist Church	10,063,046	10,063,046	935,723,000	92.99	71.92	21.07

Source: Yearbook of American Churches, data for 1973 for United Methodist, 1974 for all other denominations.

Only Florida ranks in the top ten states in percentage of citizens who are Jewish, and it is tenth with 2.27 percent. Most of Southern Judaism is Conservative rather than Reform or Orthodox.

There are many limitations and pitfalls in gathering church statistics. They are always incomplete and in flux; they pass through many hands, not all of which are exacting or objective. Church bureaucratic structures are often at variance with one another and have differing interests in reporting. Information from different denominations is often not comparable because of different definitions of membership, financial categories, reporting periods,

SELECTED CHURCH MEMBERSHIP IN THE SOUTH, 1971*

Denomination	Members
Southern Baptist Convention	12,469,706
Roman Catholic	5,529,894
United Methodist Church	4,835,954
Presbyterian Church, US	1,093,699
Episcopal	843,157
Christian & Church of God	757,673
Christian Church (Disciples)	462,376
Lutheran Church in America	314,951
United Presbyterian, USA	295,244
Missouri Synod, Lutheran	283,955
Church of God (Cleveland, Tn)	265,877
Church of the Nazarene	247,222
Baptist Missionary Assoc.	217,773
Free-Will Baptists	206,797
American Baptists Conv.	158,733
Cumberland Presbyterian	91,781
Pentecostal Holiness	79,606

THE CHURCH AS A CORPORATION COMPARATIVE SIZES, 1975†

Corporation/Church	Assets	Sales/Revenues	Emply./Clergy
Southern Baptist Convention	$6,000,000,000	$1,500,000,000	54,150
United Methodist Church	7,667,308,709	1,009,760,804	35,245
AMAX	2,480,120,000	962,090,000	13,300
Burlington Industries	1,566,525,000	1,958,092,000	71,000
CBS	1,193,110,000	1,938,867,000	29,177
Coca-Cola Co.	1,710,873,000	2,872,840,000	31,100
Dow Chemical	5,846,731,000	4,888,114,000	53,100
Duke Power	3,740,799,000	954,414,000	13,600
Genesco	507,425,000	1,095,972,000	46,000
Kerr-McGee Oil Co.	1,387,882,000	1,798,580,000	10,300
Middle South Utilities	3,634,623,000	923,023,000	10,500
R. J. Reynolds	3,528,895,000	3,294,322,000	34,700
Reynolds Metal	2,204,138,000	1,679,262,000	33,400
Southern Co. (utility)	7,237,003,000	1,998,912,000	19,000
J. P. Stevens	755,586,000	1,122,974,000	44,400
Texas Instruments	941,477,000	1,367,621,000	56,700
Virginia Electric & Power	3,871,808,000	1,033,336,000	7,400

*Source: Churches and Church Membership in the US, 1971   †Source: Fortune's 500; Yearbook of American Churches, 1976

decentralization, etc.

Nonetheless, the quantitative aspects of church life and wealth are often surprising and revealing. Clearly, the churches' impact and influence on the life of the South is not only spiritual. Its investments, property, organizational structures, communications networks, and personnel reveal a sizeable stake in the earthly security(ies) which undergird its heavenly witness. There can be little doubt that the major denominations are Southern corporations, with economic clout as well as moral sanctions.

The purpose here is not to embarrass, downgrade or moralize, but to help get a clearer picture of the South we live in and the roles of institutions that inevitably dominate its development. It is also only a modest effort to place information in the hands of church folks, and those whom the church would serve, as they seek to relate corporate religious institutions responsibly to an increasingly complex world.

Much of the information from this section was obtained from the denominations themselves. Two sources were especially helpful with the demographic information: *Yearbook of American and Canadian Churches, 1976,* edited by Constant H. Jacquet (Abingdon Press), and *Churches and Church Membership in the United States* by Douglas W. Johnson, Paul R. Picard, and Bernard Quinn (Glenmary Research Center). For a full review of shareholder resolutions concerning social responsibility, contact Interfaith Center on Corporate Responsibility, Room 556, 475 Riverside Dr., New York, New York 10027.

Southern Baptist Convention

> Undoubtedly, there are in our Southern Churches multitudes of good Christian men and women, as good as are to be found; undoubtedly, they have multitudes of good and faithful pastors, sharing with them a common lot of poverty.... The South is to rise, and for the resurrection Baptists should be preparing.
> —The Baptist Examiner and Chronicle, 1865

And rise they did. And share "a common lot of poverty" they did not. At least not for very long.

From small, anti-establishment, counter-culture beginnings, the Southern Baptist Convention (SBC) has grown to Protestantism's largest denomination, embodying virtually an entire culture. The SBC is the dominant religious group in the one region of the US where religion is still a powerful, if not the basic, ethical sanction. Its prominence in the social, political and economic life of the South is in accord with its numbers and its resources.

Government

The Southern Baptist form of church government is called congregational, as distinguished from episcopal and presbyterian. Southern Baptists believe: (1) "the governmental power is in the hands of the people"; (2) "it is the right of a majority of the members of a church to rule, in accordance with the law of Christ"; and (3) "the power of a church cannot be transferred or alienated, and that the church action is final."

The Southern Baptist Convention in the South, 1975

$1.5 billion	annual contribution
$4.7 billion	property value
12,469,706	members
28,500	churches
44,403	clergy

Each congregation has complete local autonomy to hire and fire its minister, and to emphasize, preach, and teach as its minister and people wish. Thus, local churches have great latitude in adapting their message to fit the local situation. Coupled with their interpretation of the "priesthood of all believers" (each individual is given the responsibility to read the Bible and interpret it for himself), good Southern Baptists can hold a variety of positions and views. National or state convention votes have no practical effect on autonomous local congregations. This loose structure has cushioned the Southern Baptists against controversies that have wracked other denominations.

The local churches also retain power of the purse over the one and a half billion dollars they raise each year. There are no binding apportionments; churches dissatisfied with any Convention program simply exclude it from their donation. Since much depends on voluntary cooperation, only the most acceptable programs are put forward.

These local churches form the broad base of a pyramid: churches from an area the size of a county or two unite to form associations; Baptists within bounds of a single state form state conventions; and the Southern Baptist Convention, the apex of the pyramid, coordinates denominational efforts for the entire South, nation, world. A de facto hierarchy that has some subtle control over local churches has nevertheless emerged from the expansions of the huge Southern Baptist organizations dealing with missions, publishing, institutions, and other denominational programs. As one ex-Baptist put it, "The pressure for conformity is a great deal less obvious than that of the Roman Catholic hierarchy, but it is just as real and just as effective. God and his wooing spirit must play ball with the system or get out of the stadium."

In the past few years, church bodies including the Catholics and Baptists have been debating the question of economic centralization versus decentralization. The Catholic Church, which prides itself on unity in matters of dogma, deliberately strives for maximum disunity in matters of finance and administration. Because the One True Church has no one economic neck for a single sword stroke to sever, Catholicism has out-lived wounds over the centuries that would have bled dry tighter-knit organizations. Similarly, the congregational, decentralized Baptist and sectarian Protestant churches operate on a "principle of subsidiarity," so every church and agency is financially self-sufficient and autonomous. They have not only survived, they have flourished.

Baptists in the South (partial list only)*	Date of Organi- zation	Number of Churches	Members
American Baptist Assoc.	1925	3,295	790,000
Baptist Missionary Assoc. of America	1950	1,408	187,246
Christian Unity Baptist Assoc. (In Tenn. & Va.)	1934	5	345
Conservative Baptist Assoc. of America	1947	1,127	300,000
Duck River Assoc. of Bapts.		81	8,492
Evangelical Baptist Church (Free Will Baptist in NC)	1935	31	2,200
Independent Baptist Church in America	1893	2	30
Natl. Assoc. of Free-Will Bapt.	1935	2,163	186,136
National Baptist Convention of America	1895	11,398	2,668,800
National Baptist Convention, USA, Inc.	1895	26,000	5,500,000
National Primitive Baptist Convention of the USA	1907	2,196	1,523,000
Pentecostal Free-Will Baptist	1855	150	13,500
Primitive Baptists	ca.1830	1,000	72,000
Progressive National Baptist Convention	1961	655	521,700
Regular Baptists (22 assocs.)		266	17,186
Separate Baptist in Christ	1758	84	7,496
Southern Baptist Convention	1845	34,340	11,628,032
Two-Seed-in-the-Spirit Predestinarian Baptists	ca.1826	16	201
United Baptists	1838	586	63,641
United Free-Will Baptist Church (South)	1870	836	100,000

* prepared from *A History of the Baptists* by Robert G. Torbet (Valley Forge: Judson Press, 1973)

But decentralization also means, denominationally speaking, a dilution of authority, lack of direction and efficiency, duplication of effort, etc. Efforts to modernize finances, management practices, and investment policies have caused some unrest within the professional church.

In the Southern Baptist Convention, a highly successful fundraising device known as the Cooperative Program has been the lifeline of everything Southern Baptists have done as a denomination for almost fifty years. It raised thirty-five thousand dollars in its first year in 1923, and today raises well over one hundred and eleven million dollars for all causes annually. In 1927, an executive committee of the SBC was formed to administer the Cooperative Program and bring responsible fiscal procedures to the church. Its success over the years has made Southern Baptists, by self-description, "the mightiest force for world evangelism on the contemporary scene." But it is also gradually changing the Southern Baptist motif from autonomy to efficiency. As one Southern Baptist explains, "Unobtrusively, the flow of power is being altered to flow *down* from duly elected official representatives, rather than up from the individual church members." Checking centralized power and keeping it invulnerable to the church's foes is difficult because of the instinctive Baptist refusal to admit that in a "democracy" power can concentrate at the top without anyone deliberately running for "Pope."

There are almost eleven million Southern Baptist members in the South, in 28,500 churches, served by 44,400 clergy. While their largest numbers are in Texas (almost 2.5 million), their greatest strength in proportion to the total population is in Alabama, Mississippi, Georgia and South Carolina, where a third to a half of the people in almost every county are Southern Baptists. They are weakest in West Virginia, although in the last fifteen years they have more than doubled their membership and increased contributions in the state by eightfold. There are 245 Southern Baptist churches in Houston, Texas, and 152 in Dallas compared to only 65 in West Virginia. The bulk of the church's wealth is now found in the large city and suburban churches, but more than sixty percent of all members are still in rural churches of less than 200 members.

Property and Prosperity

Being congregationalists, *official* SBC opinions hardly exist. The difficulty of determining "the Baptist position" on a given topic is obvious. However, because of the necessity of voluntary cooperation, all reports, resolutions, and editorials are designed to elicit favorable responses from grassroots Baptists. Indeed, the institution probably responds more amenably to social pressures than to any heavenly vision.

The Southern Baptist doctrine of property is fairly clear and traditional: a property owner is a trustee in charge of a portion of God's property; the basis of possession is the dominion over the earth which God bestowed upon man in the creation. The church itself owns property now conservatively valued at almost five billion dollars. They take good care of it, and always have. Legend has it that General Sherman, fresh from marching through Georgia, dispatched a lieutenant with a squad of soldiers to the heart of Columbia, S. C., with one order: "Destroy that Baptist church where the first secession convention was held!" Arriving at the stately but unidentifiable building, the soldiers accosted the old caretaker and demanded to know, "Is this the First Baptist Church?" The loyal caretaker pointed to another church two blocks up the street and answered, "No, sir! No, sir! That's it up yonder!" The neighbor church was blown to bits, and the First Baptist Church, scene of the historic secession convention, stands to this day.

The Southern Baptists believe in the old Puritan idea that "righteousness has the promise of material prosperity." Since God rewards righteousness, the church has more to do with material prosperity than any other earthly agency. On the other hand, the hungry and poor are not suffering so much from a lack of proper distribution of goods, as a lack of evangelism and the willingness of Christians to share with "those less fortunate." Therefore, the need is not for new laws and social programs; the need is for *revival*!

Baptist Families

Some of the righteous Baptist laymen who have prospered and served as leaders of the church include the late millionaire-oilman, Senator Robert Kerr of Oklahoma, a chairman of the Baptist Foundation; tobacco king R. J. Reynolds, a strong bulwark of the Baptist's Wake Forest University; Owen Cooper, a president of the Southern Baptist Convention, vice-president of the Baptist World Alliance, director of the Federal Reserve Board in Atlanta, president of Coastal Chemical Corporation for twelve years, executive vice-president of Mississippi Chemical Corporation and an appropriate member of the Baptist's Missions Challenge Committee.

W. Maxey Jarman, currently the chairman of Genesco's executive committee and director of the Nashville City Bank and Trust Co. and the Mutual Life Insurance Co., is also a trustee of the Moody Bible Institute, vice-president of the American Bible Society, author of *A Businessman Looks at the Bible*, and a former vice-president of the Southern Baptist Convention. W. Gordon Hobgood and Duane Geis are both trustees of the Southern Baptist Annuity Board and bankers in Dallas. John Justin of the Justin Boot Co. is a major fundraiser, and the Fleming Oil Company family is an important Baptist contributor.

The list could go on and on. Suffice it to say, this happy coincidence (blessing) of wealth and faith lies at the heart of the Convention. Witness the Norton family (G. W. Norton and Company; Eckstein Norton, president of the L & N Railroad). They were bankers, businessmen, and financiers. G. W. was the first treasurer of the SBC and the first board chairman of Southern Baptist Theological Seminary. G. W. II was the second treasurer of the SBC and chairman of the building committee of the Southern Baptist Theological Seminary. G. W. III was the third treasurer of the SBC and a member of the Seminary's executive committee. The family contributed well over a million dollars to the Convention.

Texas Baptists have traditionally furnished financial leadership for Baptists. They emerged from the Great Depression without the loss of a single institution and with more than seven million dollars in *new* assets. They increased their gifts to the Cooperative Program over the Depression and World War II from $548,694 in 1929 to almost three million dollars in 1945, to nineteen million dollars in 1974. Texas cattleman Christopher Slaughter prayed, "Master, give me a hand to get and a heart to give." He gave over a million dollars to Baptist causes, paid the mortgage on *The Baptist Standard*, erased the debt on the First Baptist Church in Dallas, and became president of the Baptist General Convention of Texas at the turn of the century. Texan George Washington Bottoms and his wife Ida made a fortune in the lumber industry. They set up a trust fund for the Home Mission Board and produced around a million dollars for work in Cuba. They also built churches in Palestine and Brazil, and supported Baptist orphanages and colleges with well over two million dollars. A director and president of the Texas Baptist Foundation for 18 years until his death, Herbert Lee Kokernot was a cattleman, business executive, organizer and director of the First National Bank of Alpine, Texas, and National Finance Credit Corporation of Ft. Worth. He gave over $15 million to Baptist schools. John G. Hardin, Texas oilman, gave over $6 million to Baptist schools and a large trust to be administered for Convention interests.

Imbedded in the political and economic history of the South are such leading Baptist names as Joseph E. Brown, industrialist and governor of Georgia; Leondus L. Polk, editor of *The Progressive Farmer*; Basil Manley, Jr., president of the University of Alabama; James P. Eagle, governor of Arkansas; Isaac T. Tichenor, president of Alabama Polytechnic Institute; the Broadus and Jones families of Virginia; Mercer and Cobb of Georgia; Fuller, Elliott, and Furman of South Carolina; the Loweries of Mississippi; and on and on.

Educational Institutions

Southern Baptist schools have absorbed an incredible amount of wealth to train their young. The church has 43 senior colleges and universities, ten junior colleges, four Bible schools, seven academies, and seven seminaries. Three of the seminaries—Southwestern, Southern, and New Orleans—are the largest schools belonging to the American Association of Theological Schools. Baylor and Richmond are the two largest Baptist universities with about 10,000 students each. Samford has an enrollment of over 7,000 and Wake Forest over 5,000. (Samford changed its name from Howard College when it moved to a new Birmingham campus built largely with contributions from Tennessee Coal and Iron Company (US Steel) and the Alabama Power Company.) Richmond has the largest endowment, almost seventy-one million dollars but Wake Forest has the highest valued property, fifty-nine million dollars. All told, the Southern Baptist Convention has right at one billion dollars in school endowments and property in 70 institutions, training 130,000 young people at a cost of two hundred and fifty million dollars a year.

Investments

How is five billion dollars worth of property, almost a billion dollars in other assets, securities and stocks, and another one and a half billion dollars in yearly income distributed, invested, and raised?

The local church raises most of the annual revenue to support itself, its clergy, and its particular interests. Each Baptist contributes an average of $108 per year with $90 going for congregational expenses and $18 for "benevolences." Two "special" offerings are taken: the Lottie Moon offering for foreign missions, which raised over twenty-two million dollars in 1974, and the Annie Armstrong offering for national missions, which raised eight million dollars in the same year. The Cooperative Program receives "benevolences" and distributes the income to various agencies. In 1974, it took in over ninety-six million dollars from the Southern states, with sixty-one percent going to foreign missions, twenty-two percent to home missions, and one to three percent to seminaries, Convention agencies and institutions.

Total receipts from all sources for Convention activities beyond the local church in 1974 was one hundred and fifty-four million dollars, up twenty million dollars from 1973. The largest portions of that go to the Sunday School Board (fifty-three million dollars), the Foreign Mission Board (forty-eight million dollars), the Home Mission Board (twenty million dollars), and the Annuity Board (fourteen million dollars). The total assets of these agencies and programs come to six hundred and twenty-four million dollars. More than half of that is in the Annuity Board (three hundred and forty-one million dollars); other large holdings are in the Foreign Mission

Board (fifty-eight million dollars), Home Mission Board (sixty-four million dollars), Sunday School Board (fifty-seven million dollars), Southern Seminary (twenty-seven million dollars), and Southwestern Seminary (twenty-seven million dollars).

Among the chief financial sources outside the local church is the estate or endowment. "The preparation of a Christian will is an important matter," advises a brochure from the Southern Baptist Foundation. "Pray about it. Talk it over with your family. You may want to consult with your pastor, or your Baptist foundation." The Southern Baptist Foundation was established in 1947 "to encourage and motivate the making of gifts," for programs "fostered by the SBC." Its total investment portfolio in September 1975, was valued at fifteen million dollars, with earnings exceeding one million dollars a year.

The Foundation offers services to individuals, churches, and all Baptist agencies, and assists the formation of state foundations. The Texas Baptist Foundation would not respond to inquiries, but supposedly has over eighty-one million dollars in assets. In March 1976, the Louisiana Baptist Foundation reported a total investment of five million dollars, mainly in utilities, oil and gas, metals and mining, etc. The Baptist Foundation of South Carolina had assets in June 1976, of slightly more than nine-and-three-tenths million dollars in preferred stocks, common stocks, first-grade loans, and church real-estate loans. The Alabama Baptist Foundation reported six million dollars in assets.

These foundations liberally distribute publicity brochures and pamphlets offering their advice in estate planning, writing wills, and establishing living trusts, "designed to promote Christian stewardship." In one brochure, the Southern Baptist Foundation, referring to Cuban refugees and the African chieftains, testifies: "These people, poor as they may be, are as greedy as the man who lovingly fingers his stocks and bonds in the quiet of the bank vault. . . . God gave us this tendency, but he means for us to keep it under control. . . . Man's place is under God as a steward accountable to the owner. . . . He calls us to responsible management over the world."

"Responsible management" apparently does not quite extend to meddling in the affairs of private corporations where large sums of Christian stewardship are invested.

By far the largest portion of Southern Baptist invested wealth is in its Annuity Board which administers the pension funds for the church's clergy and the protection of their dependents. The money is entrusted to the Board by churches, individuals, agencies, and institutions for safekeeping and management; and the investment policies that govern its use reveal, as nothing else can, the Convention's power and philosophy. On 30 April 1975, the Annuity Board reported owning 3,217,140 shares of 164 companies, but it declined to update the value of this stock from the 1974 figure of over three hundred and fifty million dollars. Among others, the investments are in five of the South's top 30 corporations:

Coca-Cola	18,000 shares
Burlington Industries	23,000 shares
Genuine Parts	7,000 shares
Knight-Ridder	13,000 shares
Southern Railway	16,500 shares

Other investments include holdings in 15 of the top 30 industrial corporations in America:

Exxon	29,000 shares
General Motors	20,500 shares
Ford	12,000 shares
IBM	34,875 shares
Gulf Oil	17,000 shares
General Electric	6,000 shares
Standard Oil of Ind.	19,800 shares
US Steel	12,000 shares
Continental Oil	7,000 shares
Procter & Gamble	24,700 shares
Union Carbide	12,200 shares
Phillips Petroleum	28,000 shares
Bethlehem Steel	20,000 shares
Caterpillar Tractor	10,000 shares
Eastman Kodak	44,500 shares

The Annuity Board adopted guidelines in 1975 prohibiting investments, leases or loans in liquor, tobacco or motion picture industries, airlines, motels, hotels, restaurants, foreign companies, apartments, funeral homes, small businesses, rest homes, or hospitals. No leases or loans could be made to single family residences, apartment houses, day-care centers, oil and gas reserves, religious or charitable institutions, or office buildings (except to a major tenant).

The guidelines go on to say that "there should be no investments in, nor loans to companies known to be non-cooperative with fair-employment practices, improvement of pollution problems, and generally recognized social, health, and other national issues." However, the Annuity Board has 6,000 shares of AMAX, one of the biggest strip mine operators in the world and a frequent violator of water pollution standards. The Board also has 7,000 shares of Abbott Labs and 21,000 shares of Bristol Myers, both involved in proxy fights over nutritional and promotional questions about their infant formula. It has 10,000 shares of the J. P. Stevens textile company, known

as the worst labor law violator in the country. It has 24,000 shares of Avon, 40,000 shares of Gillette, 32,000 shares of Merck, and 36,000 shares of Warner Lambert—all challenged by shareholders because of their refusal to disclose Equal Employment Opportunity data. It has 19,800 shares of Standard Oil of Indiana, involved in a fight over stripmining on the Northern Cheyenne Reservation, and 12,200 shares of Union Carbide, the first US company to break the UN embargo on Rhodesian chrome.

There can be little doubt that the major denominations are Southern corporations with economic clout as well as moral sanctions.

Out of a total portfolio of 237,933 shares worth over $10 million, the Foreign Mission Board has 4,320 shares of Mobil, 4,000 shares of Phillips—all receiving shareholder resolutions dealing with foreign political contributions—and another 4,000 shares of Union Carbide. It also has 9,700 shares of General Motors, where 15 different church groups have submitted shareholder resolutions regarding the rights of auto workers in Chile; and 2,684 shares of IBM, where resolutions are questioning the company's support of apartheid in South Africa.

The investments and social questions are much the same throughout Baptist portfolios, investment policies notwithstanding. All of them are very big on Coca-Cola, chemicals, utilities, oil and gas.

It is small wonder that the executive secretary-treasurer of the Southern Baptist Foundation in his 1975 annual report, writes: "[Energy] development is being hampered by ecologists who seem to overreact in their effort to save humanity from destroying itself. . . . Nuclear power—which many think will be the ultimate solution to the energy crisis—has been slowed because of the scare tactics of some of the bleeding hearts seeking headlines for their own personal gain, monetarily or otherwise. . . . The main ingredient needed today, in many people's minds, is greater confidence in their fellowman, and the system under which they work, live, and have their being. This can best be accomplished by the return of man to God through the true principles of Christianity."

United Methodist Church

The General Rules of Methodism restrain extravagant and reckless expenses, and demand energy in work. Such a system is no less economical than it is spiritual. So the outcome is a Church that a century ago assembled the poor and outcast under spreading oaks, today brings together bankers, merchants, manufacturers, Senators and chief rulers in large temples. Methodism owns much of our bank, railroad and factory stock, government bonds, real estate and every form of legitimate wealth. Our people have been workers and savers, and great wealth has come to them. Such men as Cupples, Scruggs, Duke, Pelzer, Cole and Williams show that Southern Methodism is no hindrance to material success on the largest scale. We are going into the twentieth century with immense resources—running banks, factories, railroads, ship lines, city property and governments. For all this we are thankful.

—Methodist Bishop John C. Kilgo, 1900

In 1784, the Methodist Episcopal Church was organized in Baltimore with about sixty preachers. John Wesley had insisted that his "societies" remain just that, but after the American Revolution, the Church of England could no longer function in the states, and the Bishop of London refused to ordain Wesley's preachers. No doubts of national allegiance remained when the 1784 Baltimore meeting adopted articles of religion which included the commitment, "As good patriots, the Methodists should vow allegiance to the new US government." For many Methodists, however, loyalties were torn between church and state.

The United Methodist Church in the South, 1975	
$446 million	annual contributions
$2.9 billion	property value
4,449,780	members
19,147	churches
11,700	clergy

Sixty years later, Bishop James Andrew of Georgia had inherited slaves which Georgia law forbade him to free.

The 1844 General Conference meeting in New York City asked him to surrender his office as Bishop until he gave his slaves their liberty. The Southern Methodists rebelled and went home to organize the Methodist Episcopal Church, South. At about the same time, another group of Methodists were organizing the Freedmen's Aid Society and starting a number of colleges, including Central Tennessee College in Nashville, Clark University in Atlanta, Rust College in Holly Springs, Mississippi, and Meharry Medical College in Nashville.

The Southern Church returned to the fold in 1939 after years of bitterness and negotiation. A racial compromise was struck which placed all black Methodists in a single, segregated national unit called the Central Jurisdiction (now abolished). Bishop John M. Moore, who represented the Southern Church in the 1939 plan of union, reflected on the divisive racial segregation: "This philosophy of race relations was deep-seated and stronger than any church affiliation."

Structure

The importance of structure to Methodists dates back to the church's founding. The emphasis on mission—"going out into all the world," "the world is my parish"—led John Wesley to set up the structure called the "appointive system." Ministers are sent by bishops to preach, teach, administer and raise budgets. In the early days when a person became a Methodist, he was not joining a church, he was joining a "society" in order to better his spiritual condition. The rules of the society were strict and discipline tight. Indeed, the book of rules and laws which govern the United Methodist Church is still called *The Discipline*.

Several dozen local churches, or "charges," form a district, presided over by a district superintendent. Districts are joined together into annual conferences, which in turn are grouped into five large jurisdictions. One of the five is the Southeastern. The general conference is the all-encompassing, law-making body which convenes every four years.

Methodist government is called episcopal, but it is largely governed by this series of conferences, with lay and clergy delegates elected up the ladder of charge, district, annual, jurisdictional and general conferences. In this connectional system, the annual conference is the primary "connector"—where the Presiding Bishop appoints clergy to local churches for the upcoming year, where elections and ordinations take place and clergy membership reside.

Assets

President Theodore Roosevelt once remarked that he would rather address a Methodist audience than any other in America. "You know for one thing that every one there is an American," he observed. Methodists are per-haps the country's most representative middle-class denomination. It is a national church in ways that Southern Baptists and Southern Presbyterians are not. Nevertheless, Methodists are the second largest Protestant denomination in the South and they wield great influence in the United Methodist Church at large.

Of the 39,400 United Methodist churches nationally, 19,100 are in the South, involving four and a half million members, four hundred and forty-six million dollars in annual contributions, and almost $3 billion worth of property. In 1975, Methodists gave a little over $100 per member and $23,300 per church.

In the Southeast Jurisdiction, seventy percent of Methodists worship in congregations of under 200 members; fewer than one percent of the churches have memberships between 1,500 and 2,000. Nonetheless, the great temples of Methodism are Southern: The First Methodist Church of Houston has almost 11,000 members, eight and a half

Photo by David Massey

million dollars worth of property, and a pastor who is paid a salary of $31,750, plus housing and the usual clergy dispensations. Highland Park Methodist Church in Dallas has almost ten million dollars in property; its 8,374 members raised one and a half million dollars last year. Dallas has thirty Methodist churches with over 1,000 members, four of which have over 5,000. Peachtree Road Methodist Church, Atlanta, has 5,000 members and owns four and a half million dollars in property. Boston Avenue Methodist Church has 6,000 members, controls nine million dollars worth of property and pays their preacher $23,000 plus housing. Nashville Methodist churches utilize over thirty-five million dollars worth of property, while the figure for the Houston area is ninety-two million dollars.

In 1941, twenty-one million dollars went for new Methodist buildings and improvements nationally. By 1960, new development had snowballed to one hundred and eighty million dollars. The value of local Methodist church and parsonage property jumped fourfold between 1940 and 1960. The clergy has been doing better, too. Bishops, who are elected for life, make $26,500 a year with a $6,000 housing allowance plus office expenses. The average salary of Methodist ministers in the South is $10,000. South Carolina has the high average with $12,118; Kentucky, the low with $9,338.

Families

Southern Methodism has not been without its generous patrons to establish a long tradition of Methodist influence and training.

Cornelius Vanderbilt gave one million dollars to establish Methodism's Vanderbilt University, with the stipulation that his wife's first cousin's husband, Bishop Holland N. McTyeire, be named president of the board of trustees and given "the right to veto any injudicious appropriations or measures," select faculty, and purchase land. All his decisions were to be final unless reversed by a three-fourths vote of the Board. Bishop McTyeire discharged those heavy responsibilities until his death sixteen years later in 1889.

In 1914, Asa Griggs Candler gave one million dollars to move Emory College from rural Oxford, Georgia, to Atlanta, and his brother, Methodist Bishop Warren Akin Candler, promptly became the school's chancellor. Asa Candler was a druggist in Atlanta when he bought a new formula for curing headaches called Coca-Cola. By 1914, he was a millionaire many times over and a steady contributor to Methodist schools. Candler College in Havana, Cuba, is named for his brother, the Bishop, as is the theological school at Emory. Bishop Candler bitterly opposed unification of the Northern and Southern churches and drew an absolute line between the mission of the church and social/political/economic involve-

ment. He commanded his preachers to "let politics alone!"

The Duke family of North Carolina acquired the rights to the first cigarette machine in 1884 and six years later consolidated the five largest tobacco companies into the American Tobacco Co. "If John D. Rockefeller can do what he is doing in oil," Buck Duke asked, "why should I not do it in tobacco?" He forced more mergers and at one time controlled 150 factories capitalized at five hundred and two million dollars before the federal government broke up his monopoly. In 1924, Buck Duke moved Trinity College to Durham and created Duke University through a trust of around one hundred million dollars, the largest gift made to a Christian college up to that time. Since its inception, the Duke Endowment has contributed a total of about two million dollars to some 900 rural Methodist churches, one and a half million dollars toward salaries of rural preachers, four million dollars to orphanages, and over twenty-seven million dollars to hospitals. The elder Duke often remarked that, if he had amounted to anything in his life, it was due to the Methodist circuit riders who frequented his home and whose preaching and counsel brought out the best in him.

Joe Perkins was a Texas mine owner, rancher, banker and oil man who died in 1960. He gave about twelve million dollars to Southern Methodist University's Perkins School of Theology and contributed generously to Methodist pension funds, hospitals, children's homes, assembly grounds, Southern Methodist University, and Methodist Southwestern University. He and his wife, Lois, were often delegates to annual and general conferences, and Lois was a member of the executive committee of the World Methodist Council from 1961 to 1968.

Education

Duke, SMU, and Emory are the Southern three of Methodism's seven major universities. Together, the three schools enroll 27,000 students, raise three hundred and sixteen million dollars annually, control five hundred million dollars in physical facilities, and manage two hundred and fifty million dollars in endowments. They each have a seminary with a total enrollment of 1345 and annual income of around seven million dollars.

Methodists have eighty-one senior colleges with 122,000 students; they raise three hundred and seventy-seven million dollars annually, own one billion dollars worth of facilities, and have endowments totaling three hundred and sixty-six million dollars. Half of these schools are in the South. Fifteen of Methodism's nineteen junior colleges and half its secondary schools are in the South.

In 1975, Southern Methodist churches contributed two million dollars to ministerial education and one and a half million dollars to its Black College Fund.

In all, Methodist higher education has 234,000 students, over two billion dollars in buildings, seven hundred and fifty million dollars in endowments, and well over one billion dollars in annual income. In addition, there are 190 Methodist homes for the aged, sixty-five homes for children and youth, seventy-eight hospitals, and eight hundred and fourteen missionaries in forty-eight countries.

Investments

A recent Methodist editorial said, "When we grumble about apportionments, we rob ourselves of the joy we should feel as individual Christians participating, through our pooled resources, with other Christians in a common mission and ministry which extends across this land and throughout the world." Grumbling aside, Methodists put over one billion dollars in the collection plate in 1974, the most recent year for which complete statistics are available. Most of that was spent in the local church (seventy-nine percent). Another sixteen percent went to district, annual conference and jurisdictional programs, and to United Methodist Women. The remaining five percent (fifty-five million) went to national and international work of the church, twelve and a half million dollars to the Board of Global Ministries, six million dollars to the Black College Fund, ten million dollars to ministerial education, three million dollars to bishops, etc.

The General Council on Finance and Administration (GCFA) was recently given responsibility "in all matters relating to the receiving, disbursing, and reporting of general church funds." In 1975, it operated on a budget of over one million dollars. The GCFA manages the general investment fund of six and a half million dollars, which is the working capital for several smaller general agencies of the church; the million dollar Episcopal-World Service Fund; and the Board of Trustees portfolio of over three and a half million dollars. All of this gives the the GCFA a total investment of over eleven million dollars.

The Board of Global Ministry has investments in securities valued at ninety-eight million dollars, including thirty-one million dollars in the portfolio of the Women's Division. The Board of Higher Education and Ministry holds investments of $8.5 million in general investment pool, one and a half million dollars in a student loan fund, and endowment funds of over twenty-four million dollars. Revenues of the General Fund in 1975 came to almost fourteen million dollars.

The Methodist Publishing House started in 1789 when the Methodist Episcopal Church was five years old; it thus became the first "connectional" agency. There were 43,262 Methodists then, and George Washington had just been inaugurated. The Southern Methodist Publishing House opened in Nashville when the 1844 division occurred, making it the first major publishing enterprise

to locate south of the Mason-Dixon line. It is self-sustaining, with profits going into the Preachers' Fund—for retired Methodist preachers, their widows, and dependent children. Over the years, the publishing house and its predecessors have contributed twenty-one million dollars to the Preachers' Fund—half of that since unification in 1939. In 1975, it reported a net income of one and two-tenths million dollars on forty-one million dollars in sales.

The Preachers' Fund is now called the General Board of Pensions. During 1975, the book value of its funds increased from four hundred and thirty million dollars to almost five hundred million dollars. Among the stated investment policies of the Board of Pensions is the objective that investments be made "*in those industries, companies, corporations and funds deemed likely to make positive social, moral and economic impact on society in one or more of the following ways:*

a. nurture climates in which human communities are maintained and strengthened for the good of every person;

b. support the concepts of family and equal opportunity of life, health and sustenance of persons;

c. provide opportunities for the handicapped and for all persons irrespective of sex, age, or race;

d. support the rights and opportunities of children, youth and the aging."

However, the General Board of Pensions has $250,000 worth of Union Carbide bonds and 60,000 shares of Union Carbide stock, while stockholder resolutions are asking for Union Carbide to stop importing chrome from Rhodesia "until such time as governmental power is transferred to the African majority." The Board has $500,000 in bonds of Standard Oil of California and 66,000 shares of Continental Oil. Each company faces stockholder requests for information about its involvement in undermining the Northern Cheyenne tribal government's control of its minerals in Montana. The Board also has 85,000 shares of Schering-Plough, where stockholders are asking for pricing information on generic drugs compared to brand-name drugs. At Motorola, where the Board has 70,000 shares, a stockholder resolution questions the health and working conditions at the company's Korean plants. In all, the Methodist Board of Pensions has 500,000 shares and three million dollars worth of bonds in corporations whose social responsibilities are being challenged by stockholder resolutions.

The Board of Trustees of the United Methodist Church has a similar record, with three and a half million dollars in total securities heavily invested in power companies (Alabama, Arkansas, Dayton, Georgia, Illinois, Indiana, Iowa, Niagra, Utah, West Texas, Wisconsin, etc.) and 47,300 shares in many of the same companies as the Board of Pensions: Schering-Plough, General Electric, Continental Oil, Dow Chemical, etc. The same is true of the Board of Discipleship and the Episcopal World Service

Permanent Fund (1,000 shares of Continental Oil, 1,000 Schering-Plough, 500 Motorola, etc.).

It must be said that some United Methodist agencies have tried to be socially responsible in using their stockholder influence. The Women's Division of the Board of Global Ministries has led the way. In 1967, it sold bonds of a New York City bank as a protest over the bank's involvement in a financial arrangement benefiting the white-supremacist government of the Republic of South Africa. But over all there is really no contest between social responsibility and fiscal return. "Clean portfolios" seem impossible in this economy, so the "focus is on involvement," pleads the general secretary of the Board of Pensions. And the United Methodist Church is certainly involved.

* * *

The 1976 General Conference of the United Methodist Church was one of retrenchment. The Southern-based "Good News" movement had a great influence and sounded the compelling call to keep a firm grip on the status quo. There was a big evangelistic emphasis while minority constituencies continued to decrease. Oral Roberts and Billy Graham received awards from the National Association of United Methodist Evangelists. The General Conference withdrew commitment to Project Equality, an ecumenically funded affirmative action program in minority hiring and buying practices. The Methodists cut their funding from $20,000 a year to a token $1,000.

The Methodists have invested and consolidated those immense resources that Bishop Kilgo spoke of in 1900. Indeed, they seem to have settled back to live off the missionary advances of the free enterprise system.

Dr. Charles Allen, minister of the largest Methodist Church in the world—First Church, Houston—perhaps said it best: "25 years from now in the year 2001, I picture the United Methodist Church to be pretty much like it is today. I do believe that the church will be preserved until the end of time."

Presbyterian Church, US

The fact is that Christian churches are guided in their business transactions by the same law of supply and demand that guides the most soulless corporation . . . The world must be improved, but it cannot be improved very rapidly, nor is there any short cut to the economic millennium.
—Presbyterian Henry Farnum,
New Princeton Review, 1886

The Presbyterian Church, US (PCUS), really the Southern Presbyterian Church, is a *sectional* church—its history and outlook are clearly entwined with the history and outlook of the South. Presbyterians North and South were one denomination for 150 years before the Civil War. In Augusta, Georgia on 4 December 1861, the Presbyterian Church in the Confederate States of America was formed, later to change its name to the Presbyterian Church, US. *The Southern Presbyterian* declared that the Civil War had been "the occasion of untold profit to the Southern section of our country. . . . One stands amazed at the amount of good which through Providence has grown out of the war."

The Presbyterian Church, US in the South, 1975	
$185,275,224	annual contributions
883,185	members
4,028	churches
5,092	clergy

The new Southern Church started with 850 clergy, 1,309 churches, and 80,532 members. Among the thirty-eight ruling elders at the opening assembly were fifteen planters, twelve lawyers (including four judges), four merchants, three doctors, two teachers, one banker, and one mechanic. It has remained a predominantly upper-middle-class church with high educational standards for its clergy. The adherence to rigid formal education for its ministers and to a strict interpretation of its Westminster Confession placed Presbyterians in an unfavorable position to compete with the Baptists' and Methodists' huge evangelistic campaigns. While the Baptists and Methodists grew almost without plan, the Presbyterians stuck to their doctrines and ecclesiastical traditions. In the 1880s when sectarian churches began to replace both Baptists and Methodists as the churches of the poor, Presbyterians still made little or no appeal to this large portion of the Southern population. Nevertheless, it has maintained its third place ranking in Southern mainline Protestantism and strong influence in the country's politics and economics due largely to its long history and middle-class base. The Virginia and North Carolina Presbyteries called for American independence from England long before the Boston rebellions, and the Mecklenberg (NC) Presbytery was the first church body in the colonies to approve the Declaration of Independence. Today Presbyterians pervade the South, but only in three North Carolina counties, Mecklenburg, Hoke and Scotland, are they a numerical force.

Church Government

Each congregation has its own local "session." Churches in a limited area are grouped in presbyteries. The synod supervises the presbyteries of a larger geographical area. The highest judiciary is the annual general assembly, made up of clergy and lay delegates elected by the presbyteries on a proportional basis. The officers of the general assembly are the stated clerk, elected for five years, and the moderator, chosen annually to preside.

In 18 Southern states there are presently 880,000 Presbyterians (410,000 are female) in 4,000 churches with 5,000 clergy. The PCUS claims four seminaries, 15 colleges, five junior colleges, four secondary schools, seven mission schools, one school of religious education, eighteen children's homes, and twenty homes for the aged. The mission force for what the Presbyterians call "the overseas battle" was reduced in 1974 to 352 and will decline to 309 by the end of 1976. The church publishes twenty-nine periodicals and owns the John Knox Press.

Three-fourths of PCUS churches have fewer than 250 members. Of its 4,000 churches, 113 have over 1,000 members, but 463 have fewer than twenty-five members. Some of the larger churches are Highland Park in Dallas with 6,443 members and one and a half million dollars raised annually; First Church, Greensboro, with 3,892 members and $809,000 in total contributions; Memorial Drive in Houston with 4,580 members and $911,000 contributed each year; Ft. Lauderdale, Fla., 3,583 members and over one million dollars raised; First Church, Charleston, W. Va., 3,303 members and $506,000 raised; Peachtree in Atlanta, 3,220 members and $636,000 in total contributions. The Atlanta Presbytery has a high membership with over 40,000 and is a high contributor, raising almost ten million dollars a year.

Property and Prosperity

The Presbyterian Church has a history of controversy over capital and labor. From its fairly privileged position in the society, it claims that property and wealth entrusted to it are "matters of evangelism and mission," which imply both an individualism and a social concern. The Church's General Executive Board recently stated as policy: "God will not forget or forsake the poor or the needy; he demands economic justice for the poor, the exploited, the defenseless, the weak, the alien. . . ." On the other hand, "Biblical faith has refused to affirm that wealth is *per se* evil. . . . There is in Biblical faith no absolute human right of ownership of anything. We are stewards, not owners, of property and wealth given by God, who is its rightful owner." So Presbyterians have come to live with their Calvinist tradition of tension between a concern for stewardship of wealth, on the one hand, and a concern for more just economic relations on the other.

One of the most generous Presbyterian stewards of wealth was W. H. Belk, "the merchant prince of North Carolina," who expanded Presbyterianism greatly by having every Belk-affiliated store make annual contributions to a fund for churches, thereby assisting some 335 churches in their building programs. Belk was a director of the Committee of One Hundred formed by Presbyterians in the 1920s to elect anti-evolution candidates in North Carolina. It proclaimed, "We are going to keep up the fight until we get control of the State and maybe the nation." Other prominent Presbyterians of this group were Zebulon Vance Turlington and W. H. Sprunt. The group came to be known as the North Carolina Bible League.

Belk's sons carry on the tradition of merging economic, political, and religious interests. Irwin has been a state legislator, business executive, and Presbyterian church leader. He is the president, vice-president, or director of some 20 corporations from banks to textile mills. He is a trustee of the Presbyterian Consolidated College, and the University of North Carolina, serving on its finance committee. He represented Mecklenburg County in the state legislature two terms. He is on the home mission committee of Mecklenburg Presbytery and is chairman of its Charlotte finance committee, vice-president of his Sunday school class, president of Men of the Church and its district chairman, and chairman of the executive committee of the Historical Foundation of Presbyterian and Reformed Churches.

Thomas Milburn Belk, another son of W. H., is an officer in over 400 Belk and Leggett Department Stores and director of many corporations and civic organizations. He has been chairman of his church's board of deacons, president of Men of the Church, member of the executive committee of home missions of the Synod of North Carolina, and a trustee of the Presbyterian's Montreat Association in the Smokies.

Wealthy import businessman, James Sprunt built many Presbyterian churches, maintained a mission and hospital in China, and established a lectureship at Union Theological Seminary in Richmond, Virginia. The four brothers in the aluminum side of the Reynolds clan are also prominent Presbyterians; their business clout extends from Reynolds Metals to Jamaican Mines to United Virginia Bank to Eskimo Pies.

These are only some of the foremost wealthy Presbyterian givers. The list could be long. It is the same in politics. Just a sampling: five Southern Presbyterians serve on the US House Agriculture Committee alone, namely Richard Kelly of Florida, John Breckinridge of Kentucky, Charles Rose of North Carolina, Ed Jones of Tennessee, and William Wampler of Virginia.

Presbyterians own twenty-eight educational institutions with over $81 million in plant and endowment, and a total investment of over one hundred and sixteen million dollars. One of its prestigious schools, Davidson University, was set up with a forty million dollar endowment by James Buchanan Duke of Duke Power, American Tobacco, Duke University, etc.

In 1975, the Southern Presbyterians raised one hundred and eighty-five million dollars in total contributions or $211 per capita. Of the total, one hundred and twenty-four million dollars of that remained in local churches; thirty million dollars went to buildings and capital funds, twelve million dollars to presbyteries, six million dollars to synods, nine and one half million dollars to general assembly programs, and seven million dollars to "other." While the Presbyterians lost some 13,000 members between 1974 and 1975, their collections rose by almost ten million dollars.

Over a third of the one million dollars Witness Season Appeal was directed to evangelistic work in Brazil; theological education in Asia received $157,300; Zaire agricultural and community and development $56,500; and $85,000 went to Haiti for educational and medical work. In 1975, over five million dollars went overseas with the largest portion going to Brazil for "witness and evangelism" and missionaries' salaries.

The General Executive Board has assets of sixteen million dollars and a staff of around seventy. They have salaries mainly in the $18,000 to $22,000 range. The executive in charge of pensions makes $30,000 and the Stated Clerk, $26,000. In 1975, the GEB took in $8,745,000, but its 1977 projected income is only seven and one half million dollars.

Presbyterian publications had sales of over three million dollars in 1975 with a gross profit of $1,483,565.

The Presbyterian Foundation was set up in 1866 to "receive and manage permanent funds for the use of its programs, homes, colleges, seminaries, synods, presbyteries, and congregations." It tries to add one million dollars in new funds each year. In 1975, it topped that by adding $1,200,000. Its total assets at the end of 1975 were over twelve million dollars. One of its aims now is to gain $250 from each church each year and thus be assured of some ten million dollars or more annually. In 1974, it received a half million dollars through wills and bequests. As it says, "it is possible to perpetuate one's service."

The first life insurance company in America was called "Corporation for Relief of Poor and Distressed Presbyterian Ministers and of the Poor and Distressed Widows and Children of Presbyterian Ministers." It later was called "the Presbyterian Ministers' Fund." Now the Presbyterian Church, US, has the Board of Annuities and Relief. It had almost one hundred and twenty-one million dollars in assets in 1975, up seventeen million dollars since 1974, twenty-three million dollars of which is invested in utility companies. It has 133,700 shares worth over six million dollars of common stock in seven oil companies. Almost four million dollars is invested in banking insurance, including a million in J. P. Morgan & Co.

The Investment Policy and Guidelines of the General Executive Board states, "the church must be concerned to see that it does not by its investments, support uncritically, or without attempting to change them, institutions whose processes and products hurt more people than the church is able to help through programs supported by money earned from these investments." It, then, lists investment considerations such as: human worth and dignity in employment practices, stewardship of natural resources and environment, world hunger, and contributions toward peace.

But the GEB has $356,000 worth of General Electric stock. Stockholders resolutions are questioning GE's involvement in the production of the mammoth B-1 bomber. The GEB has $162,857 worth of Standard Oil of Indiana which has plans to strip mine Indian lands in Montana. Standard Oil of California, in which the GEB has $114,000 invested, is being challenged about strip mining, support of the racist Republic of South Africa, and political payoffs. More than fifteen church groups are sponsoring a stockholder resolution regarding General Motors operations in Chile. The GEB has $353,681 in that company. A similar listing of investments and social contradictions can be made for the Presbyterian Annuities Fund which has seventeen million dollars in power companies and utilities, over six million dollars in oil companies involved in strip mining and international intrigue, one and four-fifths million dollars in General Electric, two million dollars in Kraftco, whose marketing of processed anti-nutritional food in developing countries is being challenged. The listing could go on and on.

The Presbyterian guidelines observe that "attempts to build a 'clean portfolio' (of only 'good companies') may be highly impractical." Indeed it "may limit the possibility for the church to correct social injury," so any sale of anti-social stock "will be primarily a symbolic act."

Southern Presbyterianism's profits and its integration into the economic system are real enough, but its "symbolic acts" pale in the face of an old editorial declaration of *The Central Presbyterian* magazine: "that one class should sow seed and cultivate the growing product, while another class gathers the harvest, is a condition which a free and intelligent social order will not allow."

Case Study:
Coca-Cola
& Methodism

by Bob Hall

From the days when John Wesley first set foot on American soil at St. Simons Island, Georgia, right up to the present, the state of Georgia has continued to play an important role in the Methodist church's history. You might say the state provides an excellent example of Methodist growth and success. Georgia Methodists were the first denomination to erect their own church in Atlanta in 1848, when that city was just beginning its role as the hub of Southern transportation. By the turn of the century, Atlanta could boast more Methodist congregations and members per capita than any other city in the New World. It underwent a burst of growth when land taken from the Creek and Cherokee tribes was opened to Virginia and South Carolina settlers.

Recognizing the need to train their young, Georgians decided to establish their own Methodist school, Emory College, in 1824 at Oxford, thus following a tradition of education in the state which extended back a century to when George Whitefield, Wesley's famous colleague, founded a school and orphanage. Most of the Atlanta church money went to develop all-white Emory College or to build even larger, more elaborate churches. That's where much of Methodist Sunday school official and Coca-Cola founder Asa G. Candler's money went. Through the years Coca-Cola wealth has financed more church and school construction (particularly Methodist) in Georgia than any other source of donor capital.

Emory College and Georgia also figure heavily in the history of Methodist controversy. It was the slave ownership of a black woman by Emory's board president, Bishop James O. Andrew, that touched off the split between the Northern and Southern Methodists in 1844, the first of several splits in Protestantism over slavery.

The Bishop couldn't break the law which forbade freeing his slaves, the Southern church rationalized, so he shouldn't be faulted or asked to give up his office. Ninety-four years later, Bishop Warren A. Candler (Asa Candler's brother), a former president of Emory, presided at the meeting where the Southern church decided to rejoin the North. Bishop Candler had led the forces opposing union on the grounds that the Northern church was too rationalistic and liberal and would give too much power to black bishops.

It was also at Emory College that Professor Andrew Sledd, Bishop Candler's son-in-law, was fired in 1902 for publicizing his anti-lynching sentiments. Candler defended the young man, saying he really wasn't for Negro equality; he was just opposed to mob violence. With the sides of the controversy so astutely defined, lynching soon became one of the biggest social issues for the church in the 1920s and '30s. Many white Methodist women in the South recognized their social position in the ideology of racism "for the protection of our women" and led the fight to end lynching, often against their Methodist brothers.

The Candler Brothers

The Candlers were the sons of a prominent Georgia plantation master, slaveholder and Indian fighter (an enforcer of the "Cherokee Removal—Trail of Tears" from Georgia to Oklahoma) and a fundamentalist mother. They combined the attributes of stern religious fervor, practical ingenuity and aristocratic self-righteousness to find success after the set-back of the Civil War. Warren Candler graduated from Emory College to

Photo by Mark Lansky

become an editor of the Methodist *Christian Advocate*, then president of Emory in 1888. Brother Asa became a druggist in Atlanta and built up his capital to purchase the newly invented Coca-Cola. He transformed it from a local headache/hangover remedy and "lift-giver" (it contains caffeine, sugar and phosphoric acid) to the most advertised product in America in 1909 and a $25,000,000 company in 1919. With other relatives assisting, Warren helped his brother gain markets for his drink; he also held stock in the company. In turn, Asa helped Warren finance several major religious enterprises for Methodism.

The year 1898 was critical to this joint venture. Warren became a Methodist bishop and was given charge over starting a mission in Cuba, the first territory outside North America claimed by the US as bounty for its part in the Spanish-American War of 1898. Bishop Candler aimed to fulfill the church's ambition to expand Methodism into Latin America "with bread in one hand and the Bible in the other." Brother Asa was also casting an eye on foreign markets as he told Coca-Cola stockholders (mainly relatives) the same year "that wherever there are people and soda fountains, Coca-Cola will, by its now universally recognized merit, win its way quickly to the front rank of popularity." As in the States, the brothers shared the same program: winning new territory and new converts for the greatest of America's products—Christ and Coca-Cola!

Capturing Cuba for Methodism and Coca-Cola was not, however, a simple matter. The Bishop and his American missionaries complained of the evil effect of centuries of "Romanism." They weren't referring as much to the Cuban people's poverty or lack of freedom due to colonial rule as much as they were to the inability of Cubans to read the Bible, to what Bishop Candler called their "dullness," and to their lack of Church-sanctioned marriages and funerals. Meanwhile, Coca-Cola's agent in Cuba reported his problems to Atlanta headquarters: "As a rule the average Cuban doesn't know and doesn't care what he is drinking, and the words 'hygienic,' 'pure materials,' and 'cleanliness' have no meaning to him; but when once he learns that there is a difference, that Coca-Cola has more to it than wetness or sweetness, we have secured a steady consumer and an advocate of the drink."

To the Candler brothers, overcoming these "problems" and achieving success would require that the Cubans give up their old ways and *become like Americans*. As Bishop Candler told the press: "The North American and South American continents cannot be bound together firmly by ties of commerce alone. They will become fast friends when they *think and feel alike*. Our universities, if they are richly endowed and adequately equipped, will serve this end more effactually than all the consuls and commerical agents who have been or can be engaged to accomplish it. In this matter our commercial interests and our religious duty coincide."

The key, then, was education; but not just any kind would do. As brother Asa intoned, "it must be permeated with the type of Christianity that makes for a wholesome conservatism politically and socially and for a blessed civilization crowned with piety and peace."

And so, at the Bishop's insistence, a Methodist college was immediately begun in Havana "to implant a knowledge of the saving power of the gospel and Christian Culture in its students, and through them to make its

influence felt throughout the nation." Not surprisingly, the school's "greatest benefactor" was Coca-Cola's Asa G. Candler, donor of tens of thousands before his death in 1929. Appropriately, the school took the name Candler College.

Education of youth to develop local leaders with the right attitudes and to create a favorable cultural climate was the key to commercial/ religious success and the function of the college. Bishop Candler frequently axed those independently-minded Cubans he thought "unfit." Coca-Cola relied on Americans for its managers in Cuba for many years and when they did begin to change and use local leadership, they put the candidates through a rigorous screening process. "Every peg is made to fit some hole and every hole needs a peg to fit it," Asa Candler once told a group of graduating high schoolers. "The cry always in the business world is for first class pegs to fit first class holes. How shall we get first class fits? That's the great question." For Methodism and Coca-Cola in Cuba the answer was Candler College—or an education in America.

Emory University

Actually, Cuba was only one of many joint ventures tackled by Methodism and Coca-Cola. And coincidentally, the biggest, costliest, and the most gratifying to the Candler brothers was another church college: Emory University. In fact, in 1899, the same year Methodism and Coca-Cola entered Cuba, Asa Candler made his first recorded contribution to Emory College (which counted two of his sons as alumni); brother Warren was the board president and urged Asa to become a trustee. Within a year, Asa had become chairman of the board's finance committee; six years later, he was the board president.

Then in 1914, the Methodists lost control of Nashville's Vanderbilt University to an unyielding board of trustees who liked Andrew Carnegie's offer of a million dollars for a medical school more than they did church control. With a flurry of activity, the church appointed a special education commission to start a new university that they would own and control "in perpetuity." Bishop Candler became commission chairman and brother Asa the treasurer. The cards were clearly stacked. After Asa donated $1,000,000 to the commission (at a time, the biggest gift to a Southern college made by a Southerner) and pushed Atlanta's Chamber of Commerce to commit themselves for $500,000 more, the Commission announced that Emory College would move to Atlanta—to a 75-acre suburban plot donated by Candler—and become Emory University. Candler continued as board president until his death, and the Bishop became university chancellor.

For the next fifteen years, Asa Candler pumped money into the new campus. Emory's seminary became the Candler School of Theology in Bishop Warren's honor; nephews and in-laws, rich from Coca-Cola, financed dormitories and other buildings; the law school building featured a bust of its principal donor, brother John S. Candler, Coca-Cola legal counsel and Georgia Supreme Court Justice; Asa gave the library which became known as Candler Library; and in a move that shocked even wealthy Atlantans, Asa transplanted Wesley Memorial Hospital, which he and brother Warren had started in downtown Atlanta, to the remote suburban campus and financed construction of a medical school. By his death in 1929, Candler had pumped some $8,000,000 into Emory University. His son, Charles Howard Candler, who followed him as Coca-Cola chief, also succeeded him as Emory board chairman and chipped in another $7,000,000 before he died in 1957, not counting his wife's gift of the campus' large and prestigious Glenn Memorial Methodist Church, named for her father.

Today, Emory continues its tradition as a training ground for the South's rich—and for a number of children of Coca-Cola bottlers around the world, particularly those from Latin America. With special emphasis on its professional schools, it proudly produces more Methodist ministers than any other seminary, 60% of the doctors and 80% of the dentists in Atlanta, and over half the members of the gilt-edged Atlanta Lawyers Club.

Emory's all-white, male Protestant Board (with six Methodist Bishops) is still laced with Coca-Cola connections, including Asa's grandson, who sits on both boards, the sons of three other Coke directors, and nine directors of Coca-Cola's local bank, the Trust Company of Georgia. Emory's current money man and official "principal counselor" is Robert Winship Woodruff, son of the organizer of the 1919 sale of Coca-Cola from the Candler family to a group of New York and Georgia capitalists.

Woodruff, now 82, has been the main power behind Coca-Cola since 1923. Through his foresight, Coca-Cola expanded with another war, World War II, by following the GI around the globe at the request of General Eisenhower and others. When the war ended, Coke switched its foreign plants to civilian management with civilian markets and became a multi-national corporation overnight. Woodruff returned the favor to Eisenhower by helping his war-time friend and golf partner get nominated and elected President. Another close Woodruff friend is Billy Graham, a mass media version of the evangelists Billy Sunday and Sam Jones, who had counted Asa G. Candler among their benefactors.

Through the years, Woodruff's gifts to Emory have grown in excess of $50,000,000, primarily to finance the Woodruff Medical Center. His foundation gave the money to build the school's super-modern Woodruff Library. Over half of Emory's $177,000,000 endowment portfolio is tied up in Coca-Cola stock, making it one of the largest single stockholders; however, even its holdings (roughly one million shares are overshadowed by Woodruff's numerous foundations and pyramiding holding companies: Coke controlling ownership is still largely a one man/family affair.

It is no accident that Coca-Cola and Methodism found a common interest in religious education. Men like Asa and Warren Candler understood (and Robert Woodruff understands today) the critical importance of disciplining minds and tastes to the values of American Protestantism and capitalism. "Religious education," Asa often pointed out, "supplies restraints" which regulate ambition, discipline greed and sanctify the status quo. In turn, the Bishop testified, their brand of Christianity made capitalism a "holy" science, for capitalism plowed its excess "fruits" into Christian enterprises to train the next generation and perpetuate the cycle.

This article was excerpted from a longer pamphlet written in 1972.

Case Study:
Property For Prophet

by John Gaventa

Today it is known as Music City, USA. But long before the record discs launched it to its recent music fame, Nashville was well known for another reason. To millions of Americans, Nashville, Tennessee, has always been, and still remains, the Religious Capital of the South, if not of the USA.

Within greater Nashville alone are some 313 local churches. More importantly, Nashville is the center of religious power from which emanate policies, publications, money and missionaries that influence the lives and thoughts of Christians throughout the South and around the world.

Along Nashville's James Robertson Parkway—an area that was once a black community, but now has been "urban-renewed" into one of Nashville's prime business districts—the headquarters of the Southern Baptist Convention presides over an annual budget in excess of seventy million dollars and a lay membership of some thirteen million. In less physical settings but nevertheless similar places of authority are the headquarters of the Methodist Board of Education, Discipleship and Communication, the Presbyterian Board of World Missions, and other smaller religion-related institutions.

Every year, Nashville produces millions upon millions of religious publications—hymnals, devotional pamphlets, study materials, Bibles and magazines. The city boasts the largest religious printing plant in the nation (United Methodists), the largest religious publishing house (Southern Baptist Sunday School Board), the largest Bible publisher (Thomas Nelson, Inc.) and the largest Bible distributor (Gideons International). Six denominations have publishing headquarters in the city, feeding literature to half the Protestant churches in the country. Together, these "Good Word" industries ring up close to one hundred million dollars a year in sales and provide for approximately one-fifth of the city's total manufacturing payroll.[1]

Nashville trains religious leaders, ministers and missionaries by the hundreds in institutions of religious education such as Belmont College (Baptist), David Lipscomb College (Church of Christ), Scarritt College (Methodist), Free Will Baptist Bible College, Madison College (Seventh Day Adventists), Trevecca Nazarene College (Church of the Nazarene) and Vanderbilt Divinity College. Together the religious training schools occupy hundreds of acres of property and contribute substantially to Nashville's economy.

But it's not all give with religion in Nashville. Tourists come to the Religious Capital, not just for the country music, but for places like the Upper Room, the Methodist chapel and garden complex which last year attracted some 236,000 visitors from fifty states and sixty countries. Also to Nashville come dollars, lots and lots of dollars, collected from sales, tithes and offerings throughout the world.

In Nashville, religion, like music, is business, big business.

Nobody knows the business side of Nashville's religious institutions better than Jim Ed Clary, tax assessor of Davidson County. Church property in Davidson County, as throughout the country, is tax-exempt. In Clary's county, the exemptions take in the 313 churches, the religious headquarters, most of the publishing houses, and the religious education institutions. In fact, last time the figures were counted, forty-two percent of the property in Nashville was tax-exempt—a higher percentage than any other city in the country except Boston.

"Basically, it's a heck of a problem," says Jim Ed, looking from his courthouse desk out over an urban

[1]Some of this data is drawn from Richard T. White, "Bibles are Big Business," in *The South Magazine* (July/August 1976): 51-53.

landscape clearly in need of funds and services. "Not a day goes by that we do not receive an appeal for exempt property. The burden must then be shifted over to other taxable property. . . . You either have to increase the value of the property or raise the tax rate. But when you put a higher percentage on people who can't afford to pay, it hurts."

Critics of religious exemptions often say that while it may be all right for a local church to get a tax break, the sprawling religious superstructure—land, apartments, hospitals, publishing houses, etc.—should not. In Nashville, the focus of controversy has been the massive religious publishing enterprises, especially the Baptist Sunday School Board and the Methodist Publishing House. The prime critic has been Clifford Allen, president of his Methodist Sunday school class and Davidson County Tax Assessor before becoming Congressman of the fifth district. In 1969, with the advice of the Metro Legal Department, Allen and the State Board of Equalization hit the Baptist Sunday School Board with $5,622,200 in new assessments and the Methodist Publishing House with $4,689,400. "I believe in the freedom of religion," Allen said, "but I don't believe in giving religion a free ride."[2]

Like any good business, the publishing houses resisted the move. In announcing their intention to fight the matter through the courts, James Sullivan, then president of the Sunday School Board, said, "Further taxation of property devoted to religious purposes would be the start of an erosion process which would seriously impair the historic principles of separation of church and state and jeopardize religious freedom." Moreover, it was argued, the publishing houses are non-profit institutions, serving only to assist the denominations in spreading the faith.

Though legally non-profit, the religious publishing houses are assuredly money-making ventures, a fact which Allen and other non-denominational competitors in the publishing field have been quick to point out. Profits made by the Baptist Sunday School Board's sales are plowed right back into other non-paying Baptist programs. Profits from the Methodist Publishing House go to a pension fund for the "benefit of retired or disabled preachers, their wives, widows or children, or other beneficiaries." In 1975, out of forty-one million dollars in sales, the Methodist Publishing House had one and a half million dollars in net income, from which the ministers' fund gleaned $400,000.

After several years of legal proceedings, the Tennessee Chancery Court resolved the issue of whether the publishing houses should be exempt by ruling that the proportion of the buildings used for religious purposes should be exempt, while the proportion used for other purposes would be taxable. The publishing houses appealed the ruling to the Tennessee Supreme Court, which essentially upheld the lower court's decision. Both the Methodists and Baptists then appealed again, asking this time for

clarification of exactly how the line between exempt and non-exempt portions would be drawn. In response the Supreme Court said that it was "mindful" that "certain types of governmental review could endanger concepts underlying the separation of church and state" and left the specifics essentially up to the "good faith allocations of the religious institutions." "Usually," says a lawyer in the Metro Legal Department, "their 'good faith' places the assessments at about twenty percent for non-religious purposes."

For now Jim Ed Clary can live with the court's decision. However, he believes that the question of the responsibilities of local churches to the local government should now be raised. He suggests that maybe in lieu of taxes the churches should pay for the services they receive from the city. "It costs just as much to pick up the church's trash as it does yours or mine," he says, still looking out at Nashville's urban landscape.

"The Good Lord's not making any more land," he adds. "When it becomes exempt, we've got to make it up somehow."

If Nashville is the Religious Capital of the South, western North Carolina is its Religious Playground. There, surrounded by the Blue Ridge and Smoky Mountains, thousands of acres of land and buildings worth millions of dollars belong to religious assembly grounds, conference centers and campgrounds.

In the middle of it all, in Asheville, N.C., at least one man shares the perspective of Jim Ed Clary back in Nashville. "You've come to the right place," said Mr. Ed McElrath, Tax Supervisor of Buncombe County, when asked about the problem of tax-exempt property. McElrath has spent most of the last two years of his life attempting to list the parcels of property in his county belonging to owners who claim tax exemptions. So far, he's counted "between seven and eight thousand," and he's still got more to go.

Even without counting the numerous smaller property owners who claim a religious purpose, McElrath's county hosts many of the major assembly grounds in western North Carolina's panoply of religious recreation spots. They include:

	acreage	attendance/yr.
Montreat (Presbyterian)	3,600	2,900
Lake Junaluska (Methodist)	2,500	not available
Ridgecrest Baptist Conference	2,200	35,000
Young Life's Windy Gap	1,700	7,600
Kanuga Conference (Episcopal)	1,200	6,000
Wild's Christian Camp, Brevard	810	3,000
Christmount Assembly (Disciples)	640	6,000
Piedmont Presbyterian Camp	462	300
Our Lady of the Hills, Hendersonville	150	11,160
Camp Burgess Glen	150	9,900

[2]Quoted from Beverly A. Asbury, "The Southern Baptists: Between a Rock and a Hard Place," unpublished paper, 1970. Thanks to Bev Asbury for permission to use his research.

A special section of the North Carolina state code provides exemptions for religious educational assemblies and any "adjacent land reasonably necessary," as long as they are used for religious worship and instruction. But, it's clearly not simply religious education that annually attracts the multitudes to these assemblies. In the South, at least, religious instruction isn't a commodity exclusive to western North Carolina; nor does it need a posh assembly ground in which to occur. As McElrath says, religious instruction is something "a lot of people do in their homes everyday."

Those who come to the religious assembly grounds come for other obvious reasons—to enjoy the hiking, riding, swimming, recreation and sight-seeing of the mountains—much of which is conveniently located on the assemblies' "reasonably necessary adjacent land."

Brochures advertising the religious assemblies differ little, in fact, from those of any resort. A handout of the Ridgecrest Baptist Assembly, for instance, describes in vivid color the "sights, sounds and surroundings" to be found nearby—including a golf course, the Biltmore estates and the Blue Ridge Parkway. "Nestled in the forested mountains, exquisite during the flowering spring, colorful in the red autumn and crisp in the sparkling winter, the center consists of thirty buildings in an architectural blend of Southern charm and modern usefulness," the brochure reads. Not a word about religious worship or religious education.

Historically, the church institutions grabbed their property in the wake of the Northern entrepreneurs who, around the turn of the century, centered upon the Asheville area as a land that neatly combined recreational pleasure with financial returns. George Vanderbilt was perhaps the best-known of these entrepreneurs who bought up mountain land. He visited the area in the 1880s and quickly acquired over fifty farms, which he developed into country estates and hunting lodges—gentlemanly supplements to his vast holdings of forest land.

Missionaries to the region, too, saw that the land's recreational potential could be of benefit. Montreat, the oldest of the assembly grounds, began in 1897 as the Montreat Retreat Association. It was bought in 1905 by the Presbyterian Church for a summer conference ground. Ridgecrest's initial 850 acres were bought by the Baptists in 1907. Lake Junaluska, now the 2,500-acre World Methodist Center, was first purchased by a Methodist missionary movement in 1908.

In more recent years, the lush mountains of western North Carolina have again become the scene of a booming land-recreation-resort complex. Natives of the region have begun to wonder who benefits from the presence of industry—the area and its people or the owners and the affluent, urban tourists who can afford to pass through. The citizens' concerns touch also on a related question: are the vast religious holdings any different from the private corporations which exploit the area?

The manager of Ridgecrest, which annually has 35,000 visitors and a budget of three million dollars answered in a way that gave cryptic comment to the power of the religious assemblies in the area: "I'm unaware of the question," he said. "I have not known of any negative impact. Our whole community is built on what comes in to the conference center. If we were to pull out, the community of Black Mountain wouldn't have anything left. They (the people of Black Mountain) certainly wouldn't even raise the question."

Tax Supervisor McElrath doesn't quite agree. He doesn't object to the presence of the religious assembly grounds which, he admits, help local business. But he does question their preferential tax treatment which excludes them from the responsibility of supporting local government.

"The whole system is subject to abuses," McElrath says in his quiet manner. "It's not that I'm against religion or charities, but I've got so many things that nobody knows *what* they are."

As an example, McElrath mentions the World Evangelical and Christian Education Fund, a group which recently bought just under 2,000 acres of land in Buncombe County for an estimated two million dollars. While he expects to receive a tax-exemption request from them, McElrath doesn't have an inkling of who the World Evangelical and Christian Education is or what it will do with the property. He suspects that maybe it's a front for "either Graham or Moon."

For McElrath, its not just a question of who owns the land but also how it is used. He questions whether the thousands of acres of land owned adjacent to the assembly ground are necessary to their religious purpose. He wonders whether certain individuals aren't gaining unduly from the religious assembly law. He points to Deerfield, an organization chartered "to provide a comfortable and congenial home for aging members of the Protestant Episcopal Church" but which, in McElrath's view, is just a haven to provide homes for "good Episcopalians." He claims, and court records substantiate, that certain assemblies which have held land for years are now selling off lots to selected laymen or ministers for summer cottages. He describes the religious assemblies as if they were no different from real estate dealers or land speculators. "These organizations are going to defeat their purpose by abusing these laws," McElrath has decided.

"The Constitution talks about church and state," he continues. "But this defeats it. . . . All of these organizations are being supplied water, sewers, fire protection and the like. They're automatically tied to the state. It forces everybody to support these organizations, and the list goes on—The Elks, Moose, Eagle. . . . The guy out here who doesn't belong to anything is supporting them all through these exemptions."

So far, there haven't been any complicated, drawn-out law suits about religious exemptions in Buncombe

County, as there have been in Nashville. To Ed McElrath, there's an easier way to deal with the problem: "I think all exemptions should be eliminated," he ventures. "That would eliminate the abuse. It would help everybody. Then the Baptists would pay for what the Baptists get and enjoy."

Part Six

Religion in the South
Finale

> *"When shall I reach that happy place,*
>   *And be forever blest?*
> *When shall I see my Father's face,*
>   *And in His bosom rest?"*

A Ministry to Aliens

by Will Campbell

Let's pretend now that this was a great big stadium—
forty thousand people—
and we're in the midst of an evangelistic crusade.
Gotta dandy preacher up there,
and he's giving the altar call.
Somebody comes up here and plays the piano,
        "Just as I Am."

You know how to give an altar call, don't you?
Well, I do.
Can't grow up a deep water Baptist in south Mississippi
and not know how to do that!
I'm no good at it anymore
because I went off to a
sophisticated Ivy League theological school
and they taught that out of me.
Told me that wasn't cool
and I wanted to be cool.

But picture this preacher, now,
and he's giving the altar call,
and the choir's singing,
        "Just as I am without one plea
        But that Thy blood was shed for me
        And that Thou bidst me come to Thee."
Gonna change the words a little
        "Oh Lamb of God, I GO, I GO."

And he says,

You know, there are
three hundred thousand of your brothers and sisters
locked up tonight—
behind cold steel—
three hundred eighty-eight of them
condemned to die.
three hundred of those, by the way, within the province
of the Southern Presbyterian Church.
and, among the ten highest per capita states of prisoners,
seven of them are in your area—our area—
North Carolina being one of the very highest,
right at the top in the number of people we lock up.

The altar call goes on now.
Three hundred thousand people locked up—
every eye is closed and every head is bowed
while the choir is singing,
"Just as I Am."

Will you leave the aisle?
Take your husband or your wife by the hand.
The usher will assist—
NO,
don't come down here, now!
You're going the wrong way!
Get out of here!

The usher will take you in the room here—
if you don't know the name of a man or woman locked up,
they've got all this on file and they'll give you one.
And you go.
Won't you come—
GO
while we stand
while we sing. . . .
Yes.
I see you there in the balcony.
God bless you.

And all of a sudden you hear
thirty-five thousand motors
droning in the parking lot.
We're talking about evangelism now.
Not talking about social action.
That's a demonic term anyway.
We're talking about EVANGELISM.
Forty thousand people driving into the night.
Going to knock on the bars of prisons. . . .

And the warden calls Caesar and says,

What's going on here?

And Caesar—
by that time it's about midnight—
and he says,

Forty thousand people
beating on the doors. . . .
Well,
What do they want?

They want to see Jesus.

Well, goddammit,
tell them to go to church!

They been to church
and they say
He's not there,
He's risen,
and that
He had told his people
if they wanted to find him
to come to the jails
and there they would find him
locked up—
and they are demanding
to come in
and find
Him.

Do you want to talk about ministry to aliens?

Or do you?

"A Ministry to Aliens" is from a sermon delivered by Will Campbell
to the "Small Church Conference" at Montreat NC, the Presbyterian assembly, in July 1978,
and is printed here by permission of Will Campbell.

ON JORDAN'S STORMY BANKS

Composition by Omni Composition Services, Macon, Georgia
    designed by Margaret Brown
    typeset in Times Roman and Eurostile
    on an Addressograph Multigraph Comp/Set phototypesetter 5404,
    and paginated on an A/M Comp/Set 4510.

Production specifications (casebound edition):
    text paper—60 pound Warren's Olde Style
    end papers—Multicolor Antique, Bombay
    cover (on .088 boards)—Holliston Roxite B (51590)
    dust jacket—100 pound offset enamel, printed in PMS 906
        brown and varnished
(perfect bound edition):
    text paper—60 pound Warren's Olde Style
    cover—100 pound Riegel Jersey Plate Finish, ivory,
    printed in PMS 906 brown and varnished.

Printing (offset lithography) by Omnipress, Inc., Macon, Georgia
Binding by John H. Dekker and Sons, Inc., Grand Rapids, Michigan